The Pedagogy of Business Schools

By

Clayton Davies

The Pedagogy of Business Schools

By Clayton Davies

This book first published 2023

Ethics International Press Ltd, UK

British Library Cataloguing in Publication Data

A catalogue record for this book is available from the British Library

Print Book ISBN: 978-1-80441-232-9

eBook ISBN: 978-1-80441-233-6

Acknowledgements

I thank my family and my friends for their kind patience and understanding during times when I was less than sociable.

Also, my heartfelt thanks go to all those who contributed to my research, without their candour and honesty this book would not have been possible.

Contents

Foreword

This book has its origins in a research project that was started as a demonstration of how the interpretive phenomenology and hermeneutics of Hans Georg Gadamer could be applied to the study of business pedagogy. It became a journey that ended as a narrative of how engagement in a phenomenological enquiry changes the perception of the researcher of the matter-at-hand and an example of how a phenomenological process can unexpectedly uncover insights that transcend the original intent of the research question. The narrative moves of the research from a normative contextualisation that sought to establish how key factors in the evolution of business in general and business pedagogy, in particular, informed the positionality of the research project. Then by using a phenomenological approach to reviewing the relevant literature the narrative uncovers the contingent nature of what the Business Academy is and how there is no current unifying theoretical principle as the current normative manifestation of the Business Academy, describing how of Business Schools emerged through mimesis and contingency. Starting from the position that the epistemological congruence between key stakeholders, students, academics and employers is one possible measure of the effectiveness of business pedagogy in the higher education sector the narrative describes how an operationalisation of Gadamer's hermeneutics formed the basis of an informing methodology. Describing in detail how this was applied and facilitated through the use of hermeneutic circles that utilised an asymmetric process of reflection on texts that explicitly addressed epistemological congruence, the project unfolded and developed into a demonstration of how phenomenological enquiry can be used in practice. The analysis of this material and the reflection on the discursive and interrogative process revealed unexpected themes and essences that altered the original perception of what would constitute a valid congruence of epistemological boundaries. The expected agreements through discourse or fusion of horizons amongst participants did not take the expected form and the analysis of the material uncovered thematic concerns common to students, academics and employers that have implications for the shape, intent and development of pedagogy in the business academy. Underpinning all of these is the challenge of complexity and the need for transparency and honesty amongst key stakeholder groups to develop an effective pedagogy to effectively manage this. The key insight uncovered by the research project is that it may be possible to address the fragmentation of subject disciplines under the Business Academy through a phenomenological approach. In the instance of this research it was through the application of Existential Hermeneutic Phenomenology (EHP) which uncovered underlying themes and essences that crossed internal pedagogical differences and debates within the Business Academy. Reflecting on the unfolding of the research, the criticality of ethical honesty and an acknowledgement of the positionality of the researcher are identified as fundamental to the effective use of phenomenology as a research technique. This research journey has an implication for personal pedagogical practice as the essences uncovered by the research create a call to action. The next step in the development of this form of Existential Hermeneutic Phenomenological research will be to articulate insights from this research project on how the reflective techniques informed by Gadamer's hermeneutics can be used to enhance the process of discursive exchange amongst key stakeholders in the evolution of Business pedagogy.

Chapter 1

Origins and Context

Originally, I aimed to question our understanding of what "Business" is and to challenge the manner in which we teach students to become effective business practitioners. A question that I reflect upon daily during my teaching practice is am I doing the right thing? In more formal academic language; is the pedagogical approach adopted by the Business Academy in the United Kingdom (UK) appropriate for our students, the organisations, the enterprises and the contexts within which they wish to form careers and derive a livelihood? Do we have across the academy a coherent pedagogy that is both effective and relevant to students and other stakeholders? These are not complex questions and my original intent was to answer these through the methodological lens of Existential Hermeneutic Phenomenology, a process that I hoped would deliver a multiplicity of meaning and a unique insight. I had anticipated that the structure of the methods derived from a specific application of phenomenology a technique not commonly used as a research process in the Business Academy would deliver unique insights. What I did not anticipate was that by using this methodology was that the research would evolve as the discursive process at its heart unfolded. So, the two key research questions set at the outset of the research went through parallel evolution. The question; Is Business School pedagogy appropriate for key stakeholders? Became, What pedagogy might be appropriate for key stakeholders? and the allied question; Does the Business Academy have a coherent pedagogy? Became, what could a coherent pedagogy look like? This research became a record of a journey moulded by the unfolding insights of the methodology. I was motivated to ask the original research questions as the numerous conversations I have with students at varying stages of their passage through the higher education process seem to indicate that despite the investment in time and money involved in acquiring a business degree there is little focus or clarity regarding the end goal. This lack of clarity extends in most cases to the career destination of the student and in almost all cases to some reflective idea of what the experience of university has or will deliver in the context of personal development. My original intent was to help address these uncertainties and in order to understand the full extent of the journey, I must begin with a transparent account of where I started.

Origins

I will cover in more depth what I had believed to be the relevance of my methodological approach in the succeeding chapter. First, though, I will contextualise the memes that have dominated my perception of the business academy and in this latter part of my working life my involvement as an educator in a large business school.

I am not alone as a business academic in questioning the efficacy and purpose of the contemporary form and delivery of Business pedagogy in the context of higher education. Two prominent contributors to this debate are Marie-Laure Djelic and Martin Parker. My first degree was in History and Politics and I was drawn to Professor Djleic's article *History of management–what is the future for research on the past?* In this Professor Djelic eloquently articulates the contingent nature of what "Management" (and by extension business) means in an evolving historical context.

> When management emerged, at the turn of the twentieth century in the United States, it was a tool of power for decision makers without ownership rights. They used this tool in their interactions with both labor and shareholders. Management, hence, was a highly political instrument. Then, after the Second World War, management was clearly constructed and presented as a geopolitical weapon. Management would bring wealth and prosperity to battered countries, it was claimed. Wealth and prosperity would keep Communism at bay. In that context, management was a major weapon of the Cold War, and again a highly political tool.
>
> (Djelic, 2016, p. 7)

If we accept Djelic's assertion that "management is, in reality, neither neutral nor de-politicised" (Djelic, 2016, p.8) we should reasonably expect that contemporary business schools recognise this contingency by embedding within their curricula formal mechanisms that would aid students by inculcating, for example, a historical perspective. Unfortunately, the teaching of the history of business as a discrete subject is in decline and not a common or core part of the curriculum in the contemporary academy (Van Fleet, 2005, Wright, 2010, Murcia, Rocha & Birkinshaw, 2018). As a historian by original inclination and with an awareness of historiography and its implications, my view agrees with that of Djelic when she observes "management has reached a status of taken-for-grantedness that makes it essentially transparent and invisible to us" (Djelic. 2016 p. 1). This has significant implications for how we conceptualise business pedagogy. In many of the subject disciplines of Business, we as teachers encourage students to reflect on the nature and relevance of that which they are taught (Brunnquell & Brunstein, 2018) and yet outside our relevant academic fields we have no systematic process of holistically looking at that which we teach other than through programmatic reviews within individual schools. However, within the context of the United Kingdom (UK) Higher Education Sector there is some evidence that the advent of the Teaching Excellence Framework (TEF) has galvanised movement toward wider questioning of the pedagogy (O'Leary & Cui, 2018). This research is my contribution to this emerging reflective process and I used the interpretive phenomenology of Hans Georg Gadamer as a methodological lens and I called this project PHAEDRUS.

PHAEDRUS, in the context of this research journey, is an acronym that stands for Phenomenological Hermeneutical Analysis Extending Discursive Reach Utilising Subjectivity/Inter-subjectivity. This is indicative of the intended novelty of my research into the concerns I have listed above. The first two words are descriptive of the philosophical origins whilst the ambition of deepening discursive understanding through the medium of language and text is encapsulated in the remainder of the acronym. Gadamer outlines the potential of interpretive phenomenology to extend discursive reach through the process of hermeneutical analysis in *The Scope of Hermeneutical Reflection,* one of the essays in a collection entitled *Philosophical Hermeneutics* first published in 1977.

> Hermeneutics being confronted with a disrupted subjective understanding seeks to place communication on a new basis and in particular to replace the false objectivism of alienated knowing with new hermeneutical foundations. Just as in rhetoric and hermeneutics so also in sociological reflection an emancipatory interest is at work that undertakes to free us of outer and inner social forces and compulsions simply by making us aware of them.
>
> (Gadamer, 2008, pp. 29-30)

The methodology directly draws on Gadamer's notion of the "fusing of horizons" and the acronym itself is an allusion to the discursive process of the Socratic Dialogue as Phaedrus was, as described by Plato, Socrates' interlocutor in his dialogical method (Hackforth, 1952). In turn, the acronym also acknowledges the philosophical bearings of Heidegger and Gadamer and their grounding in classical Greek philology (Gadamer, 2008; Heidegger, 2014).

The novelty of this research proposal is in the unique application of Hans Georg Gadamer's (1972, 2000) phenomenological perspective in the examination of pedagogical discourse in the discipline. The use of Gadamer's interpretive phenomenological approach places language and its continually evolving form as a carrier and mediator of meaning at the centre of both the methodology and the method. Furthermore, it is the primacy of meaning to the individual as expressed through the discursive exchange that places the individual and their perception of the "Life-World" (Gadamer, 1972) at the heart of the analysis.

This research seeks to examine where the epistemological boundaries are drawn in the academic discipline of business. This is subject to the prejudice and perception of whether practitioners subscribe to whether Business and Management is considered a science (Anderson *et al*.., 2015) or an art (Badua, 2015) or whether it is a mixture of both (Richardson, 2008). Bauda (2015) argues that the widening of business school curricula to include "the ROOT disciplines of rhetoric, orthography, ontology, and teleology" is not only desirable but a vital balance to the dominant pedagogic narratives within the discipline. Most contemporary critical writing that examines the epistemological fit of Business Pedagogy is still predicated on either humanist or rational/positivist approaches which both focus on outcomes and procedural delivery. Academic thought on business pedagogy from the humanist, sociological perspective (Amann *et al*.., 2011, Petriglieri & Petriglieri, 2015) attempts to re-centre the core of Business School epistemology in an ontological base predicated on the contingency of social relationships arguing that business is fundamentally a social transactional process. Accordingly, pedagogical strategies must focus on outcomes that enhance students' social and transactional skills. In contrast, rational/positivist writing (Fourcade & Khurana, 2013) directly locates business epistemology in the positivist ontologies of empiricism and natural science. Conceptualising Business as a procedural discipline in this manner emphasises such skills as mathematics and analysis and promotes the desirability of defined outcomes (Anderson *et al*., 2015, Taylor, 2015). Whilst these differing ontological and epistemological perspectives may often be in conflict over pedagogical approaches, (Steiner & Gaskin, 1999) they nevertheless coexist in contemporary Business School curricula. On the periphery of this ontological battle are approaches that have the potential to offer new insights Badua (2015). Amongst the alternate ontological perspectives increasingly gaining traction in the consideration of Business Pedagogy is that of Phenomenology (Nilson, 2015; Berglund, 2015; Gill, 2014). I am suggesting thorough this research that an examination of the life-world of respondents and the merging of their epistemological horizons has the potential to resolve the bifurcation between these two dominant perspectives and bring the individual as the embodiment of meaning and the carrier of relevance into focus as the true object of pedagogical effort.

So, in order to contextualise this research, I am going to stay true to the principles and practice of interpretive phenomenology as this forms the methodological basis of my study. Drawing on the work of Heidegger and Gadamer I am accepting that my conceptualisation of the world is fundamentally a complex, historical web of pre-understanding or prejudice as Gadamer would have it. My epistemological horizon is bound by this life-in-the-world experience and my internalised interpretation of events and my perception of phenomena that have relevance and meaning to me. By engaging in a reflective, discursive examination of this set of prejudices through a process that will merge my horizon with the epistemological horizons of others I hope to accomplish two things. First to deepen and reflect on my understanding of the relevance and effect of that which I do – namely the teaching of the discipline of Business in the Higher Education sector in the United Kingdom (UK) and second to contribute to the common horizon of understanding of the Business Academy in the field of its pedagogical practice. To be faithful to this aim I must be as transparent as I can with a personal evaluation of how Business has evolved during my own experience of Business as a series of activities, normative social practices and manifest consequences. This reflective process is critical to the practice of interpretive phenomenology as a method for academic purposes. Additionally, I must acknowledge and situate my being-in-the-world or as Heidegger terms it Dasein (1996). I must with honesty locate my epistemological horizon, for without this clarity I cannot expect my horizon to be merged with others in the process of creating a new understanding. Clarity, transparency and honesty are essential in establishing my prejudice, the method demands this and requires me to set out a personal account of how I perceive the field which I am studying. The following contextual writing is an account of the memes that I judge as crucial to the construction of my prejudice regarding Business Pedagogy in the Higher Education sector in the UK is necessarily personal as it locates a personal horizon and acts furthermore as orientation in what is an area of infinite complexity and multiple perspectives. This contextualisation is inescapable.

communicate with clarity within the context of my employment to create a significant personal profile within which my skills were valued. Within this environment where most of my peer group did not possess this training, this became an advantage in a period which saw the adoption of computer-mediated communication and its supplanting of traditional media as the core process that enabled the flow of business information. Although I did not have a computer science degree or even a technical qualification I could rapidly assimilate the techniques and normative standards of the new culture and recognise the fundamental impact this would have on the nature of work. It is moot whether the rise of digital communication and the embracing of the principles of the knowledge economy are causally linked but I can make the reasonable assumption that the two have a direct correlation. Through my personal experience, the very act of moving an artefact such as a repository of knowledge from traditional media into digital media added credibility to that information. Here I want to make a distinction between the enhanced flexibility that these digital processes offered and the meaning ascribed to the new form of information. In many circumstances, the former was misunderstood or could not be understood by those not initiated into the mysteries of computer technology whereas the latter form-of-the-thing was readily embraced and accepted as meaningful. I did not reflect on this at the time and it is only now that it is clear to me from a personal standpoint that I was in some small way instrumental in underpinning the assumptions that we were making about the efficacy of adopting the new normative rules of the knowledge economy. Olsen and Peters (2005) clearly articulate this ascription of validity to the notion of the knowledge economy and its new iteration as knowledge capitalism.

> The term 'knowledge capitalism' emerged only recently to describe the transition to the so-called 'knowledge economy', which we characterize in terms of the economics of abundance, the annihilation of distance, the de-territorialization of the state, and, investment in human capital (see Figure 2). As the business development and policy advocate Burton-Jones (1999, p. vi) puts it, 'knowledge is fast becoming the

Contextualisation

I entered the world of full-time work in October 1978, starting as a "Local Assistant Manager" (LAM) based at the Gaumont State Cinema, Kilburn, a cinema, theatre and bingo hall owned and run by what was then called the Rank Organisation. I was an oddity as I was a graduate of London University with a degree in History and Politics. The normal educational level of my peer group, other LAMs as they were affectionately known was at most the possession of Certificate of Secondary education qualification and possibly an Ordinary level or two. Education per se was not prized in the context of what was seen as a "calling" a vocation to the cinema trade and what was more highly valued was a commitment to the job and an aptitude for dealing with the general public. Beyond a basic acuity with numbers and adequate literacy, it was clear that the corporation assumed that the in-house training which took place informally "on-the-job" and formally in company facilitated sessions would be used to educate new junior entrants about the culture and the mores of the managerial community that was specific to the corporation. In fact, a clear and overtly stated aim of recruitment was to find individuals that would commit themselves to the company for their entire careers, a job for life was on offer for those who conformed, worked hard, developed themselves along company lines and who remained loyal to the corporation's aims and policies. On reflection in the very act of writing these words, I realise how alien this may sound to the contemporary reader with no direct visceral experience of this culture. It was not however at odds with the normative assumptions of the time (Kalleberg, 2013). Now I work as a senior lecturer in a Business School part of a faculty in a major regional university in the United Kingdom preparing graduates for similar entry-level jobs in corporations that will avowedly not offer the same psychological contract of security and commitment as often its historical iteration once did (Kalleberg, 2013). In the intervening decades, there has a significant change in the normative values not only of corporate culture but also in the structural manner in which we anticipate that new entrants into the job market will prepare themselves and assume a greater degree of personal risk and uncertainty.

My perception is that there have been four key memetic changes in the relationship between organisations, society and individuals that have both enabled this change and in turn been reinforced by this structural shift in cultural norms. These are, the ephemeral nature of employment and the rise of the "portfolio" career, the transfer of responsibility for the development of employee's skills from the organisation to the state and the individual, the rise of the primacy of the "knowledge" economy and finally the emergence of the Business Academy in Higher Education. I will briefly contextualise these in turn but at this point, I must acknowledge that this is an arbitrary taxonomy that is keyed to my perception and is almost a personal historical interpretation that invests these phenomena with meaning that may be disconnected from other perceptions of the relative importance of these phenomena. I, therefore, warn that this is not intended to be a definitive or comprehensive historical account of this societal shift but an explanation of why I am doing what I am doing, namely attempting to make personal sense of a pedagogical culture that has arisen and come to dominate discourses around the training, skills, behaviours and attitudes required of young graduates entering the job market now as I did then.

"Jobs for Life" cannot now be found within the embrace of a single organisation (Dore, 1995). In fact, there is an embedded assumption amongst even the most high-profile corporations in the UK and other western industrialised nations that employees will move out of the corporate culture in order to pursue individual developmental needs and aims. This is often promoted as a good both for the corporation and the individual. Flexibility is inherent in the contemporary psychological contract between potential employees and the corporation and statements to this can be found in the public literature of numerous organisations. The subtext is one of the transitory nature of the relationship and the willingness of the individual to embrace the needs of the corporation and sublimate their own. Yet there is no rejoinder that this flexibility will ensure the stability of employment; the best that is on offer is personal career development. This movement of responsibility from the organisation to the individual has a consequence summarised by Creed and Hughes (2013).

> Unfortunately, choosing a career might be constrained b
> real or imagined barriers, such as believing you do not ha
> the ability or stamina for a particular course, or determinir
> that there are too few openings available after qualifyin
> Such constraints lead young people to adjust, or compromi
> on, their desired careers options, and accept ones that a
> less desirable to them... Less desirable options might inclu
> choosing a pathway that is less prestigious or interesting,
> is more demanding or challenging, than desired.
>
> (Creed and Hughes, 2013 p.

In accepting the inevitability of flexibility and individual res
sibility for "self-development" we have absolved the corpor
or the organisation from its structural need to engage in long
development and planning we accept that organisations are
to hire and fire as the demands of the environment in which
operate see fit and that there is no moral or ethical requiremen
them to consider the consequences of such actions not just on
viduals but also (and perhaps less recognised) on the commun
in which the individual is situated. Perhaps though there is a w
societal benefit to this shift, perhaps economies are better se
by self-motivated constituents whose inherent insecurity crea
competitive environment on the supply side of the labour ma
that enhances the competitive responsiveness of the entire econ
and some commentators do in fact argue that we see this effect i
major popular conurbations such as London (Turok, 2004).

The second meme that appears to act as a philosophical justi
tion for the increasing transience of work throughout the s
demographic structure is that of the rise and the inevitability of
societal move from an economy based on heavy industry, ma
facturing, mining and fishing to an economy based on the ser
industries. The rise of the "knowledge economy" was seen eve
the early 1960s as an inescapable destiny (Powell & Snellman, 20
As I progressed in my career it became apparent that I could lever
the academic skills of research, the acquisition of information
experience, the acuity to recognise key factors and the ability

> most important form of global capital—hence "knowledge capitalism".
>
> (Olsen & Peters, 2005, p. 331)

Olsen and Peters go on to allege that this embracing of knowledge as the new carrier of value and worth also gave rise to the re-evaluation on a global scale of the importance of Higher Education as the conduit for the creation, enhancement and transfer of this value. However and again on a personal level, I witnessed that removal of entire skillsets within the workplace as these flexible and evolving technologies supplanted old ways of doing things, this rapid adoption of computer-mediated communication across all levels of my working environment led to a new perception of the worth of the individual within the context I was working, those who embraced change and adopted new techniques prospered (as I did) and those that did not were simply removed. Underpinning what was often a brutal process was this narrative of the new, the digital and the new forms of knowledge it manifested. It is unclear to me whether this was used as a justification to increase the transience of the workplace or if it was a cause of it. What can be said is that the two phenomena of digital technology and the embrace of the transience created by adopting a knowledge-driven culture appeared to have evolved together.

The third meme, that of the transient nature of employment has had a personal and profound effect on my understanding of individual worth and how organisations perceive the value or otherwise of its employees. I must question whether my own acute experiences of the transient nature of employment with its attendant emotional resonance has an effect on my understanding of the impact that this has on wider society and whether others ascribe similar meaning to the contract of loyalty implied in full time, tenured employment. The current debates and commentaries, particularly in the UK over such phenomena as the "Gig Economy" and "Zero Hour Contracts" appear to confirm that stability and security remain valued aspects of employment as well as flexibility. Some quantitative studies confirm that transience in the workplace has increased over the last five decades (Stroh & Brett, 1994). It appears that we have embraced the principles of transience and change as an inevitable consequence of rapid economic change and adaptation and that this process will continue with inevitability and that we as individuals are fundamentally responsible for equipping ourselves to meet the needs of our organisations rather than the organisation taking responsibility to equip itself to accommodate the challenges of change. On reflection, this is an odd thing that we have accepted, namely that it is the right of an organisation to re-mould itself, to adapt to new competitive stress not by investing in its constituent participants – its people – but to reserve the right to itself to simply find new participants with more appropriate skills or experience. My view inclines towards the responsibility of the organisation to ensure an appropriate fit of employees' skills and it must be recognised that there is a continuum of approach where some contemporary organisations meet this expectation and others patently do not (Thorne & Pellant, 2007). What has replaced the paternalistic relationship between employee and employer in respect of training needs is the wider narrative on the need for those who are active in the jobs market to embrace "lifelong learning", Anna Tuschling and Christoph Engemann (2006) have tracked this emerging shift from societal education to individual learning across the European Union.

> The beginnings of this transition are located in the 1970s, with a phase of build-up in the 1980s and a general visibility in the late 1990s, especially in the social-democratic regimes of the so-called 'Third Way' in Great Britain and Germany. The administrative initiatives brought forward by these ruling parties made rich use of a political rhetoric asserting a profound change in the distribution of responsibilities between state and individuals, calling for a stronger utilization of individual 'resources' for the good of the society. Especially in the realm of social welfare, new arrangements were sought where individual action is increasingly invoked to ideally foster both individual chances and collective good.
>
> (Tuschling & Engemann , 2006 pp. 452- 453)

For lifelong learning, we can read an abrogation of a large part of the responsibility for the training of employees that was once assumed by the employer. Again, structurally and in terms of the innate flexibility this builds into economic responsiveness this is not an entirely bad thing. For those who can respond to this call for individual responsibility the support structures such as grants, subsidised courses and career sabbaticals enable and enhance a more fulfilling and ultimately varied career often across a variety of sectors and organisations. On those less able to cope with the admonishment to develop the self can lead to higher stress and enhance the feeling of transience and insecurity (Field, 2000). From my perspective my ability to switch between careers, from Leisure to eCommerce, to Venture Capital and finally to Higher Education I can trace directly to my educational experiences at secondary and tertiary levels. Even at "A" level I was encouraged by both the curriculum and my teachers to develop a keen sense of questioning and this process continued seamlessly into tertiary education at undergraduate level. It would be nonsensical to attribute the entirety of my resilience and flexibility to education as these ecologies of challenge, questioning and testing were part of a different social settlement in which a greater degree of inequality in society and opportunity was acceptable. Higher education found its participants through a process of exclusion whereby each level of academic measure had its quota of achievement irrespective of the "objective" level of attainment. A binary system existed not just between Polytechnics and Universities, but also in England And Wales between secondary modern and grammar schools and the process of selection was for most was irrevocably set at the end of junior education by the 11 plus examination, few beyond this escaped their classification (Taylor, 1980). This poses a significant and personal question. If I accept this new settlement of individual responsibility of "lifelong" learning as a professional educator what am I consciously doing to engage the students for whom I responsible in this process? Should I simply accept that the overt messages embedded in our programmes with their admonishment to continue to train and to learn is a sufficient discharge of my professional responsibilities or should I attempt to encourage students to in a more detailed reflective discourse on the wider political, sociological and psychological processes that this form of commitment involves? This is particularly problematic for Higher Education students for two reasons, first is the pragmatic argument that the investment in a degree in the context of the UK is already a significant commitment of time and money. There is a danger here that I could devalue their effort by pointing out that a business degree cannot constitute a final destination and further resources must be committed in an open-ended career spanning process. The second reason is one of critical acuity and resilience. Am I truly confident that at whatever stage in their academic process that any individual student has developed sufficient internal strength to look forward to more education plus the common demands of life such as work and other more personal social relationships? For some, the answer will be may be yes insomuch that I can judge resilience on the manifest evidence of the behaviours I observe and the statements I hear, but even here I cannot fully gauge the internal life-world of any individual student without a lengthy process of discursive exchange and even then the judgement would be one of an amateur rather than a professional. This is a real conundrum in higher education in the UK context as it is clear from recent research that the mental stress we place as a society on students in terms of the expectation of performance has been exacerbated by the "value" that a degree has acquired through the introduction of tuition fees that manifest the base monetary investment in achieving the qualification.

> Epidemiological studies have shown a relationship between debt and mental health difficulties and substance dependence in the general UK population. Previous research with British students has found that poor mental health is related to financial difficulties and level of debt, with greater financial concern predicting deterioration in mental health over time.
>
> (Richardson, Elliott and Roberts, 2015 p. 5)

As educators, we participate in a system that creates the debt and then we tell the students that even this will not be enough to ensure future success and prosperity as they will have to engage in lifelong learning. Responsibility for the consequences of this must lie within the Business Academy as the final meme that has re-shaped the societal context of business has been the inexorable rise of the Business Academy and its eminence within the tertiary sector in the UK.

Returning to my career to encounter a Business School graduate in the echelons of the large multi-national corporation I worked for was a rarity. More commonplace were the professionals such as accountants, economists and lawyers that were recruited either directly from professions (Accountants and Lawyers) or well-established University faculties (Economists). There were a few graduates from more technical disciplines and a few from arts disciplines but these were a rarity and often thought to be odd for choosing a career in commerce. At the end of my career with this organisation, the reverse was true, almost every new management entrant was in possession of some form of degree and this change from almost zero percent graduate entry to one hundred percent graduate entry only took two decades and most of these were graduates with some form of Business degree. The rise of participation in the rising academic discipline of Business has moved rapidly from one of a few specialist business schools to faculties that often dominate their host institutions in terms of numbers of students and revenue through tuition fees (Williams, 2010). Within the context of the HE community in the UK, this has not been an entirely easy process as the academic legitimacy of this new (and large) interloper has been challenged (Masrani, Williams & McKiernan, 2011). However, as nearly one in seven of all undergraduate students in the UK are in Business Schools (HESA Statistics, 2017/18) we have a structural commitment to Business education which would be difficult to dismantle. Furthermore, the advance in legitimacy has been supported by two critically important professional bodies both of which have been instrumental in bolstering the validity and the political reach of the academy.

Both BAM (The British Academy of Management) and ABS (The Association of Business Schools) entered an embryonic UK field contextualized by a suspicion of the quality and applicability of management education and especially of its research component. Both institutions aimed to gain legitimacy from external stakeholders through active agency by lobbying, by creating formal and symbolic structures and through the use of measurement systems in order to influence the prevailing belief systems and to alter decision making rules and regulations, e.g. those pertaining to research funding.

(Masrani, Williams & McKiernan, 2011, p. 396)

What was hitherto a technical discipline mainly rooted in further education has now almost totally transferred its education processes into the higher education sector. The justification for this can be directly related to the three other memes that have reshaped my understanding of the ecology of business.

The "knowledge" economy demands the deployment of higher-level skills and it seems to be a direct corollary of this assumption that higher-level skills should be delivered by the higher education sector. Thus Business education moves from the procedural and the focus on the task to the embedding of critical acuity and other "soft skills" such as organisational awareness and communication processes. Disciplines that had previously been academic cultures that stood alone, such as economics and accounting are moved into the domain of the business faculty and subsumed into multi-disciplinary programmes. New discourses on such phenomena as globalisation, technological change and enterprise culture become areas of study and included in the expanded curricula and new philosophical perspectives are added to improve the perceptual comprehension of those engaged in Project Management and Human resources management. The technical-commercial college that once trained typists, draughtsmen and engineers now educates analysts, consultants and executives. Some observers argue that it is uncertain that this has enhanced economic effectiveness but it is an inescapable fact that per capita wealth creation has accelerated over the last fifty years at a global level and even faster in those jurisdictions that have high levels of Business School graduates entering their economies so at the very least we can claim that this academisation of business has not had a negative effect. However, serious challenges have emerged to the pedagogic rationale that underpins the Business Schools position in Higher Education. In a trenchant critique of the current state of Business School pedagogy, Professor Martin Parker offers an alternate vision of how "management" could be taught.

> Organizing is all around us, and it is a topic of enquiry that clearly overlaps with other parts of the social sciences and humanities – sociology, anthropology, politics, history and so on. The School of Organizing wouldn't need its own building to stress its distinctiveness, because it would have to work with teachers and researchers who could show us variety and strangeness, rather than endless recitations of the supposedly similar. No form of organization would be off-limits, so we might imagine courses and research projects on the circus, families, queues, city-states, utopias, villages, sects, matriarchies, mobs, gangs, cities, clubs, segmentary lineage systems, pirates, the mafia, Occupy and the landing of Apollo 11 on the moon at 8:17 GMT in the evening of Sunday 20 July 1969.
>
> (Parker, 2016 p. 151)

Parker directly challenges the current nature of Business Pedagogy arguing for a wider more eclectic view of what management is claiming that it should be better termed as "organising" and speculating on which subject academic disciplines could or should contribute to the curriculum.

Evolution

Phaedrus written by Plato in 360 B.C.E opens with Socrates asking his interlocutor "My dear Phaedrus, whence come you, and whither are you going?" A question that is particularly relevant to this research journey. In the context of my starting understanding of Business Schools, this was framed as whether we are producing students with the right knowledge? With the follow on question, Is there enough epistemological overlap between universities, students and employers? The acronym PHAEDRUS was an encapsulation that summarised both the core intent of the research and the novelty of my approach to the research questions. However, by using a research process based on Gadamer's iteration of interpretive phenomenology and adapting this into my Existential Hermeneutic Phenomenology I created a new process of discursive exchange that changed the intent and emphasis of the original research questions. The application of phenomenological principles changed the nature and positionality of the research. I had originally sought to deliver an operationalised version of Gadamer's "Fusion of Horizons" by deconstructing the stages in this process and had sought to uncover how the life experience of key stakeholders in the Business Academy could inform the evolution of pedagogical approaches used by Business Schools. The intent of this was to determine how we could make these approaches more congruous in terms of the fusion of the epistemological horizons of the respondents and thereby more congruous in the shape of desired and effective outcomes. I had hoped that the act of research and the act of fusion could establish a new semi-autonomous structure that could be used to enable an open-ended discursive exchange amongst the stakeholders I had identified. A hermeneutic circle that would never need to be closed. The research evolved though, in an unexpected manner. The critical juncture came when I applied the process of phenomenological interpretation to the outcomes of the initial research discussions. It became clear that any attempt to operationalise any phenomenologically based methodology was both contingent on time place and circumstance and that that the true contribution of my iteration of existential hermeneutic phenomenology was in its description of the process itself and an understanding of how this contributed to (amongst others) Djelic's and Parker's challenges to some of the assumptions of Business Pedagogy. In order to understand this journey fully, I will first place the wider iterations of Phenomenological enquiry in the context of business and business research pedagogy through the literature review. I will then recount my original understanding, interpretation and application of Gadamer's philosophy and other phenomenological influences in my chapters on methodology and methods. In the chapters on the research process and analysis, I describe in detail how the discursive process and the application of phenomenological principles changed this positionality. Finally, I conclude with a discussion on the actual results of the research and it's ethical and procedural implications for my practice and that of others.

Chapter 2

Business Pedagogy; a brief history

Evidence from the Literature

The range of literature written on the origins, nature and development of the pedagogy of the business academy is extensive both in scope and in chronological reach. I must be selective in the process of identifying what is relevant and to do so I will use the informing methodology of this study, namely by utilising a phenomenological approach to identify and analyse the appropriate literature from this canon of work. A phenomenological approach to reading the literature derives from the manner in which I give primacy to my life-world and my own lived experience of the pedagogy as it has, and does, manifest itself in my own direct experience. This is part of the journey, part of the unfolding horizon of my understanding of the nature of business pedagogy and its effect on my own practice and the views of others as I perceive them. This is an integral and living part of the journey that I described in Chapter one and my analytical observations on the unfolding of the literature cannot capture with purity my sense-making of the pedagogy as it manifests itself at any time in the past. My personal understanding has changed irrevocably as my personal horizon has merged with that of others. What I can do with honesty is to attempt to acknowledge the key influences on my views of the pedagogy of the business academy as-they-were at the specific moment in time that I became aware of them. I cannot fully replicate my original sense-making of them as phenomena at that time and can only offer a palimpsest of this awareness. In this, I acknowledge the contingency of an unfolding understanding.

To inform this phenomenological approach to a history of the Business Academy I am drawing in part from the writings of Saunders (1982) and Groenewald (2004) and in part from my own interpretation of Gadamer's hermeneutical methodology to construct a framework that will enable me to coherently organise and interpret these influences. Furthermore, the description and commentary that Hart (1998,) gives on the features and nature of a literature review based on phenomenological principles was both instructive and useful in my process of framing the analysis and the criteria for the selection of literature. Adapting Hart's summation (1998 pp 103-105) on a phenomenological reading of literature I have an analytical process that I can apply to key points in the chronological unfolding of my understanding.

First, I must identify the underlying assumptions of the literature and then to reflect and recognise the consequences of this when I seek to understand the phenomenon of Business Pedagogy. Following this, I must disentangle and identify with as much clarity as possible these assumptions so that I can identify as far as is possible the essence of the pedagogy as-it-is and then reflect on the consequences of this on the influence of the development of pedagogical theory and practice in the context of business. To be clear, I am not attempting a chronologically accurate unpicking of the development of business pedagogy I am re-constructing as far as my current apprehension will allow, a reconstruction of the unfolding of my epistemological horizon and seeking to identify the moments of rapprochement that developed this. Here I am using the notion of rapprochement in the Gadamerian sense by seeking to identify the particular influences that significantly affected my emerging understanding of the pedagogy. As part of the phenomenological analytic, I will summarise at each key point in my chosen chronology my understanding of the foreknowledge or prejudice as it then stood within the academic discourse. This will also include my perception of rapprochement within the academy, how this impacted on the application and practice of pedagogy and finally the wider consequences of the pedagogy as a phenomenon in itself.

In outline, my selection of literature covers three key periods, all of which have direct personal relevance to my own life-world and experience. The first period I shall cover is that of the period up to 1992 before the "Major" reforms that ended the binary system of higher education within the United Kingdom. Up until this point, my perception of the Business Academy was largely determined by understanding of the process as described by peers and colleagues that had attended Business Schools combined with my reading and comprehension of what was published in the non-academic media. The second period will overlap the first as I will attempt an account of the period during which business studies gained traction as an integral part of the Higher Education sector in the UK a period when faculties of Business and Management became embedded both as drivers of a significant expansion of students in HE in the UK and mainstays of institutional finance. Finally, I will map out the current "state of play" in the Business Academy. Each section of this literature review follows a structure that is determined by my phenomenological stance. I will describe my foreknowledge, my prejudicial understanding as it stood at the time. Then, I will examine the accounts of the practice of pedagogy that influenced and altered my understanding of the pedagogy of this period. From this, I will be able to identify how these influences altered the practice of pedagogy in the academy and finally I will attempt to analyse the consequence of how these developments in practice alter mine and other perceptions of business pedagogy as a phenomenon. In brief, each section will map foreknowledge, rapprochement, practice and consequence. It must be acknowledged that the further back in time that I track my foreknowledge the less reliable on a personal level this becomes as I am attempting to reconstruct personal epistemological horizons that have long since been altered as my own life-world experiences have evolved. With this caveat, I will start with the period prior to the 1992 Major reforms.

1945 – 1992 Business and Management as an emerging profession

Foreknowledge

As a graduate of London University with a joint honours degree in History and Politics, I had a limited view of the value and efficacy of business school education. The perception that I had of business education mainly drew from my perception of this being a technical skillset taught primarily in Further Education colleges, Technical colleges and Polytechnics. In truth, this was simply prejudice in the colloquial sense of the word. An attitude that I took into my first steps into a career in business in late 1979. However, this view was not entirely mistaken. An article written by Stephen Black in 1971, *Thoughts on Management Education*, examined the social and cultural prejudices that influenced the structure and delivery of Management Education in the UK at that time. I have replicated below a table from that article summarising the educational background of managers within the UK at that time.

Sources of Management Education by Managerial Level

	Directors	Top Managers	All Managers
Universities	14.3%	21.1%	11.3%
Technical Colleges	35.8%	33.3%	18.0%
Consultants	14.3%	8.4%	2.7%
Internal	0	14.0%	43.8%

(Black, 1971 p.45)

It should be noted that 35.6% of the Directors of companies in the UK at that time had no form of tertiary education. What I could not anticipate though was that throughout the early 1980s the UK was to undergo a radical economic shift. Prior to the "Major" reforms observations of an American commentator Robert Locke clearly identified the social stratification that was enshrined by a division between the elite business schools of London and Manchester and their Polytechnic based counterparts.

> The social prejudices voiced within the academic community, on both sides of the binary line, are also directed at business schools: for, if they are attacked by university people in the older, established disciplines, they are also attacked by professors in the polytechnics.
>
> (Locke, 1989, p. 187)

Locke then goes on to quote Professor Newbigging of the Central London Polytechnic,

> The so-called classical or liberal education, (with its) call for

> the education of generalists, and the Anglo-Saxon model of "profession" have all promoted a middle-class professional ethic which continues to promote a dubious distinction from the world of work
>
> (Locke, 1989, p. 187)

The 1992 reforms were only a visible and arbitrary dividing line. Business pedagogy, its practice, its theory, its delivery and the social and cultural attitudes that determined its acceptability as an academic discipline, had been undergoing radical change even before the post-war period in the UK. To fully understand the present pedagogical practices, I will adopt a historical approach as I am by first inclination a historian and as Peter Mathias says in his article *Business History and Management Education,*

> In practical terms, also, it is relevant for a person to know the myths currently explaining the present, as well as to seek more objective explanation. The present is explained both by objective and by subjective interpretations of the past.
>
> (Mathias, 1975 p. 13)

Rapprochement within academia prior to 1992

The immediate aftermath of the Second world war saw a decline in the UK's global political and economic influence. This was a relative decline and was partly due to the burgeoning of American economic power and political reach that followed almost inevitably from their pivotal role in the defeat of Nazi Germany (Barnett, 1972). In the late 1940's it became apparent that critical to the economic success of the USA was its culture of enterprise and the contribution made to the effectiveness of their economy by the Business Schools present on most University campuses in the USA (Tiratsoo, 2004). In response, the UK government attempted to emulate the success of this by encouraging initiatives that would establish a similar network of Business Schools. One of the fundamental obstacles to the success of these initiatives was the attitude of both British industry and academia to the validity of and the need for these initiatives. Industry questioned the need for such training and academia the intellectual validity of the field (Ivory & Scholar, 2006). Furthermore, there was a more general societal resistance.

> The British believed leadership to be a personality trait that could not be taught in a classroom. Because of these and other social forces, few university graduates chose business as their desired career except as a last resort well into the post-war era.
>
> (Larson 1992, p. 3)

Nevertheless, the concern at policy level on the lack of a substantive response to the need for the education of managers remained and was highlighted as a critical gap in the provision of Higher Education in the UK by the Robbins report (1963). Following the establishment of the London and Manchester Business Schools the subsequent growth of similar establishments transformed both the scale of provision and the eventual academic acceptance of the validity of the discipline. As Larson goes on to say.

> The creation of the British business schools in 1965-1966 represented a turning point in the movement to professionalize management and establish it as a theoretically based discipline.
>
> (Larson 1992, p.8)

Initially, the pedagogical approach of Business Schools as informed by theory drew from a positivist and rational tradition (Mulligan, 1987) in direct emulation of the American tradition. This included the adoption of the principles of natural science as the ontological and epistemological foundation of the discipline (Simon, 1960). Whilst functional processes were efficient in delivering set outcomes (Grayson, 1973), business academia nevertheless acknowledged that humanist perspectives such as those derived from the research of Bandura (1977), Maslow (1943) and Schein (2010) had the potential to unlock a greater repository of insight into the human condition. These perspectives drew from the ontological writings of Foucault (1972) and Berger and Luckman (1966) and from other academic traditions such as Psychology, Sociology and Anthropology (Koontz, 1961). These sources influenced the rational positive strand of business pedagogy (Barney, 2002; Hunt, 2002) and whilst differing perspectives on the teaching of business remain (Datar et al., 2011) there is nevertheless evidence that these influences are continuing to merge (Mulligan, 1987; Mintzberg, 2004). In summary, this eclectic multi-disciplinary approach sets the foundations of the structure of contemporary business schools in the UK.

Pedagogical Implications

Whilst eclectic in the influences they drew upon to inform the academisation of Business as an academic discipline and flexible with pedagogic techniques they adopted there were nevertheless critical gaps in the curricula of the new Business Schools. This was highlighted in the aftermath of the financial crisis of 2008 as Wilson and Thomas describe in their 2012 paper, *The Legitimacy of the Business of Business Schools; What's the Future?*

> The failure of business schools to embrace and teach critical thinking and moral reasoning is allegedly why MBAs made the short-sighted and self-serving decisions that resulted in the current financial crisis and other organisational crashes (e.g. Enron, Parmalat, WorldCom). Thomas and Wilson (2011) neatly summarise the allegations of business school failure. They divide these into knowledge creation (schools research the wrong things); pedagogical issues (schools teach the wrong things); and ideology, purpose and leadership (schools focus almost exclusively on free-market economics, are unclear about their roles in academia or the world of practice).
>
> (Wilson & Thomas, 2012 p 373)

These aporia in the curriculum were to become wider and the fragmentation of pedagogical approach in the subject disciplines was to become even more pronounced with the end of the binary system of Higher Education in the UK.

Post-1992 Business and Management as an academic discipline

Foreknowledge

The reforming Government of Margaret Thatcher which moved the economic base of the UK economy from what was perceived to be the unsustainable traditional mainstays of the economy, heavy industry, mining and mass manufacturing to the global service economy of today (Crang and Martin, 1991). Social and academic attitudes to Business Education went through a parallel reconstruction. Business faculties became integral parts of most universities within the UK. The ending of the "binary" system of Higher Education within the UK by the Major Government in 1992 re-oriented Business Studies as a more socially acceptable form of study. Within fifteen years research by Massimiliano Brattti (2006) found that there was no identifiable class bias in the cohorts studying Business in the UK. From an external perspective Business and Management, studies seemed to have gained full acceptance as an academic discipline. However, the consolidation of the Higher Education Sector in the UK had a significant effect on Business Schools as they now began to be judged in league tables on their research effectiveness. Institutions that hitherto were well regarded fell rapidly down the league tables as the research effectiveness of host institutions became instrumental in the success or failure of Business Schools in the myriad ranking systems (Wilkins & Huisman, 2012). What did not emerge with this concatenation of business education with academia was a settled core theoretical base, the fragmentation of the pedagogy continued at an even greater pace driven by the demands of research performance (Clark, Knights & Jarvis, 2012).

Rapprochement

The rapprochement amongst Business Schools post the 1992 reforms was fundamentally a direct continuation of the pattern of evolution that had started following the Robbins report and the establishment of the London and Manchester Business Schools. The National Committee of Inquiry into Higher Education otherwise known as the Dearing Report (1997) emphasised the burgeoning impact of communications and technological innovation and it confirmed the status of Business Schools in the national strategy for Higher Education and their critical importance for harnessing these technologies for the benefit of the economy. In order to promote an assured quality in business schools the practice of "benchmarking", commonplace in business processes, was now being suggested for the new monitoring agency designed to regulate and monitor what was hoped to be a growing provision of Higher education in the UK. The language and practice of Business were now beginning to shape elements of the discourse across a wide range of academic disciplines (Holloway & Francis, 2002). Fundamentally the post-binary environment accelerated the process of the academisation of the Business School curricula without any significant challenge to its foundations and structure (Wilmott, 1994). This led to the equanimity of the provision in which the offers within this newly competitive environment had a high degree of conformity to a set structure. The focus was on outcomes and this had a consequence for the evolution of the pedagogy of business schools. Business schools embraced their mission to improve the effectiveness of business leaders and thereby the performance of the economy and developed an outcome led pedagogy that focused on the delivery of technical skills, theoretical understanding of structures and a quasi-legal grasp of regulatory instruments. Management Education (ME) as delivered by the Business Schools also drew its legitimacy from other wider societal, cultural and political influences (Grey, 2002). What seemed to be lacking was a focus that looked beyond these positivist and humanist approaches into the consequence of conformity for the individual. Even pre-Dearing there were voices that criticised this approach. Wilmott (1994) offered a critique of the pedagogy that highlighted amongst other things a lack of innovation in management education and suggested that a more critical, action-oriented approach might produce more rounded business graduates. An exemplar of this voice of dissent was the argument for re-orienting business pedagogy and centering this around critical management education which involved such disciplines as critical reasoning and moral reasoning.

> The agenda that critical management education might follow and the critical pedagogy it should employ are most clearly articulated in Grey and Mitev (1995). They argue for the need for critical management academics to contest the instrumental and unquestioned teaching that characterizes 'mainstream', 'technicist' or 'managerialist' management education. Critical academics are defined as those 'concerned to analyse management in terms of its social, moral and political significance and in general terms to challenge management practice rather than seek to sustain it' (Grey and Mitev, 1995: 74).
>
> (Perriton, and Reynolds, 2004 pps 64-64)

Despite this challenge owing to the effect of such influences as previously mentioned, league tables, the financial contribution of the business school to wider institutional coffers and the demands of engagement in research activity have led to the perseverance of mimetic conformity across the sector. (Wilson & Thomas, 2012).

The Contemporary State of Business Pedagogy

This section of the literature review, which covers current practice, does not have a foreknowledge section as this is covered in the previous two sections. What now follows is my analysis of the current rapprochement within the Business academy. At this juncture I will deal with a question central to my narrative which is; Is there a definable and distinct "Business Pedagogy" and by extension, a "Business Academy" or are Business Schools simply aggregations of teaching practices concatenated by a combination of chance, tradition and convenience? The answer to this question is complex. On a topographical level, a review of the Higher Education Institutions in the United Kingdom (UK) would inevitably conclude that most of these institutions with a broad multi-disciplinary offering have embedded in their faculties or departments a Business School, or a Management School. Also, if this topographical survey were to examine the curricula of a random selection of these business schools they would find a remarkable equanimity of structure and content, not least due to the impact of compliance with accreditation bodies such as the Association to Advance Collegiate Schools of Business, European Quality Improvement System, Association of MBAs, Association of Collegiate Business Schools and Programs and International Assembly for Collegiate Business Education that all seek to add a mark professional credibility and intellectual quality to the institution (Zhao and Ferran, 2016). Not only has the mimesis that dominated business school curricula after the post-1992 reform of the binary system persevered it has been further strengthened. So, our topographical survey would have to conclude that there is a definable Academy and that it teaches much the same curriculum across a wide variety of institutions. As most recently averred by Anderson, Thorpe and Coleman (2020).

> The scholarly community engaged in the field of management learning is now far more disparate and widespread than ever before, and the ideas of management learning are more pervasive and recognisable in other fields of management.
>
> (Anderson, Thorpe and Coleman, 2020, p. 30)

This does not mean though, that I accept this as proof of a uniform academy. One of the key issues that undermine a claim for the existence of an academy is the lack of a settled core of a universally accepted definition of what business actually is. There is no unifying theory, nor even a unifying definition. If for example, I was to ask what a department or school of philosophy taught I can reasonably start with a standard dictionary definition and then examine what particular strands of philosophical that were favoured by that school. I have no such certitude with business schools. To illustrate this contrast the definition of Business with that of Sociology from the Oxford English Dictionary.

Business -	A person's regular occupation, profession, or trade. The activity of making, buying, selling or supplying goods or services for money
Sociology-	The scientific study of the nature and development of society and social behaviour

The definition of business is sweeping, it encompasses a wide range of human activity. What is to be studied here, manufacture, procurement, occupational behaviours, professional structures? The list can be continued ad-infinitum. In contrast, the definition of sociology is succinct, it describes precisely the object to be studied and the manner of its study. Attempts to corral what business is into a definable field amenable to a particular mode of study have in the past failed, for example, the attempt by the redoubtable pioneer of British Management education, Lyndall Urwick to steer British Business Schools firmly into the school of scientific management ultimately failed (Brech, Thomson, and Wilson, 2010). It failed as the complexity of engagement of what we define as Business, or even what we define as management has such a multiplicity of forms that a single unified guiding set of ruling principles cannot and will not be useful in most let alone all circumstances. It seems almost correct that fragmentation of practice and engagement leads to a fragmentation of the curriculum. I am not going to attempt to provide a uniform theory. I will (later) claim that a phenomenological approach to the study of business does, by placing individual experience as the fundamental measure of business, provide an opportunity to anchor an analytic process in a defined and definable location. This perspective allows for the consideration of and the reflection on a multiplicity of often different and antithetical influences whilst maintaining coherence. So, for the purposes of orientation, I will accept as my definition of the Business Academy, the disparate collection of subject disciplines that are held loosely under this socially accepted entity, the Business School.

So, these twin factors the lack of a unifying theory and the mimetic nature of how business schools have been organised have led to a plethora of competing pedagogical insights that contribute to the complexity of the Business Academy. These can be a focus on specific techniques as diverse as critical reflection (Gray, 2007) mindfulness (Vu and Burton, 2020), critical discourse (Darics, 2019), or entire philosophical positions such as critical realism (Willis, 2009). Specialists in individual fields often argue for the deepening of the curriculum of the academy in their direction such as human resource management (Parks-Ledue, et al. 2018) and strategic management (Rennie et al. 2018). Added to this are the voices that advocate the importance of learning the principles and behaviours of thematic topics that cross disciplines such as the embedding of honour and integrity (Eury and Trevino, 2019), an understanding of sustainability and its application (Edwards et al, 2020) and the centrality of corporate social responsibility (Deer and Zaretsky, 2017). It is, therefore, unsurprising that there is within these debates and acknowledgement of the need for review

> A clearer understanding of the nature of the environmental and institutional factors which act as barriers to long-term and holistic approaches to curriculum review might help avoid the all too common piecemeal changes noted by Green et al. (2009) and lead to more consistent and sustainable approaches to curriculum review.
>
> (Allen & Simpson, 2019 p 355)

The problem is an epistemological one. And the issue here is where epistemology sits in the context of the pedagogical theories that inform Business Pedagogy is moot (Rippen et al., 2002). Differing ontological perspectives within the discipline; such as the rational versus the humanist, gives rise inevitably to two differing epistemological views. From the positivist tradition predicated on scientific rationalism, epistemology stops at what is measurable (Winch, 2008). Knowledge for the business practitioner is only useful as long as it can be acted upon and deployed to procedural ends (Kavanagh & Drennan 2008). In contrast, the subjectivist views of humanist sociological traditions emphasise the socially and culturally contingent nature of what constitutes knowledge (Mitchell et al., 2010). Here knowledge ceases to be fully procedural and becomes a malleable analytical tool that has the potential to yield a multiplicity of outcomes. Whilst these two perspectives have instances where they meet and epistemological boundaries that merge (Andrews & Higson, 2008) there is nevertheless a dynamic debate within the discipline on epistemological verisimilitude (Mitroff & Mason, 1980; Mitroff *et al.*, 2010; Brady, 2014; Westwood et al., 2014; Bryman & Bell, 2015). This leads to an epistemological stalemate in which no strand can gain dominance. The Business Academy and Business Pedagogy without this epistemological certainty continue to be an aggregate of different epistemological positions and this creates fertile ground for the subsuming of an ever more eclectic mix of epistemological and pedagogical positions. Evidence of contemporary Business Academia's continued willingness to draw on a multiplicity of influences can be seen in current research practices (Bryman & Bell, 2015). An exemplar of this is Sarasvathy (2011) whose work on the origins of entrepreneurship as a process of effectuation draws on anthropology, scientific analysis, empirical research and psychology. It is almost inevitable given the flexibility of the epistemological boundaries of the business academy that however modestly, phenomenology in various forms already has a place.

Phenomenology and Business Pedagogy

The current adoption of phenomenology in the context of business pedagogy is dominated by two strands. The first is in the field of Organisational Studies. Phenomenological approaches have variously been used to explore issues around how individual actors and agents perceive their roles, responsibilities and rights in the context of organisational relationships (Küpers, 2007, Cole et al., 2015; Gill, 2014, 2015 Hughes et al., 2018) and even as a mentoring technique in an organisational context (Gibson, 2004). Patricia Sanders' paper, Phenomenology: a new way of viewing organisational research (1987) is a succinct and clear exposition of some of the key processes of phenomenological research in the context of organisational studies which argued that, as the title suggested that phenomenological enquiry has the potential to deliver new insights into the nature of organisational life, but she does conclude with a warning.

> Exploring the phenomenon of human consciousness is not a simple task…One begins by learning phenomenology in a step-by-set disciplined fashion thorough reading, observation, discussion and reflection. Then one does phenomenology. It is only after doing phenomenology that one begins to understand the meaning of intentionality, intersubjectivity, eidetic reduction and how to practice epoche.
>
> (Sanders, 1987 p. 359)

So it is in the field or organisational studies that the techniques of phenomenology are mostly employed Phenomenology and its application is a difficult process and does require a sound knowledge of some of the core concepts that inform this area of methodological thinking. Nevertheless, attempts to adopt and use phenomenological techniques do occur (albeit infrequently) in the academic literature (Conklin, 2013; Gill, 2014; Antoniadou, 2018). Also, there is evidence of the use of phenomenological techniques in other aspects of research into business practice such as the structure of markets (Mancuso & Tonelli 2014) and aspects of some forms of entrepreneurship (Ainley, 2014, Keupers, 2016). In a paper entitled; A university-industry collaborative response to the growing global demand for student talent: Using interpretive phenomenology to discover life-world knowledge (Vauterin et al. 2013) explores the global marketplace for higher education in business and the critical epistemological boundary and knowledge transfer between academia and commerce. The authors of this paper succinctly argue that the exploration of the exchange of meaning and value in the life-world between actors in these spheres of influence offers the opportunity to de-contextualise socially acquired knowledge and reveal the essential nature of this epistemological exchange. This gives clear evidence that the application of interpretive phenomenology is gaining some academic traction in the discipline of Business.

The second is in the process of the execution of research within the field of business in general. As an adjunct to the reflexive research techniques, it has, with its intensely personal focus something to offer in deepening the consideration of such issues as positionality (Schipper, 1999, Segal, 2010). Furthermore, almost every compendium for students and researchers in the field of Business and Management makes mention of the influence and potential of Phenomenology (Harlos et al., 2003, Ellery Brown et al., 2008).

However, the application of phenomenological theories and research practices in the field of research into Business Pedagogy is less common, although there are some notable exceptions, particularly in recent literature. The phenomenological aspects of the use of computer-based business simulations as a pedagogical technique are explored by De Klerk (2015), whilst De Vita & Case (2014) use phenomenological theory to deconstruct and analyse the "failure" of managerialist culture in UK business schools. These examples of how phenomenology can be applied in the context of business pedagogy have a common purpose; to expand epistemological insight and deliver new perspectives into the perception by individual participants of the meaning, purpose and effectiveness of teaching as suggested in the context of research into Human Resource Development by Gibson and Haynes (2003). It is the centrality of where the epistemological boundaries lie which is the core justification of adopting a phenomenological approach (Bomboola, 2012).

It is in this discursive space that the phenomenological perspective offers the possibility of examining where these boundaries from both these perspectives impact on individual perception of worth, value and meaning within the Business context. Patricia Sanders (1982) succinctly summarised its core perspective,

> In its applied form, phenomenology can be described as a qualitative technique that seeks to make explicit the implicit structure and meaning of human experience.
>
> (Sanders, 1982 p. 353)

It is the placing of the individual at the centre of epistemological analysis rather than the procedural and processional influences that are extant within Business and its relationship to society that is one of the key methodological ambitions of this research. Key to this ambition is Gadamer's iteration of phenomenological thought and its insight into the nature of epistemology which will be discussed at length in the following chapter.

The adoption of phenomenological methodologies does mean that there a particular personal intensity to the nature of the research process. Kate Caelli in her succinct analysis of the application of the methodology in health and medical disciplines identifies the core ethical problem and offers an ameliorative solution.

> One may understand a theory but still not anticipate the full depth, breadth, and scope of the implications of that theory... Consequently, more description of actual, real-life ethical dilemmas faced by researchers can only help the situation, because it would seem that the circumstances that arose in the study under discussion might be yet another outcome of the reticence that surrounds the process of doing phenomenological research.
>
> (Caelli, 2001 p. 280)

This admonition to constantly review and reflect on not only your own experience but the experiences and accounts of others is particularly useful when considering, as I am, utilising a hermeneutical circle as the core method. Acting as the instigator and facilitator of a hermeneutical circle demands that the researches engages in a continual act of conscious reflection on the changes that may be affected by the process on the research participants and the researcher themselves (Dowling, 2004; Debasy *et al.*, 2008). This has prescriptive implications for the design of the methods to be used within a hermeneutical dialogue. Embedded in the discursive procedures must be a feedback mechanism in which a multiplicity of the participants is given the opportunity to check on the accuracy of interpretation and where necessary provide further elucidation and exposition to clarify meaning (Fleming et al., 2003, Bradbury-Jones et al., 2010). Within the discipline of business, this acknowledgement of the interpretive process is also clear. In his article, All Research is Interpretive; Evett Gummesson (2003) in discussing the role of the hermeneutic in the context of Business research makes the following observation.

> The hermeneutic circle states that in a research project we move from pre-understanding to understanding, where understanding from phase 1 furnishes the pre-understanding for phase 2, and so forth. There is thus an oscillation between what we knew and what we have learnt.
>
> (Gummesson, 2003 p. 484)

Summary

This literary history has used a phenomenological approach structured around my perception of the nature of Business Schools and their contribution to society and the practice of management in doing so I have in part acknowledged the contingency of my fore-knowledge or prejudice of the Business Academy. The recognition by successive post-war governments in the UK that the economy needed better-educated managers had two consequences. The adoption of an American model of Business Education and a mimetic effect that caused a wide-ranging similarity in the curricula offered by UK Business Schools. These curricula have been dominated by two main strands of epistemological thought, the positivist-rational and the humanist. Neither has gained ascendancy and both are continuing to be developed within the broad umbrella of business pedagogy in an ever more fragmented manner. Within this expansion of techniques, there has been some development of phenomenology as a research practice, primarily in the field of organisational studies. It is still only an adjunct to a wide range of qualitative techniques, and its application in the field of research into the pedagogy is still relatively rare owing to issues in normative acceptability in the wider business community and the difficulties associated with its implementation. But there is still considerable potential for the application of phenomenology, into an examination of the epistemological boundaries within the discipline which is the core concern of this research. Why this should be a hermeneutically based version of phenomenology is discussed in the next chapter.

Chapter 3

Existential Hermeneutic Phenomenology

Philosophical Grounding

The choice of a methodology by any researcher is primarily determined by four factors, the ontological field within which the researchers grounds their epistemological understanding, the personal epistemology, or the reach of their knowledge that derives from this, the field of study in which the object of study is located and finally their access to data directly or indirectly related to their object and field of study.

It would, for example, not be appropriate for a researcher to choose a qualitative method to examine a given phenomenon if their base ontology was grounded in a mechanistic understanding of the nature of the world, conversely, a personal ontology based on the primacy of contingent and negotiated meaning would fundamentally undermine the validity of a purely quantitative approach. Personal epistemology or the reach of the understanding of the individual also either determines or points to certain methodological approaches. Again, here it would be inappropriate for a researcher who did not fully understand the statistical techniques of, for example, regression analysis to use this as part of their research. The Field of Study also determines the environmental appropriateness of some techniques and this can be illustrated by considering the clear demarcation here between the physical sciences that can use laboratory techniques and the social sciences that cannot (Winch, 2008). Finally, the context and access to data or the physical limits of what can be obtained for the study is a critical shaper of the methodological approach. If, for example, the researcher cannot access primary data they become dependent upon the use and interpretation of secondary data. Furthermore, all these elements cannot be considered in isolation as they are bound in a cyclical relationship in which development in any one of these areas has a commensurate impact on the others.

This can be shown when considering researching the nature of the epistemological overlap between Universities, Employers and Students.

My ontological grounding is my belief that all business is fundamentally based on a network of transactional relationships (Anderson, 1995; Humphrey & Hugh-Jones, 1992; Goldkuhl, 1998), in which value or the perception of value is exchanged. Value in this context is contingent and dependent upon the perception of the actors in the transaction. An extreme example of this is a collector's market in which artefacts which are apparently of little or no value acquire a premium value within the parameters of that market. Value is, therefore, contingent, negotiated and dependent on context. This ontological base of contingency determines the way the researcher within higher education examines the pedagogy that supports the development of business graduates. Furthermore, the researcher is, by virtue of their externality to the actual process of business, epistemologically bounded by an observational rather than a participatory viewpoint. Accordingly, the field of study is wide as a multiplicity of the narratives of business processes can be accommodated into a single study. These narratives become an account of a post facto lived experience that can be used to either support or challenge the ontic notion of the transactional basis of business processes thus completing the cycle. This cyclical relationship and the factors themselves indicate that a methodological approach that can structure a multiplicity of material that is varied in form and nature is appropriate. One such of these is hermeneutic interpretation a philosophical process that seeks to uncover the true essence of social interaction through the interpretation of textual dialogue and other communicative artefacts. Here, even where the Ontological base and the field of study remain constant, it is the immersion of the practitioner in the process of Business itself that indicates that this may be an appropriate choice of methodology. This also applies where an academic has been a practitioner as I have. My life-word is still informed and rooted in the experience of business and management.

The literature review uncovers a core concern regarding the relevance and applicability of using a phenomenological approach in the context of business research in general and as a philosophical grounding for an examination of the epistemological efficacy of the Business Academy. The depth and the fundamental challenge of phenomenology as philosophy lie at an ontological level, as Heidegger observed in Being and Time.

> Ontology and phenomenology are not two distinct philosophical disciplines among others. These terms characterise philosophy itself with regard to its object and its way of treating its object. Philosophy is universal phenomenological ontology, and takes its departure from the hermeneutic of Dasein, which as an analytic of existence, has made fast the guiding-line for all philosophical inquiry at the point where it arises to where it returns.
>
> (Heidegger, 1962, p. 62)

This is directly opposite to the relationship between ontology and philosophy in positivism and the range of humanist philosophy applied to much mainstream business research. The ontological underpinning of both pre-supposes an underlying reality which is to a greater or lesser extent the fundamental substrate of reality. Accordingly, this means that there are real absolutes even if these may be insensible or incomprehensible to us as observers. This is an important distinction as the mainstream of western thought is predicated on this notion of an underlying fundamental reality; to aver as does phenomenology, that this is a misunderstanding of the manner in which the world becomes comprehensible to us, directly challenges the core idea of what is valid as knowledge. In doing do it is an epistemological challenge to the validity of current knowledge. The Business Academy as a relatively recent addition to the pantheon of higher education disciplines (Bennis & O'Toole, 2005) and it is sensitive to accusations of invalidity and superficiality despite its success in establishing itself as a popular choice for aspiring undergraduates (Oblinger & Verville, 1998). A brief review of its philosophical antecedents demonstrates how this bifurcation of western philosophical thought leads to a divergence that gives rise to a bias of attitude. On one side the positivist, rational and empirical schools of philosophy have settled the ontological question by acknowledging the existence of absolute forms (Cupchik, 2001). On the other, we have the challenge of the "continental" school of philosophy that encompasses constructivism, hermeneutics, existentialism and phenomenology whose origins can be traced to the works of Freidrich Nietzsche and Soren Kierkegaard (Warnock, 1970). Phenomenology in particular rejects "Cartesian Dualism" by focussing on the apprehension of reality as a process that can only be mediated by human agency and for which the possible existence of an alternate world of supra-human forms and rules is rendered irrelevant through its incomprehensibility. The key dispute lies in the movement of perception towards what is real, if a world of idealised forms does exist then movement towards the apprehension of these through the development and perfection of epistemology is an agreed endpoint in which disputation over competing views can be resolved by being in possession of the most valid facts. For example, in a positivist view of how an organisations performance should or could be analysed on any criteria, an analytical narrative will gain credibility through triangulating with the greatest amount of verifiable data possible. This granularity of facts, figures and views moves us closer to a truth (Dubé & Paré, 2003). In contrast a phenomenological approach is constantly moving away from an idealised form of reality, not just because it rejects the metaphysical possibility of such an idealised state, but also because an individual's reality at any given moment is subject to discourse and the exchange of meaning with other human beings. This means that we are constantly pulled away from a set reality by the necessity to accommodate, understand and absorb the understanding of the other. This too can be conducted through the medium of data, facts and figures but the critical difference is that we are moved away from the constant and the sure and not driven towards it. A phenomenological approach that acknowledges the contingency of reality presents difficulty in the realm of business communication. Case studies are a key tool of the business academy and most of these are analysed in a positivist manner (Piekkari, Welch & Paavilainen, 2009). In analysing a case study in a positivist manner, validity is predicated on a linear understanding which moves a narrative from the analysis and evaluation of a set of circumstances through to a conclusion which makes the observed actions and phenomena understandable, here we are moving towards an idealised reality which is comprehensible to the reader. A phenomenological approach has difficulty with this linearity, particularly when considering the contingency of meaning.

> The outcome of using a hermeneutic phenomenological approach is a piece of writing that explicates the meaning of human phenomena and helps to understand the lived structures of meaning.
>
> (Erich, 2005, p. 6)

By implication "lived structures" are transient, subject to variable interpretation and move away from certainty and a definable truth. The promise of the positivist approach is that organisations and individuals can learn from the analytical deconstruction of events in order to either replicate success or to avoid failure, but if we acknowledge through the use of phenomenology the unique and moveable historicity of any given set of events the value and replicability of action that is informed by these are diminished. A phenomenological approach is non-procedural and is based on an apprehension of the life-world perceptions of a participant(s) in any given event. Understanding of what the term "life-world" in the phenomenological sense is critical here.

> The all-embracing world horizon is constituted by a fundamentally *anonymous* intentionality – i.e., not achieved by anyone by name. Using a concept consciously formulated in contrast to a concept of a world of what can be made objective by science. Husserl calls this phenomenological concept of the world "life-world – i.e., the world in which we are immersed in the natural attitude that never becomes an object as such for us, but that represents the pre-given basis of all experience. This world horizon is a presupposition of all science as well and is, therefore, more fundamental. As a horizon phenomenon "world is essentially related to subjectivity, and this relation means also that it "exists in

> transiency". The life-world exists in a constant movement of relative validity. The concept of the life-world is the antithesis of all objectivism. It is essentially historical concept, which does not refer to a universe of being, to an "existent world." In fact, not even the infinite idea of true world can be meaningfully created out of the infinite progress of the infinite progress of human historical worlds in historical experience.
>
> (Gadamer, 1989, p. 248)

The life-world focusses on the immediacy of an individual's experience and applied to a research context the core of the process must be an attempt to understand how this immediacy of experience acts upon and is changed by the bounded circumstances under investigation. To further illustrate how radical a departure this is from the mainstream process of research in the academy consider the following scenario. A researcher approaches an organisation in order to examine a particular circumstance where the organisation has demonstrated a particular commercial acuity. Using traditional methods of enquiry, they may use either an inductive or deductive approach seeking to either form some post -priori theory or perhaps test a hypothesis derived from an a-priori theory. In both cases, the event or process under examination will be bounded by the theoretical structure defined by the theoretical construct. In contrast, a phenomenological approach that gives immediacy to the life-world of actors in this event cannot be bound by any given theory either anti or post priori. This does not mean that theory has no place in a phenomenological analysis as theoretical understanding is a central part of the pre-existing prejudice of any individual's life-world. It does mean that unless there is an almost impossible unanimity of individual prejudice amongst the actors relevant to the matter-at-hand the researcher will have to consciously acknowledge the individualised contingency of theory. The focus of the life-world lies with the individual actor and whilst we can reach an understanding of why this actor may have taken this action, or said this thing through a process of discursive exchange that examines the event we have to acknowledge that this understanding only applies to this individual at this time and in this circumstance. The life-world experience of this individual at this time cannot be identically replicated which does lead to question as to what utility this is for the reader wishing to acquire transferable knowledge. The aim of a hermeneutic phenomenological analysis is to uncover the "meaning of human phenomena and understanding of the lived structures of meaning" (Ehrich, 2005, p3), this affords the reader of the work access to horizons of meaning and experience that can inform their own reflective consideration of similar phenomena. In doing so this crosses the barrier of subjectivity into inter-subjectivity and fuses the life-world horizons of respondent and reader.

Using Phenomenological Hermeneutics

The adoption of a phenomenological methodology does mean that there a particular personal intensity to the nature of the research process. Kate Caelli in her succinct analysis of the application of the methodology in health and medical disciplines identifies the core ethical problem and offers an ameliorative solution.

> One may understand a theory but still not anticipate the full depth, breadth, and scope of the implications of that theory… Consequently, more description of actual, real-life ethical dilemmas faced by researchers can only help the situation, because it would seem that the circumstances that arose in the study under discussion might be yet another outcome of the reticence that surrounds the process of doing phenomenological research.
>
> (Caelli, 2001 p. 280)

This admonition to constantly review and reflect on not only your own experience but the experiences and accounts of others is particularly useful when considering, as I am, utilising a hermeneutical circle as the core method. Acting as the instigator and facilitator of a hermeneutical circle demands that the researcher engages in a continual act of conscious reflection on the changes that may be affected by the process on the research participants and the researcher themselves (Dowling, 2004; Debasy *et al.*, 2008). This has proscriptive implications for the design of the methods to be used within a hermeneutical dialogue. Embedded in the discursive procedures must be a feedback mechanism in which a multiplicity of the participants is given the opportunity to check on the accuracy of interpretation and where necessary provide further elucidation and exposition to clarify meaning (Fleming et al., 2003, Bradbury-Jones et al., 2010). Within the discipline of Business, this acknowledgement of the interpretive process is also clear. In his article, *All Research is Interpretive*; Evett Gummesson (2003) in discussing the role of the hermeneutic in the context of Business research makes the following observation.

> The hermeneutic circle states that in a research project we move from pre-understanding to understanding, where understanding from phase 1 furnishes the pre-understanding for phase 2, and so forth. There is thus an oscillation between what we knew and what we have learnt.
>
> (Gummesson, 2003 p. 484)

The key advantage of this hermeneutic approach is that it can un-mask complexity. If we acknowledge that the life-world of the individual has primacy in research then this is the most complex unit of analysis. Each individual makes sense of the world through fragmentary inputs and experiences that cannot encompass the totality of all phenomenological potential; put simply we cannot experience all things at all times. These phenomena are processed by the individual and relayed back to the external world in a similarly fragmented manner; again, we cannot say and do all things at all times. This means that we can through our research into this individual's experience of a given phenomenon gain some sense of how they understood and acted upon complex sequences of events or complex contextual environments. Complexity has been processed and made sense of by the respondent in the research and from this, we have meaning that has relevance which can be understood by the reader of the research. Accordingly, even the most challenging and complex scenarios are reduced to individual meaning. Furthermore, if we acknowledge the primacy of the life-world as the base unit of our analysis we can include in our research a wide range of respondents with differing pre-understandings of a phenomenon. We do not need to presuppose that common understanding will be a pre-requisite for the exchange of meaning. The key consideration is how that respondent absorbed and made sense of the experiences of the phenomenon into their life-world. Consider the core of this research; I do not need to ensure that employer stakeholders are using the same words in the same manner or with the same meaning as the academic respondents or the student respondents, what I am seeking to uncover is the impact of the business school environment and process on the epistemological horizons of each respondent. I am seeking a coming-together of life world horizons. In this way, the focus on the individual avoids the in-authenticity of imposing an artificial theoretical construct. The outcome of the research is the product of the shared meaning of the participants, in other words, a fusion of horizons.

As I have covered in the literature review the prime disadvantage of this approach is that it is not part of the normative language of business, nor is it part of the normative language of the wider culture.

> Sanders (1982) noted that phenomenological studies are infrequent in organizational research and dominating the field is "[t]he scientific/normative research paradigm"
>
> (Ehrich, 2005, p. 7)

The essence of Business as we currently understand it is an outcome focussed activity. This also applies to non-commercial management as success in outcomes is driven mostly by metric measurements and budgets. This embeds in stakeholders in the processes of management, commerce and organisational processes a natural suspicion of views with a theoretical bias unless those theoretical ideas can contribute directly to the "bottom line". Philosophy where it is relevant applies to the periphery of business activity in the consideration of business ethics (Moriarty, 2005, Koslowski, 2010, Miles & Munilla, 1993) or in its use as an underpinning for research methods (Bam, 1992, Baskerville

& Myers, 2004). The contention that a phenomenological approach may have utility in understanding the process of business pedagogy lies outside of this normative understanding and it is probably inevitable that it will be treated with suspicion as by its very nature its outcomes are contingent on the moment and indeterminate in effect. This is antithetical to what business wants and by extension what it wants of those who purport to educate on its behalf. As Pfeffer and Fong point out in their analysis of the early expectations of Business Schools in the United States of America (USA).

> The Gordon and Howell report and funding from the Ford Foundation and the Carnegie Council (Pierson, 1959) started business schools on their continuing trajectory to achieve academic respectability and legitimacy on their campuses by becoming social science departments, or perhaps, applied social science departments. In the process of achieving academic legitimacy, business schools took "on the traditions and ways of mainstream academia" (Crainer & Dearlove, 1999: 40). Quantitative, statistical analyses gained prominence, as did the study of the science of decision making. In both their teaching and research activities, business schools "enthusiastically seized on and applied a scientific paradigm that applies criteria of precision, control, and testable models" (Bailey & Ford, 1996: 8).
>
> (Pfeffer & Fong, 2002 p. 1)

Of more contemporary currency in the specific context of Business schools in the UK, a report commissioned by the Advanced Institute of Management had this warning for Business Schools.

> The future of UK business schools is under threat from a number of directions. Their purpose is questioned – they are accused of focusing on theoretical research at the expense of improving management practice and of turning out MBA graduates unsuited to the demands of modern-day management.
>
> (Ivory et el, 2006 p.4)

In a time when the success of Business and the reaction of business to a challenging environment is seen as critical to national survival (Jensen & Smith, 2016) it is perhaps foolhardy to challenge this normative view of Business. There may be a hostile reception to the underlying idea that theoretical constructs and practical skills designed to optimise success and produce a profit, improve efficiency and deliver effectiveness are simply peripheral to the actual experience of business and its relevance. A hermeneutic phenomenology can be viewed as pre-theory or perhaps under-theory. By this I mean that the life-world of the individual may learn, absorb and use theory to guide action and form an opinion; the manifestation of this is not-theory, it is mediated by individual interpretation. Whilst many may agree to a common glossary of understanding that appears to validate or give rise to a demonstrable agreement on terms, this is still contingent on intersubjective agreement and this must arise in first instance from the individual. This is an extension of the fundamental paradox of the phenomenological view of ontology. We cannot know exactly how any individual thinks upon theory as part of the perceptual process of their life-world we can only know what they have understood of the theory post subjectivity in the inter/subjective arena. The life-world pre-exists these intersubjective agreements and gives rise to the legitimate question, so what? If Business as practice appears to be focussed on outcome and results, then surely it will only be interested or find relevant that which has been mediated and agreed in the realm of the intersubjective. This is a legitimate challenge as a phenomenologically guided inquiry has little to call upon in terms of validity of outcome from previous usage of phenomenology in the context of the business academy. The brutal consequence may be that the results of this research into the pedagogy of business may be neither comprehensible or relevant to the intended audience or other stakeholders. This is an issue of epistemology and it is necessary to mitigate this danger.

Conversely, there are advantages to using interpretive phenomenology as a research grounding in the epistemological dimension. The research project was founded on the aim to examine the epistemological overlap between three key stakeholders in the Business Academy. As epistemology or the extent of an individual's knowledge is the core of the research then it is entirely appropriate to base the investigation on a methodology that gives primacy to the centrality of an individual's perceptions and apprehension of their life-world. The use of interpretive phenomenological approaches in the context of business research into whatever area is limited (as has been demonstrated in the literature review) but they are present and they are relevant. Returning to the insights of Patricia Sanders in 1982 she wrote, "There is a new star on the research horizon. It is Phenomenology" (Sanders, 1982, p.353). In her seminal paper on the potential of Phenomenology as a research approach, Sanders summarised the outcome of this approach and contrasted it with a normative paradigm. In the normative paradigm, research outcomes produce generalisable results that can be used and expressed and compared with similar analyses of data. The outcomes become an addition to the normative understanding of what is valid and what can be replicated in practice. In contrast, a phenomenological outcome only offers generalisable outcomes on the specific group under investigation, its datum only forms the basis for further study (ibid. p.358). Here I return to my idea of this research being pre-theory or under-theory; the generalisable outcome of Hermeneutic study is that if we examine the pre-understanding of what is valid through the facility of discursive exchange we can begin to approach the key determinates of how the subjectivity of the life-world moves into intersubjectivity of our chosen area of study – namely the pedagogic efficacy of Business School education. To determine this there must be some conduit that could encourage the research respondents to be discursive and so the method begins to suggest itself. The methodology needs to be grounded in the realm of how inter-subjectivity and language as the facilitator of understanding between the actors in any given matter-at-hand.

Gadamer's Hermeneutics

Gadamer's work and his development of the principles of phenomenology give primacy to the role of language as the carrier and transmitter of meaning. Furthermore, his hermeneutical philosophy developed in turn from Heidegger's work (and of whom he was a pupil) indicates how a workable process of phenomenological enquiry can be developed through the establishment of hermeneutical circles that can fuse the epistemological horizons of respondents in the circle. I must first start with some key ideas that will contextualise this research process and that will aid understanding. No exposition of Gadamer's work can neglect that of Heidegger and in particular Heidegger's notion of Dasein or in-being. Dasein which Heidegger introduced in his "Being and Time" lies at the centre of Interpretive Phenomenology. In her book on Existentialism (1970) Mary Warnock gives a succinct idea of what Heidegger meant by Dasein.

> Heidegger's word for human being is Dasein, literally "Being There". He wishes to emphasize, by the use of this expression, the fact that one cannot consider a human being except as being in the midst of a world an existent thing stuck there, so to speak, in the middle of other things…In Being and Time it is argued that we must approach it (philosophy) through the consideration of the nature of man, who stands in peculiar relation to Being as a whole because he and he alone of all beings can raise questions about Being.
>
> (Warnock, 1970 pp. 50-52)

Gadamer further develops Heidegger's Dasein in his own work and links this specifically with hermeneutics.

> Heidegger temporal analytics of Dasein has, I think shown convincingly that understanding is not just one of the various possible behaviour of the subject but the mode of being of Dasein itself. It is in this sense that the hermeneutics has been used here. It denotes the basic being-in-motion of Dasein that constitutes its finitude and historicity, and hence embraces the whole of its experience of the world.
>
> (Gadamer, 1989 p. 8)

Here Gadamer explicitly links Heidegger's Dasein to hermeneutical exchange as the prime repository and carrier of meaning, he further develops this primacy. In her book outlining the philosophical context of Gadamer's work, Georgia Warnke explains this.

> Hermeneutics as Gadamer conceives of it, then, is no longer to be seen as a discourse on methods of "objective" understanding as it was for the hermeneutic tradition of Schleiermacher and Dilthey. It no longer seeks to formulate a set of interpretive rules; rather, in referring to his analysis as "philosophical hermeneutics," Gadamer turns to an account of the conditions of the possibility of understanding in general...Methodological approaches to both natural and human phenomena are rooted in history: they accept certain historical assumptions as to both what is to be studied and how it is to be approached. Understanding is therefore rooted in prejudice and the way in which we understand is thoroughly conditioned by the past or by what Gadamer calls effective history. This influence of the past obtains in our aesthetic understanding, in our social and Psychological understanding and in all forms of scientific understanding.
>
> (Warnke, 1987, p. 3)

The principle carrier of meaning in the hermeneutical tradition other than an aesthetical appreciation of art is the medium of language and here Gadamer emphasises the importance of how epistemological "horizons" are predetermined by our prejudice or pre-judgements.

> The all-embracing world horizon is constituted by fundamentally anonymous intentionality – i.e. not achieved by anyone by name...Husserl calls this phenomenological concept of the world "life-world" i.e. the world in which we are immersed in the natural attitude that never becomes an object as such for us, but that represents the pre-given basis of all experience.
>
> (Gadamer 1989, p. 247)

Gadamer's contention that knowledge is contingent on prejudice and prejudgement and can only be validated through a continual process of hermeneutical interpretation, through art, aesthetics and language leads to the conclusion that Dasein is bound inevitably in a hermeneutical circle of mediated meaning which shifts and changes for each Dasein. This suggests a method based on the primacy of text as a facilitator for the reflective understanding applied by Dasein to the other. A human being reading any text uses foreknowledge to understand at a basic level the meaning of the words. But it is clear her that even at an early age in the development of human thought and language the simple literal meaning of the words is not enough. Folk tales, fairy stories, nursery rhymes also carry a wealth of emotional aesthetics that underpin the literal meaning of the words; emotions that emphasise the lessons of danger, trust, responsibility and human affection and solidarity. Each human being developing in their cultural context absorbs and carries this meaning forward into their own prejudice, used here in the Gadamerian sense as pre-judgement. The final acquisition of the ability to independently read a given text is a major developmental milestone acknowledged by early years pedagogical academics (Chapman, & Tunmer 1997, Worthy & Broaddus, 2001). At this point we can say Dasein is free and is able to with greater rapidity develop a unique prejudice. And yet we still mediate through shared speech and text a life-world that is infinitely complex and able to deliver infinite meaning. If therefore I can use a shared text to extract the underlying apprehension by Dasein of the life-world of Business Pedagogy then this pre-theoretical, raw cognition has the potential to offer unique insights into epistemological reach shorn of the post-facto theoretical assumptions that we make about the efficacy of our teaching. As Gadamer points out.

> A person who is trying to understand a text is always projecting. He projects a meaning for the text as a whole as soon as some initial meaning emerges in the text. Again, the initial meaning emerges only because he is reading the text with particular expectations in regard to a certain meaning. Working out this fore-projection, which is constantly revised

> in terms of what emerges as he penetrates into the meaning, is understanding what is there.
>
> (Gadamer, 1989, p. 280)

Gadamer avers that there is an "anticipation of completeness" which is a pre-requisite for the reader of a text. By this, he means that there is a presupposition on the part of the reader that any text can be rendered comprehensible. A shared document can, therefore, embody a hermeneutical circle of "good-will" especially if there is embedded in the reading a pre-judgment that one of the principle objectives of the text is a unity of understanding. Here I return to the idea of pre-theory as my concept of this now becomes clearer. The focus of Gadamer on the hermeneutical interpretation of Text as a carrier of meaning and his clarity on the role of Dasein's prejudice and fore-projection makes every reading of any given text explicitly unique and subject to an infinite variety of interpretation. I can uncover this uniqueness through a research process that carefully observes how pre-understanding is mediated and changed by the innate desire of the reader (Dasein) to render a text sensible and to accommodate the horizons of the other. In this way, the epistemological boundaries and accommodations of disparate research respondents can be examined, not in the out-coming text but in the process of deconstructing how this text has been rendered meaningful to the life-world of each respondent. This is pre-theory, there is no set structure or framework to be constructed or hypothesis to be tested. It is the examination of the process of understanding that reveals how Dasein moves towards shared meaning and a fusion of horizons. As expounded by Todres and Galvin (2008) shared meaning is an inescapable element of Dasein's in-being in the world. Adopting a phenomenologically based attitude to research validity makes this immersion in intersubjectivity inescapable.

> Within an aesthetically informed, phenomenologically based research into others' experiences, we do not believe that we have to stick to the same words as an informant in order to illuminate an experience like homelessness or pain. Yes, we attend very closely to the experiential world that the infor-

> mant's word-expressions open up, the horizons and lively evocative happenings that the words signify. But we also stand before such a world as an instance of something that has shareable dimensions within a meaningful world-with-others. To understand is then to understand both something of this unique individual and the shared intersubjective horizons within which any unique experience occurs.
>
> (Todres and Galvin, 2008 pps 571-572)

Here then is the unique contribution of this methodology to our understanding of the epistemological fit of pedagogic practice. I am explicitly acknowledging the primacy of the individual rather than the procedural. In this, I mean that I am not attempting to extract or impose or assume a theoretical structure that has the potential to point towards a procedural intervention. Rather, I am uncovering the process by which such theory is subsumed. In this way, I can examine the moment at which pre-judgement is altered to accommodate a new and mediated prejudicial awareness of the thing-at-hand, in this instance the epistemological boundaries of business pedagogy. This gives primacy to the perception of Dasein and the evolving Life-World. In this, I am attempting to circumvent normative terms and conventions in order to deliver new insights. It is the un-masking of complexity and the rejection of the arbitrary nature of theoretical constructs that I am challenging. The methodology becomes how Dasein perceives the evolving life-world post intersubjective discourse, but prior to the fusion of horizons. The carrier of this mediated fusion of horizons is speech and text. For replicability and comprehension, I must capture this in the form of Text so that there is an opportunity for reflection on and absorption of the perception of the other. The hermeneutical circle becomes a process of discussion, reflection, fusion and re-visitation so that the fusion of horizons becomes an arena in which Dasein and its life-world evolves and throws itself into the future.

Existential Hermeneutic Phenomenology

To distinguish the particular form of the methodology I am using from other forms of phenomenological techniques I am calling this, Existential Hermeneutic Phenomenology (EHP). Existential as it is derived from an acknowledgement of the primacy of individual experience and the contingency of that experience. It is Hermeneutic as it draws on the work and insights of Georg Gadamer and in particular his understanding of how text and language are critical to the evolution of Dasein's epistemological reach and phenomenological as it is a subset of interpretive or interpretative phenomenological approaches. What follows is a description of how Gadamer was operationalised in the method.

Chapter 4

Methods and Implementation

From Methodology to Method

I have established in my history of the Business School that a Phenomenological approach is not commonly used as a research methodology in any area of the study of the Business Academy. I also contend from my exposition of the use of hermeneutical circles that the methodology I propose to use, has the potential to uncover new understanding through unmasking complexity and exposing the pre-theory used by individuals (Dasein) to merge horizons of understanding and meaning. The methodology has developed by reflection and expansion of understanding the philology of hermeneutical phenomenology. Yet my original intention to examine the efficacy and perception of the Business Academy's pedagogical technique remains unchanged. I will now outline in detail the implementation of the methodology and detail how the hermeneutical circles operated as a qualitative technique. I use this term qualitative in an advisory manner to more easily communicate the nature of the process of discursive research that I am using.

Methodological relevance

In reflecting upon whether existential hermeneutic phenomenology is an appropriate methodology for a research project the key consideration is to reflect on whether the object of study is amenable to this form of enquiry. The proposed enquiry is into the nature of the role and contribution of Business pedagogy as manifest in Higher Education in the UK. This is one small part of a wider and ongoing societal debate into how Universities contribute to or shape the evolving structure of the economy. This relationship is one that is under constant scrutiny (Bercovitz & Feldman, 2006; Harkavy, 2006; Whitley, 2008). In the context of business and commerce, the perception of the contribution of the Higher Education sector to the development of economic activity is one in which there are polarised opinions from those who consider the influence of universities to be benign (Henderson *et al.*, 1998; Forida, 1999; Stromquist & Monkman, 2014) to those who doubt their efficacy (Bennis & O'Toole 2005; Lilley *et al.*, 2014). The central question from both ends of this debate is whether or not Universities and the Higher Education Sector are producing graduates with skills, attitudes and understanding which are appropriate for the workplace. Whilst this can be viewed from a multiplicity of perspectives this is a critical concern for Business Schools whose main purpose is to produce graduates with vocational skills that are needed by employers.

This is not a simple relationship as the Business academy has many stakeholders ranging from the particular – students to the general – taxpayers. A study that attempts to examine the roots of the efficacy of business pedagogy from all stakeholders is patently complex and such wide-ranging research would be inappropriate when testing a new method in this context. How then should I limit this enquiry I order to render the process manageable and yet still relevant in outcome and insight? Reflecting on the multiplicity of stakeholders; not all have an equal stake in the efficacy of business pedagogy. Some stakeholders have a direct and tangible concern regarding the success or otherwise of business education whilst others will only feel an indirect effect it the process is either successful or leads to disappointing results. An example of a stakeholder with a direct link is an employer dependent on the quality of graduate cohorts for succession planning, expansion and sometimes the development of new opportunities. Employers that are dependent in this manner have a clear stake in the efficacy of business pedagogy and its outcomes, A Business School that either by choice or accident wilfully ignores the needs of such employers' risks rendering its outcomes irrelevant and the value of its degrees is significantly undermined. The needs of the UK economy for good quality business graduates is increasing rather than diminishing (Minocha, Hristov & Reynolds, 2017). A stakeholder with an indirect relationship with the effectiveness of business pedagogy and its onward contribution to the success of Business and the economy would not necessarily have the same detailed interest in such matters as the content of the curricula or whether or not graduates of business schools have the skills specific to the emerging needs of the economy. So if the scope of the research project is to be bounded for the purposes of practicality then it is prudent to choose stakeholders with a direct granular interest in Business School pedagogy.

Returning to the methodological justification for the research this identification of stakeholders with a direct relationship with the academy a hermeneutic circle uncovers the process of fusion and uncovers the way Dasein changes its life-world. If the process of research is going to demonstrate clearly these aims, then it would be useful if there was a measurable difference in the prejudicial pre-judgment amongst the research participants. Therefore, stakeholders with direct interests in the object of study (business pedagogy) and different perceptions of its relevance and goals would be useful as the starting points of perception would more clearly illustrate how the discursive process enabled by the hermeneutic circle has the potential to fuse epistemological horizons. Fortunately, there are three key stakeholder groups that do have an unequivocal interest in Business Pedagogy: employers as already shown above, students whose future employability rests significantly on the relevance of the academy's curricula and business school academics whose professional engagement and contribution is central to pedagogical effectiveness. By examining the relationship of these three key stakeholder groups with differing perspectives this places boundaries on the process of research but which nevertheless has the degree of difference that is seen in other qualitative research methods such as Action Research (Brydon-Miller et al., 2003). It is necessary however to acknowledge that the critical reason that I have chosen these three groups is a personal one. I have variously been a student of the business school an employer of business school graduates and I currently work as an academic within a business school. This gives me a crucial insight into the nature of the prejudices of the stakeholder groups I am studying and this has a major advantage in that I can understand to a greater or lesser extent the languages, the cultures and the pre-understanding of each group which places me as a well-informed interlocutor between the three. Balancing this is the need to be reflective about the process and to continually consciously acknowledge that my own prejudicial understanding may colour my interpretation of discussions with each of the research respondents. It is only through the execution of the research process and the final analysis of its effectiveness will I be able to judge where this balance lies and this in turn will aid the development of the method.

Figure 1 is a graphic depiction of how I visualise this inter-relationship and illustrates how the interests of these three major stakeholders overlap and how they are related to one another. The core issue for examination is whether the epistemological boundaries of these stakeholders is in congruence, in other words how closely their epistemological boundaries overlap in a Zone of Epistemological Congruence.

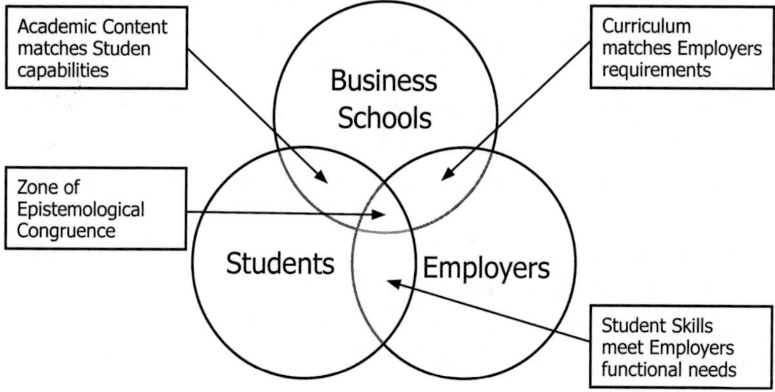

Figure 1. *Zone of Epistemological Congruence*

As can be seen from the diagram the Zone of Epistemological Congruence is where the nature of the education on offer to students and the curricula offered by The University at which they are studying coincides with employer's requirements. This means that the acquired skills and knowledge of students will match seamlessly to the needs of the employers. Ideally, this zone should be as large as possible. For some students, this is the case and the aim of Universities seeking to improve the employability of their graduates is critical to ensure as many students as possible enjoy the benefits of this congruity.

In order to more fully explain, epistemological congruity and how epistemological range affects the employability of graduates I have used my own graphic images based on research and data into various business sectors. The first is Figure 2 an illustration of how the epistemological spectrum which stretches from functional skills, such as the ability to perform simple spreadsheet calculations to speculative skills such as the creative application of complex spreadsheet functions impacts on the "fit" between the expectations of the employers and the skills of the graduate.

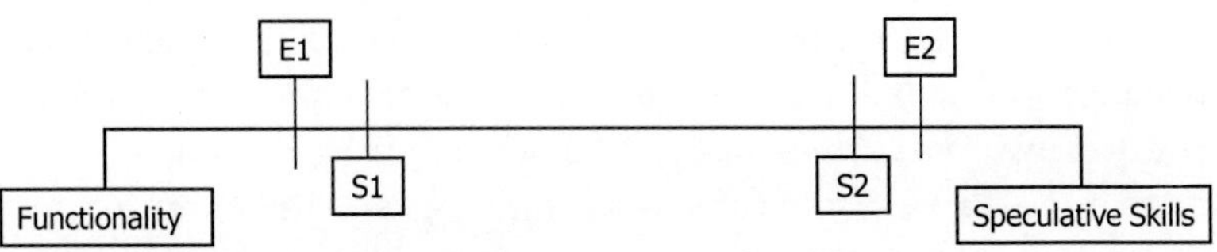

Figure 2. *The Epistemological Spectrum*

In this illustration Employer one (E1) has engaged Student one (S1) and has found that their skills and knowledge exceed the requirements of the position whereas in the second example E2, S2 the situation is reversed. It has been argued (Robinson, 2006) that both students would have benefited from a process that more closely matched workplace requirements so that their own personal resources could have been deployed to better match their chosen career. This is not though, a simple process of matching the requirements of the employment market, there is a commensurate responsibility of all stakeholders to reflect upon the right mix of skills and expertise needed and adjust expectations accordingly (Curtis & Lucas 2001). This is why the "Zone of Epistemological Congruence" will never be a perfect match. In other words, neither employers nor students can fully anticipate the skill levels needed from one moment to the next both can only make approximate judgements as to what the emerging needs of an organisation will be.

Rationale

That Business Schools attempt deliver this approximate level of skill between these stakeholders (Students and Employers) is a key concern due to the vocational origins of Business pedagogy. Originally conceived of as educational institutions established to provide students with the vocational skills needed by industry and commerce (Khurana, 2010) the business schools still retain this core purpose, to produce graduates suitable for the economy (Petriglieri & Petriglieri, 2010). One of the reasons that business schools were subsumed into the Higher Education sector was in response to the economic restructuring, the growth of the "knowledge economy" (Slaughter & Rhoades 2004). The increasing move during the 1980s from an economy based on heavy industry and manufacturing to one based on the service sector began to place an increasing emphasis on the need for the "soft skills" such as interpersonal communication and cultural awareness demanded by an economic environment whose basis moved away from functional trade skills to the more complex and nuanced requirements of social interaction. Again I have used my own illustrations and Figure 3 and Figure 4 graphically demonstrate how the demand for graduates in the economy has shifted.

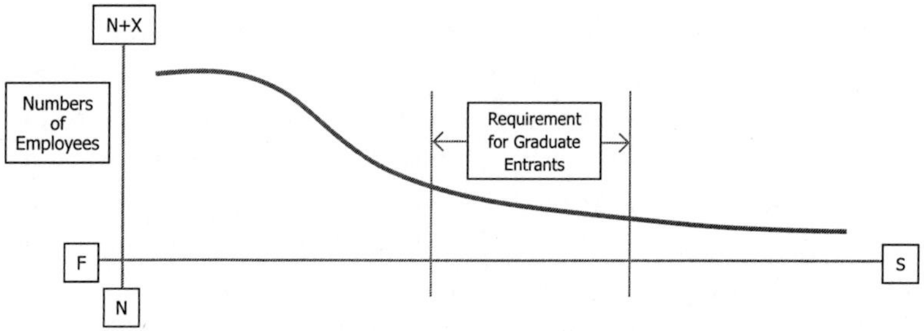

Figure 3. *Epistemological Distribution – The Classical Command and Control Economy*

Key: **F** - Functional Skills, **S** - Speculative Skills, **N** - Number of Employed, **N+X** - Increasing Numbers of Employees

In the classical command and control model of economic production (Audretsch & Thurik, 2004) the aggregated need for graduate entrants into the labour market is relatively modest. Much of the training and skill acquisition is provided by employers and the recruitment of graduates is either for specialist skills such as engineering for succession planning for the management structure. In this model, a relatively modest supply of graduates is adequate to support the needs of the economy. In contrast, when an economy moves from command and control to a knowledge-based economy the demand for graduates in all disciplines rises sharply as is shown in Figure 4.

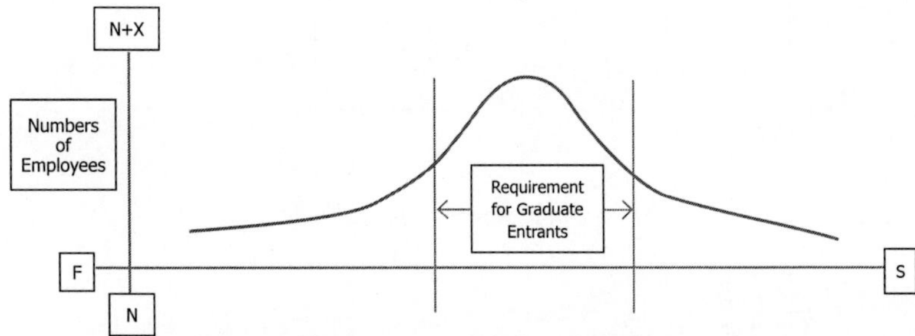

Figure 4. *Epistemological Distribution in the Knowledge-Economy*

There is still a requirement for low-level functionality and further post-graduate professional development but now graduates are recruited not just for specialist skills or succession planning but at a level where they will need a degree to fulfil the basic requirements of a job role (Brown & Hesketh, 2004). Contributing to this trend are such factors as the "professionalization" of key jobs such as nursing and teaching, sectors that moved relentlessly over the latter part of the 20th century to a graduate entrance requirement (White & Heslop, 2012). Furthermore, service industries that increasingly departed from hierarchical modes of organisation to matrices of equals developed flatter organisational structures that recognised the knowledge contribution of graduates. For example; in the Information Technology sector graduates in such disciplines as computer science and engineering graduates would often contribute vital new skills and knowledge to a sector in which technological evolution and innovation outran the capability of organisations to acquire the requisite skills to keep pace with competitors (Bresnahan *et al.*, 1999). In this context the role of Universities in producing graduates with the right skills and epistemological reach is vital. These are however aggregated models and there remain significant differences in the need for graduate entrants across different economic sectors. Figures 5 and 6 illustrate the difference between Investment Banking and

Mass Retail.

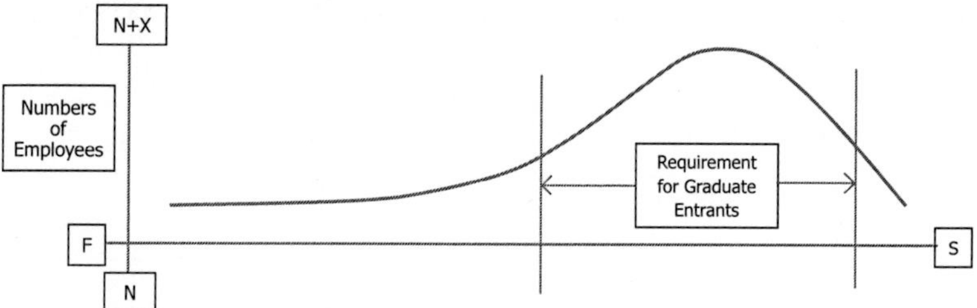

Figure 5. *Epistemological Distribution – Investment Banking*

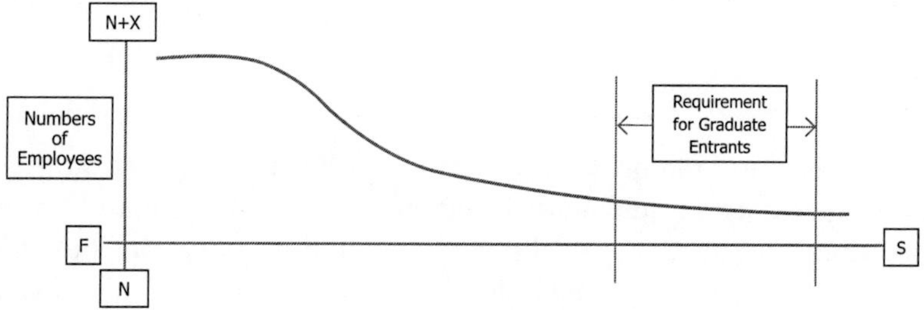

Figure 6. Epistemological Distribution – Mass Retail

In Investment Banking where there is a specific need for new employees to have a high level of technical expertise and knowledge before engagement (Jayawardhena & Foley, 2000), graduates are accordingly essential to the organisation, in contrast as the bulk of employees employed by supermarkets are engaged in functional roles the graduate entrants form a relatively small number of the total number of employees (Grugulis et al. 2011). However even here the requirements are complex, the number of graduate entrants into mass retail on an annual basis far outnumber the graduate entrants into investment banking (HESA, 2013). This makes the challenge for the Higher Education sector equally complex raising the question as to whether the epistemological reach of business school curricula can, or should, encompass the expectations of all business sectors? Whilst this may seem to external observers that the requirements of such professions as accountancy and banking would appear to be relatively straightforward the increasing interconnectedness and interdependency of an advanced economy demands that organisations embed "soft skills" as well as technical and professional knowledge (Andrews & Higson, 2008).

Returning to the "Zone of Epistemological Congruity" it is clear that given the fluid and malleable nature of the requirement of different sectors of the economy, the evolution of the economy itself and the interconnectedness of advanced economies that this zone can never fully extend to meet the exact expectations of students and employers and that the curricula of business schools can never fully predict what the economy in general, and industry sectors in particular, will require. However, research and dialogue can be used to ensure that this overlap is maximised and that the overall epistemological relationship between these stakeholders remains connected. The question is what methodology is appropriate to examine this relationship? Can interpretive phenomenology adequately examine this issue?

Using Existential Hermeneutic Phenomenology

It is the three-way relationship between employers, students and universities that adds a level of complexity that many iterations of the research process, including, for example, Action Research, would find almost impossible to untangle, particularly when examining areas of perception and understanding. A simple quantitative analysis of skill requirements could indicate (through metrics) whether students have the right Excel spreadsheet skills needed by employers and whether these have been acquired at university. At more speculative levels however where graduate entrants contribute such unquantifiable skills as creativity simple metrics cannot yield a useful or accurate judgement as these are skills that are subject to individual interpretation and perception which are almost infinitely nuanced and contextually contingent. Unfortunately, then, from the perspective of the researcher into the epistemological overlap between these stakeholders' quantitative techniques have limited utility. What is required is a research process that can untangle these complexities of intercommunication, expectation and interpretation. One such model is phenomenological hermeneutics where a multiplicity of contextual understandings can be drawn into what Gadamer (1960, 2008) terms a "fusion of horizons" and this may be of use in understanding the underlying processes of communication and how closely or otherwise the epistemological boundaries of these stakeholders overlap. This process acknowledges that the researcher brings their own history and internal prejudices to the examination of the phenomena which they seek to examine and understand, as Gadamer puts it,

> The horizon of the present is continually in the process of being formed because we are continually having to test all our prejudices. An important part of this testing occurs in encountering the past and in understanding the tradition from which we come. Hence the horizon of the present cannot be formed without the past
>
> (Gadamer, 1996, p. 306).

Nevertheless, through a process of acknowledging what Gadamer terms (with others) as "intersubjectivity" (Gadamer, 2000) or shared experiences accessed through the interpretation of text and dialogue, these horizons may be drawn together in a composite understanding which can lead to a shared interpretation or explanation of a phenomenon or phenomena. In the context of establishing the nature and extent of the zone of epistemological overlap between Universities, Employers and Students this mechanism of reaching common epistemological ground through the acknowledgment of unique perceptual viewpoints is particularly useful as the "fusion of horizons" demands that this conflation is sensible within the epistemological parameters of all three stakeholders. In other words, the outcomes of the research should be accessible to validation by all.

Figure 7 is an illustration how the Hermeneutic Circle, the methodological approach of dialogue, reflection and analysis has the capability to fuse such a multiplicity of horizons moving the pre-understanding of the researcher to an evolving understanding and from assumed meaning to negotiated meaning.

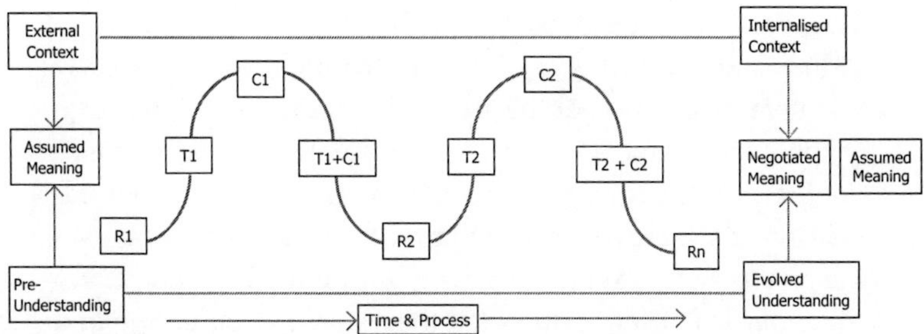

Figure 7. *The Hermeneutic Circle*

Key:

R1 – The initial pre-understanding of the researcher
T1 – Interpretation of textual or dialogue
C1 – Initial conversations with stakeholders determined by initial analysis
T1+C1 – Conflation of textual and dialogic evidence
R2 – Reflection on new evidence altering the pre-understanding
T2 – New textual sources indicated by evolving understanding
C2 – Revisited and additional conversations with stakeholders
T2+C2 – Re-conflation of evidence
Rn – Indicator of continuing and evolving process

It can be seen through the unravelling of the circle into a sine wave that the process can be continued ad infinitum and that this is a particular strength of this methodological approach as long as the instigating researcher grounds the evolving understanding of the process in the core aim of the research. Furthermore, this methodological approach allows for the inclusion of a variety of methods including the deconstruction and analysis of textual data, qualitative interviews that can be used to more closely examine and deconstruct themes and issues arising out of the initial textual analysis, and further discursive communication with key stakeholders/participants. The use of this variety of methods is intended to create a structure of discourse and re-examination, establishing a cycle of communication and reflection. The quality both of conduct of the unfolding circle and the validity of its outcomes is largely dependent on the selection of participants as their insights shape both discussions and provide the material for thematic analysis. Engaging in a hermeneutic process places this methodology EHP, directly under the umbrella of interpretive phenomenological analysis (IPA).

> The IPA researcher thus starts either by examining an individual and producing a case study or moves to an equally attentive exploration of the second case, and so on. This idiographic commitment is unusual even among qualitative methodologies. If the researcher wants to study a group of individuals, he or she moves between important themes generated in the analysis and exemplifies them with individual narratives (how particular individuals tell their stories), comparing and contrasting them (i.e., showing similarities and differences).
>
> (Pietkiewicz and Smith, 2014)

Selection of Participants

I assumed at the outset that the selection of participants for the hermeneutic circles would be critical to the success of the research process. In this, I am indebted to the observations of Thomas Groenewald in his article *A phenomenological research design illustrated* (2004). Within this article, he specifically describes how he selected participants for his own phenomenological enquiry into the unfolding of a cooperative education initiative. I have paraphrased his approach and the assumptions he made as this formed the structure of my own selective process.

I adopted the practice of "purposive sampling" or "theoretical sampling" to recruit respondents for the circles.

> ...theoretical sampling means selecting groups or categories to study on the basis of their relevance to your research questions, your theoretical position and analytical framework, your analytical practice, and most importantly the argument or explanation you are developing. Theoretical sampling is concerned with constructing a sample (sometimes called a study group) which is meaningful theoretically and empirically because it builds in certain characteristics or criteria that which will develop and test your theory or argument.
>
> (Mason, 2002 p.124)

The respondents I selected all met the criterion of "theoretical meaning" as through a combination of personal knowledge and the careful preparatory consideration of each participant's personal history and life experiences I knew that each had a direct connection with Business Education in the Higher Education sector. Once I had selected the initial participants for the first hermeneutical circle I then extended the sample of respondents through snowball sampling. In this, I followed Groenewald directly. As he describes.

> In order to trace additional participants or informants, I used snowball sampling. Snowballing is a method of expanding the sample by asking one informant or participant to recommend others for interviewing… I requested the purposive sample interviewees to give, at their discretion, the names and contact details of persons based in commerce, industry and/or government who a) were co-responsible for the educational programmes; and b) who had participated in the programme presented.
>
> (Groenewald, 2004 p.46)

Groenewald's approach has more recently been validated by a similar approach which also adopted a hermeneutic research technique used by Elley-Brown et al. to examine the careers of professional women in education.

> Purposive sampling technique (Bryman & Bell, 2015) was used which meant that participants were selected guided by the research questions posed and to fulfil the primary criteria: to have experienced a career in the education sector and be willing to talk about their experience and what career means for them. The potential sample was invited to participate by responding to the advertisement in a popular women's magazine. Additional participants were recruited using a snowball technique through contacts of the researcher and supervisors.
>
> (Elley-Brown et al, 2018 p.174)

Accordingly, I drew initially on my own contacts made in my prior professional career as a senior executive in a multi-national corporation to select respondents to represent employee stakeholders. I used my current contacts as an academic to select respondents for the student and academic stakeholder groups. In this, I was fortunate as I had (and have) extensive networks in every one of these groups through professionally facilitated social networks. In order to give an idea of the range of interests and experiences of the respondents, I have detailed below in a suitably anonymised format the nature and range of participants that this purposeful/theoretical sampling and snowball recruitment yielded.

Hermeneutic Circle One	
Employer Stakeholders	1. Senior Manager in the NHS 2. Owner/Manager Medium sized manufacturer
Academic Stakeholders	1. Lecturer in Marketing 2. Senior Lecturer in Strategy
Student Stakeholders	1. First-Year student, Business and Management 2. Third Year International Business Student
Hermeneutic Circle Two	
Employer Stakeholders	1. Senior Corporate Human Resource Executive 2. Owner and Founder Entertainment Chain
Academic Stakeholders	1. Senior Lecturer in Accounting 2. Postgraduate (Hourly Paid Lecturer)
Student Stakeholders	1. Second-year student, Business and Management 2. Third Year student, Business and Management
Hermeneutic Circle Three	
Employer Stakeholders	1. Senior Executive Car Manufacturing 2. Chief Operating Executive - Leisure Sector
Academic Stakeholders	1. Senior Lecturer in General Business 2. Lecturer in Enterprise and Operations
Student Stakeholders	1. First-Year student, Business and Management 2. Third Year Student Accounting and Economics

Notes.

- Only two of the academic respondents and two of the student respondents were drawn from the institution at which I am employed.
- Although my key practice as a professional business practitioner was in Entertainment and Leisure I was able through direct recommendation able to reach out to other organisational sectors

Figure 8. *Stakeholder Participants*

This process of purposive sampling aided by snowball sampling added a contextual richness to conduct of the phenomenological investigation and its outcomes. Furthermore, this richness formed a solid basis to the material marshalled and shaped by the research design.

The Research Design

Figure 9 (below) is a diagrammatic representation of how I operationalised Gadamer's phenomenological insights within the framework of the hermeneutic circles and engaged the respondents I had selected in the hermeneutical circles. The core of the process is are the series of interviews that attempt with each discussion to unravel the key elements of how Gadamer deconstructed the manner in which horizons become fused. Any interlocutor in a process that fuses horizons carries their own horizon which is constructed from their own prejudices or foreknowledge. It is essential to understand the origins of this foreknowledge and so the uncovering of the sources of this knowledge, textual, or otherwise is required. This enables the researcher to establish the epistemic boundaries of the respondent of the matter-at-hand, in this instance their understanding of the pedagogy of the business academy. The unfolding interview then turns to where the respondent has commonalities with the views of others where the fusion of horizons can be detected. Finally, a further uncovering of rapprochement or the specificity of what persuaded the respondent to move their epistemological position and fuse their personal horizon with that of others is essential for the final thematic analysis. What is illustrated below is a single "turn" in this interrogative technique.

Figure 9. *Operationalising Gadamer – A single hermeneutic turn*

The turn as is shown above follows four distinct stages. The promulgation of and initial statement or summary text that allows the respondent to reflect on the matter in hand. This is followed by the interviews with the respondents which yields a number of transcripts that can be analysed. This analysis results in a summative document that distils the transcripts of the interviews into a single accessible document that aims to capture the key themes on the matter-at- hand raised by the discussions. This is a critical juncture in the analytic, it is this hermeneutic process that is key to the identification of themes. This is a direct development of earlier suggestions for the application of interpretative phenomenological techniques in research.

> Smith and Osborne (2008) outline four key stages of inductive analysis for researchers underlying which is the double hermeneutic, whereby a researcher attempts to make sense of the participant's sense making activity. First, a researcher reads one transcript closely for familiarity and then looks for emerging themes, annotating significant points. The researcher then develops their notes into concise themes that capture the 'essential quality' of the respondent's comments. Second, a researcher clusters together connected or related themes to create master (superordinate or over-arching) themes. Third, a researcher uses the emergent themes from the first transcript to orient the analysis of subsequent transcripts, in an iterative fashion. Once each transcript has been analysed, a final table of superordinate themes is constructed. Fourth, the outcome of the analytical process is a narrative account where "the researcher's analytic interpretation is presented in detail with verbatim extracts from participants" (Smith et al., 2009, p. 4).
>
> (Gill, 2014 pps. 16,17)

Applying these procedural principles proved essential. As will be illustrated in the following chapter as the careful reflection on the transcripts and the inclusion of material from these in the summative documents was a matter of careful and often lengthy consideration. The subsequent reaction by the respondents to the summative documents became a validation of the editorial and analytical choices I made.

A single turn does not however constitute a hermeneutic circle. The respondents whilst remaining anonymous are now engaged in a specific dialogue on the matter-at-hand and a dialogue implies an opportunity to reflect and respond. The summary text becomes a medium of asymmetric exchange. The text is then re-circulated and each respondent re-interviewed to gauge their reaction and analysis of the collated text. This cycle of response-collation-promulgation-interview could carry on ad-infinitum. In the instance of this research, I decided to stop the circle at three turns. As will be seen in the subsequent chapter this was prudent as there was significant convergence of outcomes at the end of all three circles. The unfolding of this research process is shown below in Figure 10 – The Research Structure, this illustrates how every single hermeneutic turn fits into each hermeneutic circle

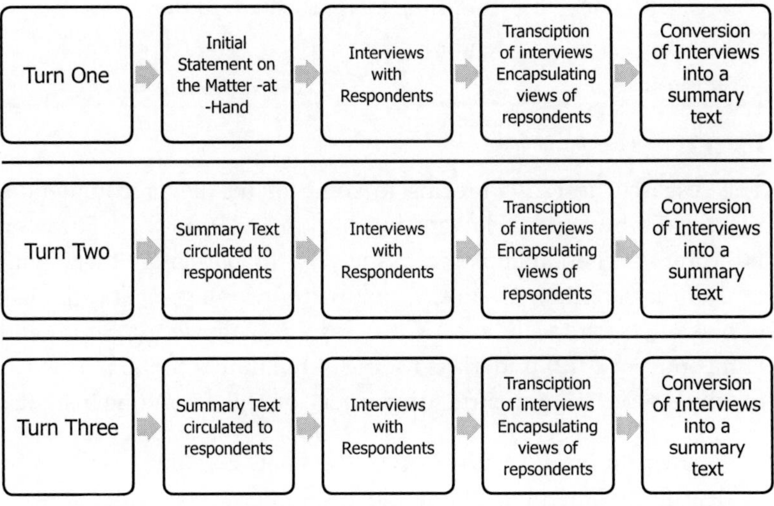

Figure 10. *The Research Structure*

Although my original intent was to progress through the cycles in an even and timely manner the vagaries of professional commitments and the practicalities of access to two of the key stakeholder groups (students and academics) in the cycle of the academic year delayed the research at key junctures. This meant that the circles unfolded unevenly. Figure 11 – timings and numbers of participants illustrate this.

Hermeneutic Circle One: February to November 2017		
Turn One: Feb-March 2017 6 Participants	Turn Two: May-Sept 2017 6 Participants	Turn Three: Sept - Nov 2017 6 Participants
Hermeneutic Circle Two: February to June 2018		
Turn One: Feb-March 2018 6 Participants	Turn Two: April - May 2018 5 Participants	Turn Three: May - June 2018 5 Participants

Hermeneutic Circle Three - September to November 2018		
Turn One: September 2018 6 Participants	Turn Two: October 2018 6 Participants	Turn Three; November 2018 6 Participants

Figure 11. *Timings and Numbers of Participants*

The research design conforms to some of the key recommendations made by Smith, Flowers and Larkin (2009) in their guide on Interpretive Phenomenological Analysis. In particular the identification of participants with communality of interests and the use of a semi-structured interview process. In a later work, Smith and Shinebourne (2012) underlined some of the fundamental reasons as to why a series of semi-structured interviews yield unique insights.

> The assumption in IPA is that the analyst is interested in learning something about the respondent's psychological world. This may be in the form of beliefs and constructs that are made manifest or suggested by the respondent's talk, or it may be that the analyst holds that the respondent's story can itself be said to represent a piece of the respondent's identity (Smith, 2003). Either way, meaning is central, and the aim is to try to understand the content and complexity of those meanings rather than measure their frequency. This involves the investigator engaging in an interpretative relationship with the transcript. While one is attempting to capture and do justice to the meanings of the respondents

> to learn about their mental and social world, those meanings are not transparently available – they must be obtained through a sustained engagement with the text and a process of interpretation.
>
> (Smith, 2012, p.66)

As will be discussed in more detail in the subsequent chapter, the more practical experience I gained through conducting the process led to greater efficiency in unfolding each turn and so Circle Three took just over three months in contrast to Circle One that took ten months to complete. One of the key reasons for the slow progress in circle one was the care I took to conduct the research in as ethical a manner as was possible. Ethical reflection and observation are critical features of any phenomenologically based research.

Ethical Considerations

The use of a hermeneutic circle which is rooted in the phenomenological method is relatively little used research process in the field of Business Pedagogy. It is almost a new method in this context. This means that much of the ethical considerations or route maps must be drawn from other disciplines that have used this approach more widely and where evidence of ethical issues has been acknowledged and resolved. Prime amongst these is the discipline of nursing that uses the dialogic basis of phenomenological enquiry to examine core relationships in medical practice such as the patient/practitioner one. Of use here is Walker's (2007) summation of the core ethical issue.

> Adherence to ethical standards is arguably heightened when researching the lived experience, calling for creative strategies in the research design and careful deliberation of the potential risks involved. In striving to achieve a quality research culture, measures to promote safety and wellbeing undoubtedly include preparation and support for both the researcher and those who have consented to be researched.
>
> (Walker, 2007, p. 43)

Walker clearly identifies the "lived experience" as a critical concern. Nevertheless, she provides some key areas which form an ethical structure that informs phenomenological research. In particular, she talks of two concepts which are of particular use when dealing with the "Lived experience" these are, Beneficence and non-maleficence or the admonition to do no harm and the phenomenological interview in which it is incumbent on the researcher to maintain the most rigorous standards of confidentiality and to be transparent in obtaining consent. Whilst Walker is referring to the discipline of nursing and its intense interpersonal relationships these guidelines can and should be transferred into the business context as, although businesses may not be dealing with matters of life and death, they are dealing with issues of livelihood and prosperity which in certain circumstances a breach of ethical practices could be seriously detrimental to an individual participating in research.

However, whilst these admonitions are critical an ethical issue lies at the core of all phenomenological methodologies and it returns to Gadamer's assertion of the essential nature of subjectivity in any process that acknowledges the primacy of language as a carrier of meaning. In her article on phenomenology and ethics, Häggman-Laitila reaches this conclusion.

> Concerning the authenticity and ethics of the research, it is of crucial importance that the researcher should identify and describe his or her own view in every phase of the research process. The identification of this view allows the researcher to meet the participants as individual human beings and enables him or her to respect the participants' individual expressions of the research subject.
>
> (Häggman-Laitila, 1999, p. 20)

So, bound up in the phenomenological method is a process of overt reflection which clearly identifies the voice of the researcher in the process. In this respect, it is not too dissimilar to Action Research.

Discussion & Conclusion

One of the key features of Phenomenological Hermeneutics is the centrality of the voice and role of the researcher as an active participant, a co-constructor of meaning. The very nature of epistemological congruence or the conditions at which universities, employers and students agree that the range of knowledge is congruous and appropriate necessitates a methodology that reaches beyond the controlled conditions of a bounded intervention into open dialogue and examination on factors and issues that may be unknown at the outset of the enquiry. Whilst the outcomes of Phenomenological enquiry cannot in this sense be predicted it does have the potential to uncover new perspectives.

The major challenge to the use of this methodology is that of validation and credibility which is overtly acknowledged in the discipline that makes the best use of this approach; Nursing. Here the advantage is that many of the pitfalls and the safeguards have already been identified and can be readily transferred to the discipline of business, namely that methods are to be strictly confidential and that the active engagement of the researcher must be transparent, reviewed and reflected upon in order to achieve credibility. If this is done well the investigation has the potential to widen discourse outside academia with stakeholders, students and employers not hitherto directly engaged in research into the academic processes and pedagogy of the discipline of business. The willingness of the discipline of Business to adopt new methodologies was recently highlighted in a series of articles in the Academy of Management Journal of Education and Learning which reflected on Epistemological Beliefs and Dialogical Pedagogy in Management Education (Egri, 2014) This indicates that the adoption of a methodology predicated on Gadamer's iteration of the hermeneutic circle indicates may form the basis of a suitable structure for engaging the critical stakeholders in the evolution of business pedagogy.

Chapter 5

The Circles of Discourse

In order to justify the claim that EHP could be an appropriate vehicle for research and enquiry it is useful to illustrate how the Hermeneutic Circles used unfolded. These are the outcomes of the methodology and method. Embedded within this evidence is the discursive process that is at the core of the application of EHP. What follows are the documents that were shared amongst the three hermeneutical circles. I have indicated how each document fits within the relevant hermeneutical circle so that the reader may orient themselves in the unfolding narrative and the research process.

Circle One – Document One – Initial Statement – Interview Cycle One

Dear ___________

Many thanks for agreeing to participate in this research.

All you have to do now is read the following statement and consider if you feel from your own personal experience that the statement is accurate.

Business Schools produce graduates with appropriate knowledge

At your convenience I would then like to hold a brief conversation with you about this statement. The manner in which you want to do this is entirely at your discretion. You may wish to do this by phone in which case you can email me with your preferred time and number and I will call you. If you prefer we can hold a Skype interview or even a face to face interview. Again, if you email me I will endeavour to accommodate your preference. Alternatively, you can elect to send a written response to my email address.

The interviews will be audio recorded for research purposes only and all material will be anonymised, kept securely and destroyed when the research project has ended.

Once you and the other participants have been interviewed I will collate the views on this statement into a single short document and recirculate this for your consideration.

I sincerely appreciate your help on this.

Circle One – Document Two – Collated Response – Interview Cycle Two

In this document I have edited out the introduction and the concluding paragraph as these follow the format as indicated above in the initial communication to the research participants. This is a collation and summary of the interview responses from the research respondents.

Dear ___________

Again, many thanks for participating in this research.

I have now interviewed participants from three stakeholder groups with direct connection with the Business Academy and the canvassed their views on the efficacy and relevance of the way we teach business. Throughout these interviews the emphasis has been on direct and personal experience. I have now collated these interviews into a single set of responses that summarises the main issues and concerns raised.

The next stage in the research process is to ask you as a key participant to read this document. When you are available I will call you again and ask you to comment on what you have read and amend the text as you want. I will interview all the other participants and follow the same process to produce a new document for your perusal.

Here is the text.

Business School Education

The perspective of the employer.

The key issue from the perspective of the employer is the lack of any meaningful engagement with the teaching processes employed by Business Schools. Feedback or other communication with academics working in Business Schools is often indirect and limited to ad hoc communication through networking and serendipitous events and there is little evidence of a formal and systemic process by which the key concerns and needs of employers can influence or inform the curriculum of the Business Academy and the manner in which this is taught. Nevertheless, Business School graduates do generally qualify with skills that are appropriate to the workplace and which have direct utility from the onset of employment. There is a caveat here. There are two features of Business School education that seem to determine both the skill level and the utility of the graduate. First, students who have been on placement generally have a higher skill level and have a greater facility to acclimatise to organisational culture. Second, this is also true of graduates from Business Schools with preeminent reputations in the world of Business and there does seem to be a direct correlation between Business acuity and the reputation of the Business School. What is uncertain is whether this is a cause or an effect, is this a self-fulfilling process in which the naturally more able students are recruited by or attracted to the more prestigious institutions. Irrespective of this there are gaps in the knowledge of all Business School graduates. These can be summarised as a lack of cultural awareness and social empathy for the organisational process in which they find themselves. This manifests itself in a number of ways including a lack of commitment to medium and longer term organisational goals and a lack of social empathy for the existing organisational community. These are not issues caused by a lack of theoretical or technical knowledge but by a misunderstanding of the wider social context within which they work. Again, though this does appear to be less of an issue with graduates who have experienced a placement.

The perspective of the student

Business Schools are attractive to students as they offer either the promise of direct advancement into organisational life or skills and knowledge essential to following an independent entrepreneurial route. The belief that Business Schools are an appropriate route to career success is largely derived from peer-based opinion, information from the internet and anecdotal narratives from a social circle of friends, acquaintances and relatives. Opinion which is critical of the validity of a Business degree as encountered in some main stream media is both accepted as true in some instances but cannot be generalised to individual circumstance either within the context of the students' own experience or across different institutions. In other words, there may be some students that they know for whom the degree will be of no utility and that their Business School is not one of the poor ones. Experience and opinion of what is taught by the academy is largely positive with criticism levelled mostly at that which has seemingly been covered at secondary level, particularly amongst those that have studied A level business or its equivalent. Students who have been on placement find that much of the curriculum is actually relevant to the experience of work and some actively apply theoretical knowledge in a practical context. Of greatest utility however are hard skills such as time planning, spreadsheet familiarity and a knowledge of business mathematics. The key gap is that of social awareness and a lack of preparedness for the cultural aspects of organisational life. The key failing of the business school curriculum is a failure to challenge and stretch the critical acuity of the best students and to hold attention and demonstrate relevance. However, it is acknowledged by students that there are two factors at play, the individual attitude and responsibility of the individual student and the attitude and enthusiasm of the teaching staff. When both are positive then the results are commensurately positive when either is lacking then the experience of the teaching process and its contextual relevance can spiral downwards and lead to non-engagement.

The perspective of the academic staff

Universally academics believe that Business Schools are of great utility and that the curriculum largely delivers what is needed by the individual student, the organisations that employ them and the wider society that these organisations serve. This is common across those academics with a great deal of wider organisational experience and those who are "career" academics. The involvement of stakeholders such as employers in the formulation of curricula is welcomed but of limited utility due to the density and granularity of knowledge that contributes to the overall curriculum of programmes. Much of the theoretical and research based material that is used in constructing teaching strategy, materials and lessons is simply unseen and unknown to those outside the academic community. The corollary of this is that it is the responsibility of the individual academic to interpret these sources and make them relevant. What engagement there is with employers is driven by outcomes and not by the structural processes of a successful pedagogic approach. In other words, there is a lack of understanding on the part of both students and employers as to what needs to be done in order to reach the desired outcome. One of the prime concerns of the Business academic community is the lack of opportunity to challenge student's perceptions and acuity; moving the curriculum too far in this direction may compromise the vocational promise of a business degree. Accordingly, this need to balance the development of critical awareness against the demands of practical skills compromises the potential of what a business education could be and what it could achieve. Of particular concern here is the lack of student engagement in modular materials that are seemingly a matter of process. Whilst students largely acknowledge their utility they fail to grasp that creative and critical engagement is still key to higher level learning in this context. Internally within the Business Academy there is a view that the balance between teaching and research in all fields needs to be addressed so that more research can be used to inform research led teaching.

Again, at your convenience I would like to hold a brief conversation with you about the text above. The manner in which you want to do this is entirely at your discretion. You may wish to do this by phone in which case you can email me with your preferred time and number and I will call you. If you prefer we can hold a Skype interview or even a face to face interview. Again, if you email me I will endeavour to accommodate your preference. Alternatively, you can elect to send a written response to my email address.

The interviews will be audio recorded for research purposes only and all material will be anonymised, kept securely and destroyed when the research project has ended.

Once you and the other participants have been interviewed I will collate the views on this statement into another single short document and recirculate this for your consideration.

Circle One – Document Three – Revised Response – Interview Cycle Three

This is the final document shared with this circle, following the circulation of this a further round of interviews was conducted in order to gauge response.

Dear ___________

Again, many thanks for participating in this research.

I have now interviewed participants from three stakeholder groups with direct connection with the Business Academy and the canvassed their views on the accuracy of my summation of their views. Again, throughout these interviews the emphasis has been on direct and personal experience. I have now collated these interviews into a revised document that should now more accurately reflect the main issues and concerns raised.

Once more the next stage in the research process is to ask you as a key participant to read this document. When you are available I will call you again and ask you to comment on what you have read and amend the text as you want. I will interview all the other participants and follow the same process to finally collate and analyse the responses that will be used in the overall research analysis.

Here is the text.

Business School Education

The perspective of the employer.

An important issue from the perspective of the employer is there is insufficient engagement with the teachers in Business Schools and the curriculum used by Business Schools. Whilst there is some evidence of communication with academics working in Business Schools this is often indirect and limited to ad hoc communication through networking and other events. Some organisations such as the Institute of Directors provide formal and systemic means by which the key concerns and needs of employers can influence or inform the curriculum of the Business Academy and the manner in which this is taught this is fragmented and there is no feedback on the effectiveness of this communication.

Business School graduates do generally qualify with some skills that are appropriate to the workplace and which have direct utility from the onset of employment. There is a caveat here. There are two features of Business School education that seem to determine both the skill level and the utility of the graduate. First, students who have been on placement generally have a higher skill level and have a greater facility to acclimatise to organisational culture irrespective of whether or not they did their placement in the organisation which employs them following graduation. Graduates from Business Schools with good reputations also do well. What is uncertain is whether this is a cause or an effect, is this a self-fulfilling process in which the naturally more able students are recruited by or attracted to the more prestigious institutions.

There are gaps in the knowledge of most Business School graduates. These can be summarised as a lack of cultural awareness and social empathy for the organisational process in which they find themselves although again, placement students are better at acclimatising themselves. This manifests itself in a number of ways including a lack of commitment to medium and longer term organisational goals and a lack of social empathy for the existing organisational community. These are not issues caused by a lack of theoretical or technical knowledge but by a misunderstanding of the customs and practices that have evolved in the working environment.

The perspective of the student

Business Schools are attractive to students as they offer either the promise of direct advancement into organisational life or skills and knowledge essential to following an independent entrepreneurial route. A key driver though, for students is the participation in University itself.

The belief that Business Schools are an appropriate route to career success is largely derived from peer-based opinion, information from the internet and anecdotal narratives from a social circle of friends, acquaintances and relatives. However, for a significant number of students Business as an academic discipline was (is) a safety net option following the failure to obtain good enough grades for other first choice options. Opinion which is critical of the validity of a Business degree is therefore accepted as true by some, but cannot be generalised to individual circumstance either within the context of the students' own experience or across different institutions. In other words, there may be some students that they know for whom the degree will be of no utility and that their Business School is not one of the poor ones.

Experience and opinion of what is taught by the academy is positive with some concerns regarding the basic skills covered in the curriculum. This is split between those who think that not enough provision is made and those who think that too much provision is made. Students who have been on placement find that some part of the curriculum are relevant to the workplace and some actively apply basic theoretical knowledge during their placement. Of greatest utility however are hard skills such as time planning, spreadsheet familiarity and a knowledge of business mathematics. One of the issues that could be addressed by Business Schools is that of cultural understanding and better preparation for the social aspects organisational life.

The key failing of the business school curriculum is a failure to challenge the best students and to hold attention of the rest of the class and demonstrate relevance although this is often due to the skill and attitude of the individual class tutor. The individual attitude and responsibility of the individual student is however important in this respect. A positive attitude on the part of both can lead to rewarding experiences for both teachers and students. If there is a negative attitude on either side of the teacher –student relationship then the experience of the teaching process and its contextual relevance can spiral downwards and lead to non-engagement.

The perspective of the academic staff

Most academics believe that Business Schools have a critical role to play in the education of the wider business community and that the curriculum largely delivers what is needed by the individual student, the organisations that employ them and the wider society that these organisations serve. This is common across those academics with a great deal of wider organisational experience and those who have entered the academy directly from their degree courses although it should be noted that many of these have direct experience of business through such initiatives as Knowledge Transfer Partnerships (KTPs).

The involvement of stakeholders such as employers in the formulation of curricula is welcomed but there is a time lag before this can be practically deployed due to the density and granularity of knowledge that contributes to the overall curriculum of programmes. Much of the theoretical and research based material that is used in constructing teaching strategy, materials and lessons is simply unseen and unknown to those outside the academic community and this is perhaps a failing. The corollary of this is that it is the responsibility of the individual academic to interpret these sources and make them relevant. What engagement there is with employers is driven by outcomes and not by the structural processes of a successful pedagogic approach.

The Academy should make a greater effort to improve understanding on the part of both students and employers as to what needs to be done in order to construct a valid and relevant curriculum. One of the prime concerns of the academic community is that it may not in all cases challenge student's perceptions and acuity; moving the curriculum too far in this direction may compromise the vocational promise of a business degree. Accordingly, this need to balance the development of critical awareness against the demands of practical skills compromises the potential of what a business education could be and what it could achieve. Of particular concern here is the lack of student engagement in modular materials that are seemingly a matter of process. Whilst students largely acknowledge their utility they fail to grasp that creative and critical engagement is still key to higher level learning in this context.

Internally within the Business Academy there is a view that the balance between teaching and research in all fields needs to be addressed so that more research can be used to inform research led teaching. There is some scepticism that the resources to improve the feed from research to teaching either are available or will be made available to rectify this.

Summary

The key issue for the development of business school pedagogy is to ensure that the delivery of the academy's curriculum takes account of the intergenerational issues that arise in the context of wider societal development. The changing values of cohorts of students as they successively progress through business schools are not fully understood by either academics or by those that will employ them. Commensurately there is a lack of comprehension on the other side of this equation. This indicates that the study and understanding of individual values, how they are acquired, how they are formed and whether or not they could be in conflict with others should be a critical challenge to the business academy both through research and how that research informs pedagogy.

Again, at your convenience I would like to hold a brief conversation with you about the text above. The manner in which you want to do this is entirely at your discretion. You may wish to do this by phone in which case you can email me with your preferred time and number and I will call you. If you prefer we can hold a Skype interview or even a face to face interview. Again, if you email me I will endeavour to accommodate your preference. Alternatively, you can elect to send a written response to my email address.

The interviews will be audio recorded for research purposes only and all material will be anonymised, kept securely and destroyed when the research project has ended.

Circle Two – Document One – Initial Statement – Interview Cycle One

In the second circle I decided to start with an initial statement that contradicted the first in order to gauge whether or not this would stimulate a different set of responses.

Dear ___________

Many thanks for agreeing to participate in this research.

All you have to do now is read the following statement and consider if you feel from your own personal experience that the statement is accurate.

> *Business Schools do not produce graduates with appropriate knowledge*

At your convenience I would then like to hold a brief conversation with you about this statement. The manner in which you want to do this is entirely at your discretion. You may wish to do this by phone in which case you can email me with your preferred time and number and I will call you. If you prefer we can hold a Skype interview or even a face to face interview. Again, if you email me I will endeavour to accommodate your preference. Alternatively, you can elect to send a written response to my email address.

The interviews will be audio recorded for research purposes only and all material will be anonymised, kept securely and destroyed when the research project has ended.

Once you and the other participants have been interviewed I will collate the views on this statement into a single short document and recirculate this for your consideration.

Circle Two – Document Two – Collated Response – Interview Cycle Two

Commentary

I have only replicated the core text document here as the accompanying communication is identical other than the dates. Circle two attempted more closely to uncover the pre-theoretical voice of the respondents. In the initial turn, the collective horizon was similar to that of the first circle, but the outputs of the second and third turns began to significantly diverge. By focussing on emotional response and immediacy to experience rather than the reflection on the utility of that experience the fusion of epistemological horizons between the three stakeholder groups becomes far more problematic and interesting. Nevertheless, even in this instance, there was a demonstrable drift towards a communality of goals amongst the respondents and a desire to reach a fusion of understanding.

The Shared Text

> *The perspective of the employer.*
>
> *Overall employers are largely satisfied with the skills and aptitudes of business graduates. It is irrelevant to the employer as to where some of these key skills are acquired and some are fully aware that many basic and technical skills are acquired prior to university in earlier employment or secondary education. There is an acknowledgement that training and education specific to the organisation must be undertaken as part of a process of enculturation or socialisation in order to acclimatise the new graduate employee to the particular normative values of the organisation. On this issue of cultural attitudes, some are affected by significant differences in cultural understanding across generations but this is largely accepted as a product of wider social pressures and developments rather than a failing of the Business School curriculum. Some employers have*

noticed a noticeable difference in the quality of business graduates but the consensus is that this is due to differences in individual acuity rather than the business school itself. This, however, may be due to a tendency in some instances to restrict recruitment to a fairly narrow band of institutions often based on physical location rather than wider academic reputation. Contact with academics in Business Schools is limited and sometimes takes the form of visits of students to premises. The prime form of contact, however, is in the confirmation of the details of prospective graduate employees through the writing of references. Primarily these are used simply to confirm chronological records rather than the academic evaluation of an individuals' ability. Work-based experience is valued as is wider evidence of a graduate's engagement with extra-curricular activities with the exception of "gap years" which some see as a societal rite of passage and not a developmental tool that adds to an employee's work place utility. In contrast placements and shorter-term internships are seen as useful. All agreed that better channels of communication should be established with business schools in order to both influence the development of the curriculum and also to understand why the academy believes certain subject disciplines are important.

The perspective of the student

The quality of teaching varies across the business school and is an unexpected feature of university life. Whilst most students have experienced significant variations in the attitude and aptitude of teachers in secondary education there was an initial expectation that these differences would not be so pronounced in Higher Education owing to the anticipated guarantee of professionalism. This is one of the early challenges to positive engagement with course materials as some tutors do not appear enthusiastic about the curriculum content although most are perceived to be knowledgeable. The choice to study business as an academic discipline draws in a surprising number of students for whom this appears to have a second choice after the failure to achieve grades needed from a first-choice degree course. There is some resentment at this amongst those for whom business is/was a first choice discipline.

It is accepted however that there is little the academy can do about this other than offering a variety of opportunities for more able and committed students to deepen and extend their understanding. There are some concerns that business as a default safety choice does diminish the reputation of business degrees making the attainment of a higher grade, an upper second or a first an absolute necessity. There is broad agreement that the scope and the content of the curriculum are appropriate at all levels but there is some concern that some subject disciplines fail to fully "stretch" students and also concern that technical skills such as the ability to use business-oriented software are not fully addressed. Campus culture came as a surprise to some students particularly in respect of the lack of monitoring of attendance and engagement with teaching. Amongst key groups, the consumption of alcohol is perceived as a problem but here it appears that academic disciplines other than Business have a more serious problem, particularly as a significant number of business students work through term time to support their studies. Here some institutions were more accommodating than others in timetable flexibility. Placements are valued and seen as difficult to secure but there is unanimity in the value of these for positive career pathways even amongst those who decide not to engage in the placement process.

The perspective of the academic staff

Each subject discipline (Management, Marketing, Human Resources etc.) within the Business Academy has an unshakeable conviction that the theories that inform the discipline and the research that underpins this, is of critical importance to a sound economy. This belief extends outside the immediate specialisation of the individual academics with a recognition that the full range of subject specialisms is necessary for the rounded education of business school graduates. The educational contract between faculty academics and the students is largely seen as positive and supportive. There is an acceptance that the varying levels of engagement of students with course materials is only partly within the control of the business school and that the lower levels of engagement as manifest through such factors as poor class attendance is a direct consequence of the move to "student-centred learning". There is some unease at the balance between the delivery of essential technical skills and the higher-level intellectual skills. Here there is recognition that this may not yet be appropriately weighted and that there needs to be cross-disciplinary communication on this. External engagement with private commerce, government agencies and other third sector organisations is positive, if fragmented and primarily mediated through the medium of research and consultancy. Finally, there is a discernible difference in teaching style and attitude between those academics that are "career academics" those that followed a path from graduation straight into postgraduate study and teaching and "practitioner academics" those who had substantive experience of business prior to an academic career. The main differences lie in the perception and use of academic business theory as there is a more sceptical attitude towards its efficacy and relevance amongst "practitioners" when compared with the approach of the "careerists". This difference is not sufficiently substantive to be destructive and can be viewed as a positive part of the debate on the balance and composition of the curriculum.

Summary

The quality of the teaching experienced in Business Schools varies considerably. From the perspective of students and alumni from a variety of Schools, this appears to be a function of the individual skill, experience and knowledge manifest by the academic in the classroom or the lecture hall. The academic view is that different disciplines warrant or demand differing teaching styles as more technically demanding fields require a greater emphasis on the transmission of knowledge and assurance that students have understood the material. Employers find this less problematical as there is an expectation that important gaps in an individuals' knowledge of technical or theoretical issues will be rapidly corrected by workplace practice and knowledge. All agree though that this is not entirely satisfactory as there should be a greater congruence between student expectation of good quality teaching and the employers need to recruit appropriately informed graduates.

Circle Two – Document Three – Revised Response – Interview Cycle Three

The perspective of the employer.

Employers are satisfied with the skills and aptitudes of those business graduates who adapt and embrace the culture of the organisation. It is irrelevant to the employer as to where some of these key skills are acquired and some are fully aware that many basic and technical skills are acquired prior to university in earlier employment or secondary education. However, those new employees, particularly graduates that acquire new skills on their own initiative are particularly valued. There is an acknowledgement that training and education specific to the organisation must be undertaken as part of a process of enculturation or socialisation in order to acclimatise the new graduate employee to the particular normative values of the organisation.

Cultural attitudes can be affected by differences in cultural understanding across generations but this is largely accepted as a product of wider social pressures and developments rather than a failing of the Business School curriculum. This can be ameliorated by the individual attitude and approach of key managers to the development of infra-organisation talent. This can be problematic as there are no reliable indicators as to which managers will be adept at this nor are there any reliable means to be certain that new graduate employees will also have an appropriate attitude. Some differences in individual acuity can be identified through such measures as psychometric tests and the final grade achievement of graduates but these are not entirely reliable.

Recruitment of graduates is sometimes determined by physical location especially where short term internships are used by organisations to cover seasonal gaps in workforce strength. The academic reputation of their business school is not often a critical factor as there is a perception that the curriculum is fairly standard across the country. Contact with academics in Business Schools is limited and sometimes takes the form of visits of students to premises. The prime form of contact, however, is in the confirmation of the details of prospective graduate employees through the writing of references. Primarily these are used simply to confirm chronological records rather than the academic evaluation of an individuals' ability. Work-based experience is of particular importance in enabling graduates to understand the critical links between theory and practice and a graduate's engagement with extra-curricular activities adds to an employee's workplace utility.

There is some agreement that more effective and frequent channels of communication, particularly in the area of work-based research should be established with business schools in order to both influence the development of the curriculum and also to understand why the academy believes certain subject disciplines are important.

The perspective of the student

The quality of teaching varies across the business school and is an unexpected feature of university life and also seems to be a feature of teaching in other faculties. Whilst most students have experienced significant variations in the attitude and aptitude of teachers in secondary education there was not an expectation that these differences would wider in quality and nature in Higher Education owing to the anticipated guarantee of professionalism. This is one of the early challenges to positive engagement with course materials as some tutors do not appear enthusiastic about the curriculum content although most are perceived to be knowledgeable.

The choice to study business as an academic discipline draws in a surprising number of students for whom this appears to have a second choice after the failure to achieve grades needed from a first-choice degree course. There is some resentment at this amongst those for whom business is/was a first choice discipline. It is accepted however that there is little the academy can do about this other than offering a variety of opportunities for more able and committed students to deepen and extend their understanding and there seems to be a commensurate response from tutors who recognise this engagement in the form of additional assistance both in the classroom and informally outside it.

There are some concerns that business as a default safety choice does diminish the reputation of business degrees making the attainment of a higher grade, an upper second or a first an absolute necessity and this seems to be confirmed by the stated preference of employers for these grades as necessary for entry into graduate schemes. There is broad agreement that the scope and the content of the curriculum is appropriate at all levels. There is concern that some subject disciplines fail to fully "stretch" students and also concern that technical skills such as the ability to use business-oriented software are not fully addressed but this is countered by the belief that for "senior" posts these basic skills may not be essential.

University culture came as a surprise to some students particularly in respect of the lack of monitoring of attendance and engagement with teaching. Although the consumption of alcohol is almost ubiquitous it appears that academic disciplines other than Business have a more serious problem, particularly as a significant number of business students work through term time to support their studies. Here some institutions were more accommodating than others in timetable flexibility. Placements are valued and seen as difficult to secure but there is unanimity in the value of these for positive career pathways.

The perspective of the academic staff

Each subject speciality within the Business Academy is part of an important mix of the theory and practice that informs Business as an academic discipline. Furthermore, the research that underpins this, is of critical importance to a pedagogical approach that is responsive to contextual changes. This belief extends outside the immediate specialisation of the individual academics with a recognition that the full range of subject specialisms is necessary for the rounded education of business school graduates.

The educational contract between faculty academics and the students is largely seen as positive and supportive and is continually being enhanced with the establishment of new support services and the extension of existing support services that operate along-

side the academy. There is a growing concern that the varying levels of engagement of students with course materials is only partly within the control of the business school and that the lower levels of engagement as manifest through such factors as poor class attendance is a direct consequence of a number of factors including the rise of "student-centred learning" and the need to adjust tariff scores to maintain student numbers.

There is some unease at the balance between the delivery of essential technical skills and the higher-level intellectual skills and this is mainly expressed by returning placement students. As a consequence, there is recognition that this may not yet be appropriately weighted and that there needs to be cross-disciplinary communication with students and employers on this. External engagement with private commerce, government agencies and other third sector organisations is positive, if fragmented and primarily mediated through the medium of research and consultancy. Finally, there is a discernible difference in teaching style and attitude between those academics that are "career academics" those that followed a path from graduation straight into postgraduate study and teaching and "practitioner academics" those who had substantive experience of business prior to an academic career. The main differences lie in the perception and use of academic business theory as there is a more sceptical attitude towards its efficacy and relevance amongst "practitioners" when compared with the approach of the "careerists". This difference is a positive part of the balance and composition of the Business School.

<u>*Summary*</u>

The perception of the quality of the teaching experienced in Business Schools varies considerably. From the perspective of students and alumni from a variety of Schools, this appears to be a function of the individual skill, experience and knowledge manifest by the academic although this may be predetermined by student understanding of what is valuable. Academics recognise that different disciplines warrant or demand differing teaching styles as more technically demanding fields require a greater emphasis on the transmission of knowledge and assurance that students have understood the material, however, there is a commensurate responsibility on the part of students to engage with the material they may not understand that they need. Employers find this less problematical as there is an expectation that important gaps in an individuals' knowledge of technical or theoretical issues will be rapidly corrected by workplace practice and knowledge. All agree though that this is not entirely satisfactory as there should be a greater congruence between student expectation of good quality teaching and the employers need to recruit appropriately informed graduates and this should be facilitated through more open and frequent communication.

Circle Three – Document One – Initial Statement – Interview Cycle One

In the second circle, I decided to start with an initial statement that was neutral again to order to gauge whether or not this would stimulate a different set of responses. Circle three in process, execution and outcome was a direct development of circle two in that it more confidently explored the visceral effect of the demands and assumptions of the normative values of business pedagogy. The final turn in outward form was not dissimilar to that of circle two but there was a deeper recognition amongst all the respondents of how wider indirect influences that impinged on their personal perceptions of what they needed from the business academy and how this influenced the fusion of horizons.

Dear ___________

Many thanks for agreeing to participate in this research.

All you have to do now is read the following statement and consider if you feel from your own personal experience that the statement is accurate.

It is not certain that Business Schools produce graduates with appropriate knowledge

At your convenience, I would then like to hold a brief conversation with you about this statement. The manner in which you want to do this is entirely at your discretion. You may wish to do this by phone in which case you can email me with your preferred time and number and I will call you. If you prefer we can hold a Skype interview or even a face to face interview. Again, if you email me I will endeavour to accommodate your preference. Alternatively, you can elect to send a written response to my email address.

The interviews will be audio recorded for research purposes only and all material will be anonymised, kept securely and destroyed when the research project has ended.

Once you and the other participants have been interviewed I will collate the views on this statement into a single short document and recirculate this for your consideration.

I sincerely appreciate your help on this.

Circle Three – Document Two – Collated Response – Interview Cycle Two

I have only replicated the core text document here as the accompanying communication is identical other than the dates.

> *The perspective of the employer.*
>
> *Business School graduates are in the main suitably ready for employment following graduation. Most employers are impressed with the manifest work ethic of new graduate entrants although it is uncertain whether this is a result of wider contextual changes rather than their education. Exposure to the culture and work ethic of the workplace prior to employment seen by most as a universal good even if this cultural exposure is at odds with that of their new employer. Engagement with staff in Business Schools is random and sporadic and even where there is an effective and consistent approach on an administrative level there is a feeling amongst employers that they are not in contact with those academics that control or direct the content of the curriculum in anything other*

than an indirect manner. Nevertheless, what contact there is seen as positive and many long term and rewarding relationships have been established, particularly where there are strong personal connections between visiting academics and key members of the organisation. Where these connections create a long term attitude of trust and confidence between organisational staff and academic visitors there have been frank exchanges regarding the problems of maintaining relevance in Higher Education due to the rapidly evolving business environment. This challenge is characterised as an issue that can only be dealt with by attitudinal skills rather than technical skills and that this may be an issue that reaches beyond the recruitment and engagement of graduates into the ongoing training of existing the wider workforce. This awareness of the need for "life-long" learning is partly driven by the cultural impact that successive intakes of graduates have on the workplace particularly in the arena of technological change and differing economic priorities. Examples of these are the adoption of social media as an increasingly important conduit for marketing campaigns and the perception that new graduates embrace the fluidity of the job market not as a challenge but as an opportunity. This can have an unsettling effect on the existing workforce.

The perspective of the student

University education is viewed as essential if a student wants a career in management at any level. The anecdotal and observational information from students starting their business degrees was that the number of graduates in the workplace in relatively junior managerial and supervisory positions meant that a degree is now perceived as an entry-level requirement for management in most sectors. Students that had done internships and placements confirmed this belief was commonplace and supported by further exposure to working environments other than the customer-facing retail or leisure sectors that normally employ student labour. In general, the curriculum in Business Schools is seen as strong on most of the essential skills for the workplace although there are gaps, particularly in the area of Information Technology skills and interpersonal skills. In this respect, there is some suggestion that academics should more closely liaise with students returning from placements and employers to more accurately determine what is needed for inclusion in the curriculum. There is a sense that the academics are more focused on their own specialities and interests to the detriment of what students will actually need to be effective in the workplace. However, this perception was at odds with the general perception of academic staff which was that they were generally empathetic and supportive towards students. Although there is some concern regarding the varying effectiveness of some tutors in the classroom, those who were prepared even briefly, to engage in one-to-one communication with students were found to be perceptive and knowledgeable. In terms of the overall culture on campus the key obstacles to a positive experience included the "drinking culture", unenthusiastic staff, focus on research that is perceived to have no direct practical utility and finally the expectation that students must engage in extra-curricular activity in order to establish personal distinctiveness. This last point was more fully explored as there was a polarised view on this. Some students believed it was essential to have a wider record of engagement and others thought that the time spent doing this detracted from academic effort. On this last point, there was agreement that the faculty should give stronger and more precise guidance on this.

<u>The perspective of the academic staff</u>

Academic staff do not actually have a firm idea of whether or not they are contributing effectively to the success of the business community. A number of assumptions are made on the relevance of the structure and content of the business curriculum and often these are predicated on custom and practice rather than a process whereby this is checked with employers, statutory agencies and students. Research is acknowledged to be largely driven by academic interest rather than industry requirements although some forms of knowledge transfer partnerships can enable effective two-way communication. The key issue is that there is no consistent or effective means by which research outputs are accessible to a wider audience and hence no feedback on impact for most published research. An exception here is research that is specifically targeted at compliance with the criteria set down by the current iteration of the Research Excellence Framework for research with impact. A more holistic view of the wider impact of the pedagogy of business schools would be useful as this might help to locate the subject disciplines within a larger framework. Relationships with students are seen as positive particularly with those who engage consistently and who challenge teaching staff formally in the classroom and informally outside the classroom on matters of content, theory, relevance and application. A crucial challenge to both students and staff is the extension of this positive relationship to as wide a range of the student cohort as possible. From the student side this is an issue of engagement and from the staff side one of pedagogic design and delivery. Wider societal views of business being seen as a second class discipline are seen as less than helpful to the morale of students and morale of business schools particularly in challenging economic and social contexts. Finally, whilst most believe that the professional standards of teaching in business schools have improved and are improving these could be enhanced by more frequent communication with the wider business community.

Summary

There is a feeling amongst these three stakeholders groups that overall the relationship between employers, students and academics is largely "fit for purpose" and that there is a mutual understanding that all face a challenging contextual environment. If there is unease here it is centred on the response rate of the academy to new technological and sociological developments which are not covered in the core curriculum of business schools as it is recognised that the private sector is the main source of innovation. Business Schools need to be better at identifying these trends, analysing their impact and embedding the lessons in the appropriate subject discipline. If we are to effectively improve the sharing of knowledge amongst stakeholder groups we must identify instances in which our teaching has been less than effective for the students or their employers. This, however, has consequences that reach beyond the Business School into post-academic environments. It may be that employers and graduates in employment have not effectively communicated their needs or failings. Academics cannot deal with problems that they either, don't know exist or which have been unacknowledged by those affected by them. Honesty and transparency are required by all.

Circle Three – Document Three – Revised Response – Interview Cycle Three

The perspective of the employer.

Some better motivated Business School graduates are ready for employment following graduation and there is a discernible difference in the quality of graduates across different business schools; some are much better prepared than others. The work ethic of new graduate entrants is nevertheless laudable irrespective of their institution although it is uncertain whether this is a result of wider contextual changes rather than their education. Exposure to the culture and work ethic of the workplace prior to employment seen by most as a universal good even if this cultural exposure is at odds with that of their new employer. Engagement with staff in Business Schools sometimes sporadic but there are signs that this is improving. Where there is an effective and consistent approach on an administrative level there is a feeling amongst employers that this contact needs to be widened so that employers can contribute to the direction and the content of the curriculum in an indirect manner. Nevertheless, positive and many long term and rewarding relationships have been established, particularly where there are strong personal connections between visiting academics and key members of the organisation. Connections that create a long term attitude of trust and confidence between organisational staff and academic visitors there have been productive exchanges regarding the problems of maintaining relevance in Higher Education. This has a balancing effect on the attitude of key staff involved in liaison with academics as it highlights the relevance and usefulness of academic research.

The challenge of dealing with volatile environments is characterised as an issue that can only be dealt with by developing attitudinal skills rather than technical skills and that this may be an issue that reaches beyond the recruitment and engagement of graduates into the ongoing training of existing the wider workforce. This awareness of the need for "life-long" learning is partly driven by the cultural impact that successive intakes of graduates have on the workplace particularly in the arena of technological change and differing economic priorities. Examples of these are the adoption of social media as an increasingly important conduit for marketing campaigns and the perception that new graduates embrace the fluidity of the job market not as a challenge but as an opportunity. This can have an unsettling effect on the existing workforce but this is a diminishing problem as the workforce ages and older employees retire.

The perspective of the student

University education is viewed as essential if a student wants a career in management at any level and the focus of the business school curriculum on vocational skills is understood and appreciated. The anecdotal and observational information from students starting their business degrees was that the number of graduates in the workplace in relatively junior managerial and supervisory positions meant that a degree is now perceived as an entry-level requirement for management in the most desired sectors. Students returning from internships and placements confirmed this belief was commonplace amongst the wider cohort and confirmed that there was some truth in this belief from further anecdotal evidence from working environments in which they had been involved.

In general, the curriculum in Business Schools is seen as strong on most of the essential skills for the workplace although there are gaps, particularly in the area of Information Technology skills and interpersonal skills. In this respect, there is some suggestion that academics should more closely liaise with students returning from placements and internships to more accurately determine what is needed for inclusion in the curriculum. There was also some argument for more formal lines of communication with employers to monitor the need for skill changes.

There is a sense that some academics are more focused on their own specialities and interests to the detriment of what students will actually need to be effective in the workplace. However, this perception is only a minor criticism as the general perception of academic staff which was that they were generally empathetic and supportive towards students. Although there is some concern regarding the varying effectiveness of some tutors in the classroom, those who were prepared even briefly, to engage in one-to-one communication with students were found to be perceptive and knowledgeable. In terms of the overall culture on campus the key obstacles to a positive experience included the "drinking culture", unenthusiastic staff, focus on research that is perceived to have no direct practical utility and finally the expectation that students must engage in extra-curricular activity in order to establish personal distinctiveness. Some students believed it was essential to have a wider record of engagement and others thought that the time spent doing this detracted from academic effort. On this last point, there was agreement that the faculty should give stronger and more precise guidance on this by ensuring that they themselves have an up to date view of what is required by the wider business community.

The perspective of the academic staff

Academic staff do not have an overarching mechanism to establish whether or not they are contributing effectively to the success of the business community. A number of assumptions are made on the relevance of the structure and content of the business curriculum and often these are predicated on custom and practice rather than a process whereby this is checked with employers, statutory agencies and students.

Research is acknowledged to be primarily driven by academic interest rather than industry requirements although some forms of knowledge transfer partnerships can enable effective two-way communication. This is not necessarily seen as a negative issue as there is a role of leadership for the Business Academy in its contribution to the wider business community. In this respect, there is a need for an effective means by which research outputs are accessible to a wider audience and enable feedback on impact for published research. Research that is specifically targeted at compliance with the criteria set down by the current iteration of the Research Excellence Framework for research with impact is an important indicator of how this might be accomplished.

A more holistic view of the wider impact of the pedagogy of business schools on the employability of students would be useful as this might help to locate the subject disciplines within a larger framework. Relationships with students are seen as positive particularly with those who engage consistently and who challenge teaching staff formally in the classroom and informally outside the classroom on matters of content, theory, relevance and application. A crucial challenge to both students and staff is the extension of this positive relationship to as wide a range of the student cohort as possible. From the student side this is an issue of engagement and from the staff side one of pedagogic design and delivery. Wider societal views of business being seen as a second class discipline are seen as less than helpful to the morale of students and morale of business schools particularly in challenging economic and social contexts although this is more of an issue with less high profile institutions. Most academics believe that the professional standards of teaching in business schools have improved and are improving and that these could be enhanced by more frequent communication with the wider business community.

Summary

There is agreement amongst these three stakeholders groups that the relationship between employers, students and academics is currently working and effective. There appears to be a mutual understanding that uncertainties in the developing world of business and organisational life is probably an insoluble problem. Unease is centred on the response rate of the academy to new technological and sociological developments which are not covered in the core curriculum of business schools as it is recognised that the private sector is the main source of innovation. The velocity of change is a factor that creates an emotional strain on the student, on the business community and anxiety amongst the academics who must teach them. It may be impossible to understand this perfectly and the best we may able to do is to just understand the difficulties of comprehending this. Business Schools need to be better at identifying these trends, analysing their impact and embedding the lessons in the appropriate subject discipline. However, this demands a commensurate response on the part of the business community.

If we are to effectively erode the boundaries of knowledge that divides stakeholder groups from each other and from the Business School, we must identify instances in which our teaching has not been effective for the students or their employers. This, however, has consequences that reach beyond the Business School into post-academic environments. It may be that employers and graduates in employment have not effectively communicated their needs or failings. Academics cannot deal with problems that they either, don't know exist or which have been unacknowledged by those affected by them. Honesty and transparency are required by all.

Commentary

At the conclusion of the three circles, the follow-up interviews and the shared texts replicated above formed the material used for the overall analysis. From this collation, the three themes of the phenomenological analysis emerged.

Chapter 6

The Unfolding Analysis

Introduction

I will describe in detail in the following chapter how the research was conducted, the results of each phase of the hermeneutic circles, the analytical process that arose from the execution of the existential hermeneutic methodology and the key themes and essences that the investigation uncovered. To aid understanding of the unfolding of this complex analytic I have tabulated in Figure 12, a summary of how the research processes are connected. Starting with the base text and interviews this led to the analysis of the transcripts from the respondents and their responses to the summary text documents shared and reviewed by the respondents in each hermeneutic circle. In the first column, the "Gadamerian structure of Research" follows the interrogative structure used in the interview process. This is detailed in the previous chapter (Figures 9, 10 and 11). What became apparent to me as the research unfolded was that the material needed to be more fully analysed and evaluated with the application of phenomenological principles of reflective understanding (Sanders, 1982). Columns two to five show how the research material produced by the interviews, the shared texts and the subsequent fusion of horizons which was facilitated by the process of discourse was used to generate a phenomenological analysis of the research data.

Gadamerian structure of research	Phenomenological analysis of data			
	Stage One **Description of Evidence**	**Stage Two** **Invariants and Themes**	**Stage Three** **Subjective reflections on themes**	**Stage Four** **Essences present in themes**
Establishment of Hermeneutic Circles	Promulgation and dispersal of documents to the three Hermeneutic circles	**Noematic recounting** – the experience of participation in the discursive process of the hermeneutic circles; the reading of the text; discussion with the facilitator of the circles as the author of the texts, the asymmetric space for reflection on text and its meaning.		
Evidence of Prejudice	Semi-structured discursive process	**Disappointment -** as an initial feeling shared amongst the participants that the pedagogy of business is at best a fragmentary response	**Noetic Correlate** - business schools must be collaborative beyond their current boundaries to develop effective curricula.	**The sharing of dissatisfaction** amongst key stakeholder groups is a necessary precursor to the uncovering of what must be done to improve
Synthesis of Text **Epistemological boundaries**	Uncovering of the sources of participants pre-knowledge The embedding of the summaries of epistemological understanding into the shared texts.	**Belongingness** as the texts are shared and the respondents "see" traces of their own pre-knowledge within the texts	**Noetic Correlate** - no single group of stakeholders holds primacy regarding contextual relevance.	The primacy of knowledge regarding the epistemological relevance of business school pedagogy lies **a shared process of renewal**
Fusion of horizons	Post text interviews with participants	**Angst** in the Heideggerian sense as a validator of shared concern and an underpinning of the fusion of horizons and rapprochement.	**Noetic Correlate** complexity cannot be managed by the individual and the current structures of collaboration are inadequate.	The Academy must continually renew itself and its pedagogical approach through **un-bunkered contextual understanding.**

Notes on the Mapping

- Column One – Gadamerian structure of the research. The structure used to facilitate the "fusion of horizons on the matter-at-hand.
- Column Two - Description of Evidence – Initial marshalling and organising of the research material based on a simple textual analysis
- Column Three - Invariants and Themes –Noesis, the consideration of the underlying themes of the research material and the discourse.
- Column Four – Subjective reflections on themes – Distilling and defining the implications of the noetic analysis
- Column Five - Essences present in themes – the essential call to action revealed by the implications of the noetic analysis

Figure 12. *Mapping the research and its phenomenological analysis*

As can be seen from the above the work of analysis moves beyond the structural framework provided by Gadamer's insights into the fusion of horizons. Applying an Existential Hermeneutic Phenomenological method forces a noetic turn as a simple textual analysis, even if it is based on Gadamer's idea of process does not uncover the emotional underpinning of personal epistemological understanding, to change one's beliefs is a partial surrendering of self and, however modest it may be, a reconfiguration of the comprehension of Dasein's life-world and perhaps an intimation of authenticity. What now follows is a detailed account of how the journey from a simple interpretation of text and discussion into a phenomenological insight was accomplished.

New Insights

The essence of the unique contribution to knowledge that I am claiming is the development and application of Gadamer's iteration of interpretive phenomenology and its operationalisation in the context of research into the pedagogy of business schools. At this stage in the narrative account of this project, I could have given a simple description of the chronology of the process with a commentary on the various stages of the hermeneutical circles as they unfolded. I have appended an account of this nature to this thesis (Appendix 1) but having written and reflected on this I feel that it does not fully explain how the influence of phenomenological practices and perspectives gave rise to a fundamentally different analysis of the role of the academy. The primary research, the process of which has been described in the previous chapter took place over a period of eighteen months. This was a much longer timeline than originally envisaged as the demands of work, other personal commitments and social events made the execution of the method far more disjointed than originally intended. In this, I am grateful to the respondents involved in the first circle for their forbearance and understanding. The first hermeneutical circle took almost eleven months to complete and this was not an even process. The timing of the interviews was affected by the rhythm of the academic term and the absence of the student respondents at critical junctures. This was taken into account in the following two circles, Circle 2 and Circle 3 were opened and closed in four and three months respectively. However, none of the circles was "closed" with finitude as some of the transcripts of the interviews needed further clarification on critical points. This meant that some respondents were re-interviewed on points of detail during the analytical process that sought to make sense of the material. This was important in the second and third circles as the nature of the discourse moved away from simple thematic exchanges to those of meaning and experience. To illustrate this here is a direct comparison between circles one and three on the same point. In seeking to uncover a fusion of understanding on the nature of external involvement in the academy the following question was asked of respondents in both circles; Do you think that Business Schools engage effectively with external agencies? In the first hermeneutical circle this question was posed directly and here is a sample response from an academic respondent from each of the circles.

> Phaedrus: Do you think that we as academics do as much as we can to take account of external perception of the academy?
>
> Respondent: Yes, we have several ways in which we bring the outside in. I mean we have outreach with schools and colleges, external speakers in classes, knowledge exchange and guest speakers at conferences and other events, yes, I think we do.

Phaedrus: But what effect does this have on the way we teach?

Respondent: (Pauses) (Silence) Well, I think that when the students hear the experiences of the real world it gives them an idea of the reality of business…

Phaedrus: Sorry to interrupt, I am sure that's true but how does it affect your teaching?

Respondent: (Longer pause) Do you know I don't think it does, I've never thought about this some of the speakers on my module I've inherited and they've all seemed appreciated by the students.

Phaedrus: Sorry I didn't mean to be rude.

Respondent: No, don't worry, it's just not something I've thought of before, well not at length. Considering it now I suppose we should reflect on this more but the students in their end of year feedback seem to sincerely appreciate these external interventions.

In the third circle the interrogative process had evolved in intent and meaning.

Phaedrus: How do others see us? Do you use external speakers? Do you ever ask them what they think of us?

Respondent: I instigated a process of external engagement through some site visits, it was a relatively small cohort and so it was manageable.

Phaedrus: I'm impressed, where did you take them?

Respondent: I thought it would be useful if they visited a call centre, so I took them to xxxxxxxx.

Phaedrus: Why did you think that that would help with the

teaching of this module?

Respondent: Well we wanted to expose them (the students) to the reality of how psychological contracts have a motivational effect even in task-oriented environments.

Phaedrus: How did that work, surely you didn't wander around a call centre floor?

Respondent: No, as it turned out we were all ushered into a room and given a standard corporate spiel by a couple of their senior managers, they then allowed the students to cross examine a couple of the floor supervisors. That was the most interesting part, the supervisors initially trotted out the company line and then as the session went on they relaxed.

Phaedrus: In what way?

Respondent: It became obvious that one of the supervisors was a recent graduate in journalism I think and seemed a lot more cynical about the company line than the other guy. But by then the end I think they (the supervisors) agreed that we as business school teachers and students should have a clear understanding of the exploitative nature of the call centre environment.

Phaedrus: I'm not sure I understand?

Respondent: I got the impression that they were looking to use for guidance, solutions if you like that would make the call centre work a little more human.

Phaedrus: How did the students react to this?

Respondent: I think they agreed, especially the couple that had worked in call centres themselves.

Phaedrus: I'm a little lost here, what did they expect us, the Business School to do.

Respondent: To think of better ways of treating people.

Phaedrus: So it got quite emotional?

Respondent: Yes, it did and quite depressing really.

Phaedrus: Why?

Respondent: We don't have the answers.

In the second extract the discursive process has moved out of the arena of the procedural and the technical into an emotional space. This a movement from simple thematic analysis to the uncovering of experience and an admission that there are unexplored gaps in our pedagogy that perhaps should be explored in more detail with a reflective process. So, this narrative of the execution of the research has become a description not of chronological events but the evolution of a more challenging discursive process.

This is critical to placing this research as a unique contribution to the development of understanding the nature of business pedagogy and is part of the movement from the technical and procedural origins of the pedagogy of the academy to a more profound perspective of what "business" is and what it means to the individual and society. This is a developing debate that is primarily argued along with the balance between theory and application.

> A continuing debate concerning pedagogy in colleges of business has been the appropriate mix of theory and application in management classroom instruction. If we are to entirely follow the application approach, and present only application, we run the risk of reducing students' understanding of "why" applications work while minimizing the myriad seminal contributions of academic scholarship to our discipline. On the other hand, should we entirely take the theoretical approach, we may produce students without practice in the important applied techniques developed by both scholars and management practitioners. There is probably an optimal balance of theory and application in

> our classroom instruction which may facilitate our goal of producing well-rounded students who contribute to organizational success.
>
> (Wren, Halbesleben & Buckley, 2007 p. 484)

What is missing from this debate is an exploration of what business actually is. Returning to Martin Parker's "Shut Down the Business School" this is a critical observation by Professor Parker on the nature of "management."

> Distilling the practice, occupation and form of knowledge down a bit then, what are the key elements of management as a form of organising? First, the idea that there is a distinct set of activities that can be called "management" and that these are different from the sort of things that ordinary people do in coping with most of their lives, when dealing with the with the troubles and anxieties the world throws at them. This is a slightly puzzling claim, because many of the things that that are done as part of management are just the same things that most human beings do – talking, paying attention to things, making sense of things, counting things, writing things down. Unlike someone who makes shoes, plays a musical instrument, or replaces corneas in an eye operation there doesn't seem to be anything that particular about the things that are involved in management such that it would be possible to say to someone else "Look I'm doing management now", "This is what management should look like." So, the claim must be that it is not the practices themselves but the ways in which they are done which make them particularly special. To do management must mean that you talk in a particular way, count certain things using specific methods, or make sense of the organization in a way that other people cannot.
>
> (Parker, 2018 pp. 105, 106)

This challenge to the role of management in business approaches more closely the nature of what the essence of business is by challenging the assumptions that we make when we teach "Business and Management". The two seem inextricably linked and yet Professor Parker's observation on the generic nature of management skills inevitably leads to a further problem. If we are unable to establish the precise nature of management skills, we could answer by pointing to a specific definition of business that identifies with more clarity which of these skills and aptitudes are appropriate in this specific context. Yet when we seek for a definition of business, this too is generic and unhelpful. There are numerous definitions offered by the Oxford English Dictionary on the meaning of "Business" and the most apposite for this discussion is as follows.

> Trade and all activity relating to it, esp. considered in terms of volume or profitability; commercial transactions, engagements, and undertakings regarded collectively; an instance of this. Hence more generally: the world of trade and commerce.
>
> (OED, 2019 Entry 14 [Accessed online])

I turn here to Peter Drucker and his seminal work on Management for a more useful definition.

> A business…has two and only two, basic functions, marketing and innovation. To discharge these functions, the enterprise must make productive the wealth-producing resources of people, capital, natural resources (including time), and management.
>
> (Drucker, 1973, p. 67)

So, management in the context of business is a "wealth-producing resource" but this does not bring us any closer to the specificity of business means nor what management qualities are required for the effective discharge of wealth-producing activities. Nor are more contemporary definitions helpful. Here is one example from an article in the journal *Philosophy of Management* where the author John Kaler attempts a definition to situate the role and meaning of ethics in the context of business.

> It is financial dependence on sales revenue or, put another way, the fact of being what official statistics call a 'trading organisation'. That is to say, a situation in which an organisation has to finance its operations by selling what it produces be that product goods or services. The significance of this is that it sets up a specific sort of relationship between the organisations and those in receipt of the goods or services which it produces: they exist as customers of the organisation. In being dependent on sales revenue, the organisation is dependent on having customers. That is, people (or other organisations) who buy whatever it is the organisation produces. A business is, we can say, a productive organisation with customers.
>
> (Kaler, 2003 pp. 61-62)

Kaler goes on in his article to cover the particular circumstances of other organisations such as charities and governmental agencies and demonstrates how these also qualify as Business. Yet this does not bring us any closer to answering Parker's challenge of what is it other than what other people already do? And this is critical to any research that examines the pedagogy of business. The process - business - for whose execution we claim as a business academy to teach essential skills is not in itself defined, clear or specific and is subject to a multiplicity of interpretation and practice. Yet in this indeterminacy leads to opportunity. A phenomenological enquiry does not seek to uncover generally applicable rules that could constitute a universal theory, it seeks to uncover the life experience of the participants in its discursive exchange so that it can say for this circumstance this particular thing held meaning and was important. Therefore, it is inclusive and has the facility to encompass a multiplicity of perspectives and make them intelligible in its extraction of meaning and significance. In the context of a field whose boundaries may be wide, indeterminate and undefinable I will demonstrate that it delivers new insight into not only the efficacy of business pedagogy but a re-definition of what business actually is and I will return to this in my final chapter.

The account of the research, the unfolding of the hermeneutical circles and the gathering of data is best accounted for in the description of its evolution in execution rather than a description of its chronological unfolding. There are four parts to unwrapping this evolution. I cannot escape the actual mechanics of discourse, how the circles were instigated, how the interviews took place and what form they took. The next identifiable stage is the uncovering of meaning from the shared texts of the circles, the reaction of the respondents to these texts and my reflection on what this meant. Reflection on my part led to a journey beyond the superficiality of simple exchange which finally led to the emergence of noetic insight as framed by Gadamer's "fusion of horizons."

The Mechanics of Discourse

I will start with a simple gazetteer of the research materials. As indicated previously the research was structured around three vehicles of hermeneutic exchange. In total fifty-six interviews were conducted most of which exceeded the brief exchanges I originally envisaged when designing the research. This was mainly due to the development of social connections between me and the respondents. Some of these were re-awakenings of old relationships, particularly amongst the employers as most of these were known to me from my previous career as a business practitioner. However, to some extent, social bonds that crossed the strict remit of the research intruded into the interview process. This is not surprising as there was a similar effect with the academic respondents where I have a common cause as a fellow practitioner in the academy. Also, social bonds are established with the students they naturally exhibit the desire to understand the motivations and drivers of an academic working in their field of study. To facilitate the progress of the primary research I decided to keep only audio recordings of the interviews and contemporaneous notes made during these. In retrospect, I should have sought ethical consent for the keeping of video transactions of the interviews and this will be a key learning for future iterations of this research process. Whilst the audio recordings and the notes constitute an accurate account of the exchanges some of the subtle emotional nuances of these encounters may have been lost. In total there were thirty-two telephone interviews, eleven face to face interviews and fourteen Skype interviews. Of these, most of the Business respondents were interviewed via the telephone whilst the students and academics had a broader mixture of the mode of contact. In all cases, I kept contemporaneous notes which were of vital utility in capturing the subtleties of emotional responses during the interviews. It must be noted that these were of diminishing utility according to the richness of contact. By this, I mean that the face to face interviews captured the most contextually rich data, the Skype interviews less so and the telephone interviews least of all. Even in the case of telephone interviews the moderation form that gave structure to the interviews was nevertheless invaluable and based on a structure suggested by Gadamer's iteration of the fusion of horizons. A copy of the moderation form can be found in Appendix 2 but here is a brief exposition of its textual structure and its intent.

The first section consisted of an introductory discussion that attended to the social etiquette of initial engagement with the respondents in the initial interview and re-engagement in subsequent interviews. In almost all cases this exchange always extended beyond the desired or planned brevity and in terms of time always exceeded intent and expectation. In retrospect, this was necessary to build a personal connection between me and the respondent and to establish trust and common cause in the subsequent conversation. As phenomenological enquiry seeks to uncover the personal and the intimate experience of phenomena these introductory "social" discussions were vital to establishing the level of intimacy required particularly in circles two and three when connections are being re-established. Evidence of Prejudice (or pre-understanding of the issue) was the next section and this I used to briefly sketch out the initial interviews my assumptions on epistemological congruence and potential understanding between the stakeholder groups. In subsequent interviews, I largely used this to re-check prior assumptions and to sense check the respondent's understanding of the documents shared with the hermeneutical circles. Synthesis of text or the identification of prior sources of knowledge was problematic and, in all cases, other than with the professional academics, as those outside a professional academic culture needed more supplemental closed questions to identify original and ongoing sources of knowledge regarding the role of business school pedagogy. Unsurprisingly it was the business practitioners that struggled with this most initially but on subsequent interviews, some had conducted supplemental reading and enquiry to better understand the shared texts. The next section explored epistemological boundaries or nature of each respondent's understanding of what knowledge business school curricula should seek to deliver and in the initial interviews with all respondents this was task and skills focussed and only in the second and third turns of the all the circles did the discourse turn to more abstract and conceptual matters. I had anticipated that the next section where I sought to establish a Fusion of Horizons would be the most problematic as I had anticipated difficulties in reconciling views. In practice, this was not the case as there was almost an eagerness amongst the respondents to understand and accommodate the views of others. This may have been a function of my own intercessory influence and I have reflected on this in a subsequent chapter. The process of "Rapprochement" and the evidence for this proved to be the most difficult. This is the stage beyond the acceptance of the views of the other where these views are used by the individual to gain new personal insights into the issue-at-hand. Evidence for this is close in nature to acceptance but is distinguished by the uncovering of the emerging synthesis by referring to previous reactions by the respondent to the same questions earlier in the hermeneutical cycle of discourse. Here is an example of this. The respondent here is a third-year student on the issue of an employer's perception of graduate qualities.

<u>Circle Two – Turn Two</u>

Phaedrus: Are you surprised at how employers evaluate the quality of graduates?

Respondent: Yes, I guess so, I expected them to be more interested in grades and things like the (extracurricular activity) certificate.

Phaedrus: Will this change your approach to securing a graduate job?

Respondent: I don't know I'm not sure that this is right.

Phaedrus: Why?

Respondent: Well I don't know how they can look at anything else. I mean, qualifications and what you've done is all they can see.

Phaedrus: Except for assessment centres, interviews, internships.

Respondent: (Pause) Yes, I suppose that's true

Circle Two – Turn Three

Respondent: I can see why employers get worried about new recruits.

Phaedrus: Why?

Respondent: It's a risk isn't it, I mean you're going to take on someone you don't even know and you're going to pay them to run something you've built up.

Phaedrus: I'm not absolutely clear what you mean?

Respondent: I was thinking about managers that work in big organisations and I used to think that who they took on didn't really matter to them as they were on salaries but I see now that this is a big risk for them.

Phaedrus: Even more than the risk taken by a "one-man band" or a small company?

Respondent: Yes, probably even more.

Phaedrus: Why?

Respondent: Well if you're an entrepreneur or your own boss there's no-one looking over your shoulder, I mean you could just sack someone if you find you've made a mistake!

Phaedrus: How have you come to this conclusion?

Respondent: From the last document you sent out.

Phaedrus: It would really help me if you quoted the appropriate extract.

Respondent: Ok, hang on (pause) "Employers' key issue with business school graduates is not the level of academic attainment, but the unknown factors that are not revealed by certificates or statements of achievement. It is whether the individual identified thorough a relatively short selection process will have the right emotional and attitudinal temperament that will fit with their organisational culture. This seems to more of an issue as organisations grow larger. Their culture becomes more complex and sub-cultures emerge for individual functional processes that can be critical of individuals, managers empowered to recruit, that pick the "wrong people" either through mistake or wilful intent." That seems right to me.

Phaedrus: So, what does that mean to you?

Respondent: I'm going to try and find a company with a culture I like.

Finally, the last section of the moderation form was concluding observations that afforded the respondents the opportunity to comment on the discourse, the process of exchange, the documents that had been circulated and any other relevant issue that occurred to them. There were three purposes to this. The first was to cover any issue or comment that they wanted to make if I had failed to cover this previously in the interview. The second was to afford an opportunity to extend the discussion untrammelled by my own interlocutory perception of what was relevant. Often, as will be seen from the extracts below some of these changes did add to the content of the shared documents. Third and last, this final less formal section did give both me and the respondents a chance to reaffirm social bonds and interests where they existed both in the sense of those that had previously been established prior to the research and those that developed during the research. Below are some sample comments from respondents from this stage of the interview process and I have also given an indication as to which circle and which turn these comments occurred. Some details I have redacted in order to safeguard anonymity.

Circle One – Turn One

Employer respondent – It's good that you're doing this, I'm interested in how these apprenticeship degrees will work out, ****** keeps badgering me about the cost of the apprentice levy, I'm not sure we're going to get a good return on this. Not directly anyway.

Circle Two – Turn One

Academic respondent – Do you get support for this? They've cut our research allocations here it's difficult to get funding now, internally I mean, not even in time.

Circle Three – Turn Two

Academic respondent – I went to a networking event last Thursday with some local business luminaries, we do the same things you do. Everyone seemed worried about Brexit especially the engineering firms, there are so many Europeans working in these small but prosperous firms. I'm not sure we're geared up (as a higher education sector) to fill the gaps.

Circle One – Turn Two

Student respondent – I actually come from Bristol, well ****** anyway. It's not so hot around here for jobs and some of my friends are thinking of moving to Bristol when they finish, or London. I suppose that I'm lucky my Dad can always sort a job out for me.

Circle Two – Turn Two

Student respondent – We've got a member of staff doing something like you're doing, research into how well they teach. I think it must be getting tough to recruit students. I mean it didn't seem to me that they cared that much about that when I started, I think things have changed. Oh, and there's less staff around but less PhD students at least everyone seems to already be a Doctor now.

Circle One – Turn Three

Employer respondent – You know this isn't the first time that I have been interviewed by academics but it never does seem to go anywhere. What are you going to do with all this work? I don't read academic journals, well not often anyway, that article you suggested (Small, Shacklock, & Marchant, 2018) was interesting, but I just read the abstract and the conclusion, made me think about recruitment, but that's an aside. Where does all this stuff go?

Circle Three – Turn Three

Academic Respondent – I think that student expectations are changing. A couple of years back it was all customer focus, where's our value for money? What are you doing for me? Now I think a lot of them are a lot more cynical about the whole university experience (laughs) it's as if it's all an extension of taking a year out with no real connection to what they really want to do!

Much of the material, whilst not directly related to the central question of the research did add some interesting contextual insights into the drift of academic culture as perceived by the respondents. One aspect of this was the assurance that most of the respondents that engaged in the hermeneutical circles felt enough confidence in the assurance of anonymity to be confident enough to express some of these opinions. This could have been due to the nature of the process itself or the personal relationship that they had developed with me. In brief, this was an added and welcome emergent feature of the discursive exchanges. The moderation form was essential to controlling the length and nature of the conversations held with the respondents. I had anticipated that the initial interviews and the re-engagement process that followed the dissemination of the shared documents would take approximately twenty minutes each. In practice, each interview took at least forty minutes and some interviews/discussions ran over ninety minutes. In total, over forty hours of interviews had to be transcribed. This is where the utility of notes made contemporaneously became critical. Digital recording allows for the facility to time mark key points of interest and using these in combination with the notes allowed the analysis of the material to commence independent of the full transcription of the material. This meant that I could author, edit, and check the documents to be read by the hermeneutic circle without having to force the respondents to wait too long. I must confess that the first circle took far too long to execute and the delay in each turn did cause some frustration amongst the respondents as they would have to refresh their understanding of the documentation prior to each interview. This was a key lesson for the subsequent circles. To speed the process of exchange I used the digital time-stamping technique to extract key points with greater acuity and speed. By the execution of the third circle, this experience telescoped the time from start to finish from eleven months to three months, a more manageable and acceptable time frame. Another key learning was the method in which documents were shared amongst respondents. In the initial stages, I experimented with a secure website secured with encrypted access. Again, this caused some frustration amongst participants, some had the technical skill to access this with ease whilst others struggled. Realising that I had over-engineered this process I switched after the first turn of the circle to a simple email. This had the added advantage of personalisation in each message which helped to build social connections and confidence.

The mechanics of discourse as bounded by the operationalisation of Gadamer's idea of how hermeneutical circles can be used to facilitate the fusion of horizons and the transmission of meaning through shared texts improved with practice and execution form circle one to circle three. What became even clearer was the centrality of personal connection throughout the process. In discussing with all respondents' responses to trends, opinions, movements in fashion, intellectual influences and how business contextualises itself in a wider societal context, I found that a purely rational response could not be extricated from the emotional and unanalysable psychological vectors of any issue. Each moment of discussion is laden with an emotional substrate and in reflecting on this, this is inevitable. Business its practice, its execution, forms the basis of the livelihood or will form the basis of the livelihood of all of the respondents myself included. To analyse it, to challenge it, to deconstruct its pedagogy is a challenge to this emotional almost visceral investment in the process of business. And this works for all respondents. For the employers actively engaged in Business, it is a significant part of what-they-are, their in-being in the world. For academics, those that have been practitioners and those that are purely academic observers the field is dependent upon the social consensus that business is a discernible field of study, something that can be identified, something that has social significance and value. And for students, it is an investment in something that has value now and will continue to have value in the future. Challenging this through the critical examination of pedagogy and epistemological boundaries has the potential to create emotional stress. This is not to say that through this study the entire edifice of business will collapse but that even to challenge peripherally the foundation of belief in which so much is invested warrants care and the realisation that this will produce an emotional as well as a rational reaction. This realisation was critical in engineering improvements in the mechanics of discourse, the centre of the exchange of meaning moved significantly from the first circle where it focussed on the rational to the emotional which became more central in circles two and three. In the next section, I will illustrate this when I will address the uncovering of meaning in this research process.

The Uncovering of Meaning

The meaning I originally sought to uncover was to demonstrate that a "fusion of horizons" could be facilitated by adapting the interpretive phenomenology of Gadamer through creating a framework of hermeneutical circles that would demonstrate how text and language as carriers of meaning facilitate understanding between individuals through discourse and reflection. By this means, I sought to uncover epistemological differences and congruity and seek to uncover the roots of this so that I could improve my pedagogy at a personal level and in some small way at an institutional level. In the execution of the first hermeneutical circle this seemed a reasonable goal as the process seemed simple to deliver, comprehensible to the respondents and the final result, the document produced after the third turn had a positive reception from the members of the circle. I have reproduced a full copy of this in Appendix 1 and here is the conclusion.

> The key issue for the development of business school pedagogy is to ensure that the delivery of the academy's curriculum takes account of the intergenerational issues that arise in the context of wider societal development. The changing values of cohorts of students as they successively progress through business schools are not fully understood by either academics or by those that will employ them. Commensurately there is a lack of comprehension on the other side of this equation. This indicates that the study and understanding of individual values, how they are acquired, how they are formed and whether or not they could be in conflict with others should be a critical challenge to the business academy both through research and how that research informs pedagogy.

After I had shared this document I started to prepare the materials for the next circle and recruited the participants/respondents. Whilst the first circle had started with the primer statement that business school did have an effective pedagogy the second as to start with a negative one, namely that the business schools did not have an effective pedagogy. Prior to starting the next circle, I decided to write up some reflective notes on the research process to date and in doing so I reviewed the conclusion as above. Part of my reflection was to pose the question to myself, what would I do with this information, how would I do something different in my practice as a professional academic that would acknowledge this finding? It was at this point that I realised that I had used the word "values" in an anodyne manner that did not fundamentally address what values actually meant to the individual. On a superficial level, I could point at the differences in the manifestation of organisational loyalty, but this could just be symptomatic of a deeper cause that lay outside the narrow remit of the research. And this perhaps would have been acceptable on this superficial level. However, this is a phenomenological study and it must, if it is to be true to its philosophical origins embrace the lived experience of the individual, in brief, I had to explore the notion of what is valuable in its deeper emotional state and I would need to change the nature of the discursive process. The first circle had been a successful demonstration of the efficacy of the structure and produced solid conclusions and outputs that had been hypothesised at the outset of the research process. But the feeling remained that this was a superficial achievement and that it had not fully reflected the unfiltered life-world perception of business pedagogy. I did not feel that it would be productive to simply repeat this process another two times as the outcomes would be fundamentally similar. What I felt was needed was not a change in the structural approach but a change in the quality and nature of the interrogative approach. The discursive process between myself and the respondents would need to change in an attempt to more profoundly explore the nature of personal experience. Moving the emphasis of the questioning process from a rational/objective basis to an emotional/instinctive one was not an easy task and there were immediate consequences. First and foremost was the establishment of rapport in the initial phase of the discussion. When talking about process rather than feeling respondents can call upon the normative rules of exchange when talking about, for example, their experience of business school pedagogy. The question; was your class on accounting useful or not? is significantly less challenging than how did you feel about your class on accounting. The former question elicits a functional response framed in the experience of professional utility, the latter challenges the respondent to re-live their emotional response to the phenomenon of being taught accounting. The former draws out the utility of outcomes the latter takes the individual back to their visceral response to the moment. This is more challenging and subject to interpretive ambiguity. Whilst I can with some confidence evaluate the different outcomes described by respondents it is another challenge entirely to examine where a description of emotional amounts to a possible fusion of experience and horizons. Here is an example. In the first circle, I talked with all respondents on the usefulness of their business qualifications, whether these were obtained in universities or not. In the second I altered this question to explore how they felt about the value of their degrees. Here are two sample exchanges each with employer participants.

> Circle One – Question: What was your most useful course (in Business)?
>
> Phaedrus: Going back to your own formal business education, what in your opinion have you found most useful?
>
> Respondent: (Long pause) Hmmm, some basic stuff I think, spreadsheets and the like.
>
> Phaedrus: I find that a bit surprising, I know you graduated with a very good degree so you must have been quite good at theory and analysis?
>
> Respondent: Ah, but when I got into my first job all they wanted me to do was fill in data on spreadsheets.
>
> Phaedrus: Didn't they want you to analyse the results?
>
> Respondent: As I recall a lot of the analysis as it was, was embedded in the software, you typed in the figures and out came the results. I found the knowledge of how spreadsheets worked very useful though as it enabled me to uncover and correct data entry errors.
>
> Phaedrus: So all that theory was not so useful?

Respondent: Well, not at first, I guess it helped me challenge things when I needed to but that was more to do with the way you thought than any actual theory.

Phaedrus: Can you remember the level and name of the module?

Respondent: I could look it up?

Phaedrus: Just an indication will do.

Respondent: Computers in Business, something like that, back in the day computers were exotic, like science fiction so we (as students) were all quite excited by the module.

Phaedrus: And the level?

Respondent: Final year I think.

<u>Circle Two – Question: What did you feel at the time was your most useful course?</u>

Phaedrus: Forgive me if I've got this wrong I think you said that you did a HND in Business at xxxxxxx. Can you cast your mind back and tell me, at the time, what did you think in your studies was going to be of most use to you when you left college?

Respondent: (Without hesitation) Oh, I felt that the module we did on managing people would be the best for me, it was because I knew that I wanted to be manager, I didn't just want to be an office worker.

Phaedrus: Did it actually turn out that way?

Respondent: Well not until later on, but I thought it was really important at the time.

Phaedrus: Why?

Respondent: It was the assumption that you were going to be important, I felt that I was going to be important. It was trust really the feeling that you could one day be trusted to look after other people. I didn't go to a grammar school like you and I felt that it was always thought that we would follow, you know.

Phaedrus: Can you give me a specific example of something from that module that actually helped you in a tricky personnel situation.

Respondent: (Pause) Well, it wasn't an actual thing from the module, it was the attitude of the teacher in class, it was like confidence, a feeling that you needed to be confident in yourself and that others would expect you to know things and be confident. I started to think I should be confident and that I could know more than others and that they would see me as a competent person.

Phaedrus: Did it turn out that way?

Respondent: Right up until the time I actually became a manager! (Laughs)

Phaedrus: It's a good line, but really?

Respondent: Some ways yes, and some ways no. I don't think that unless you show that you are confident, or you have some belief in yourself before you won't get picked out from the rest for that first step. I can't honestly remember any of the bloody theory but I remember the feeling that I had that there was something else. Some other possibility.

The first exchange is easier to interpret as it yields a functional result, spreadsheets are useful and demonstrably so in the execution of job-related tasks. The second exchange is far more problematic. There are a number of possibilities here. To be generous to the pedagogy and content of this half-remembered module it could be argued that the intent of the module had achieved its desired outcome and that the student had developed the requisite confidence to be a manager through the explanation that the effective management of other was a learned technique rather than an inherited skill. To be less generous we could say that the outcome in engendering confidence was almost entirely coincidental and that the change in attitude was a correlation rather than causality. In this interpretation, the respondent would perhaps have been already on course to develop the confidence to manage others through the simple medium of an emerging maturity. Another interpretation is that this was a post-facto justification on the part of the respondent, a validation of confidence that already pre-existed and was simply given form by the module. The ultimate truth of this cannot be uncovered and the best that can be said is that there are probably subtle combinations of each of these interpretations at play. What is important for this study is not so much the outcome but the moment at which the thought that personal competence was a critical factor in potential success emerged. Whilst I cannot claim that the actual materials used in the module are directly responsible for this respondent's subsequent career success I can say that this was a fundamentally important moment that was facilitated or enabled by the Business School in which the respondent studied and as such established an emotional bond to that moment and at that time. The respondent as a participant in the pedagogical process established a visceral bond with the Business Academy and as such enters, a wider community and value system predicated around not only the notion of business pedagogy but also of business as a discernible practice in a wider societal context. This emotional memory creates belonging. The memory of this lesson and the demonstrable truth of the tutor's words had a real resonance that was confirmed by the respondents' subsequent experience of the working environment. In this instance, the assertion of the tutor having been memorable at the moment of delivery in the classroom acquires a new truth and emotional resonance. For the respondent, this hints at a distinct cultural tradition, a heritage of knowledge being passed down from tutor-practitioner to practitioner. A particular community that spans temporal location and which shares experiences and concerns.

It was the embedding of emotive words within the questioning exchange such as feeling, empathy and regret, which moved the discursive process from one of superficial exchange into one of the uncovering of meaning, but this posed another challenge for the structure of the research. If the use of a framework predicated on the operationalisation of Gadamer's thought was not sufficient to uncover the underlying processes that governed the fusion of horizons I had to ask myself if the study could simply be pursued through a more direct interpretive phenomenological approach. The answer was that I was looking for the congruity of attitude and feeling amongst the participants in the processes and outcomes of the Business Academy and that Gadamer in his focus on the exchange of meaning and the emergence of new normative understanding through subjectivity/intersubjectivity provided gave form to the interpretive process. This meant that the method was further developed from circle two to circle three.

In circle three the method crystallised into a mature process that consisted of three stages; exchange, interpretation and fusion. Again the overall structure as laid out in the moderation form remained the same as did the questions with their re-alignment to feeling and experience, this provided the structure for the discursive exchange. Overlaid on this in the analytical process was the interpretation of the material along phenomenological lines and finally, the outcome, the shared document, represented the fusion of horizons mediated by the instigator and author of the research. Here is an example of similar questions posed to student respondents in circles two and three that illustrate this evolution.

> <u>Circle two: Question: Do you feel that your degree will be valued by employers?</u>
>
> Phaedrus: The degree is as you say a big chunk out of your life, do you feel its worth it will it get you the job you want?
>
> Respondent: I wouldn't be doing it if I thought I was wasting my time, I've been to some employers fares and the people on the stalls seem genuine when they talk to you. If you get

chatting with some you realise that they've been through it too.

Phaedrus: Through it?

Respondent: Through University, getting their own degrees.

Phaedrus: Do they ask you about your course?

Respondent: Not really most seem interested in what you are interested in outside college, sport, hobbies, gaming and the like.

Phaedrus: Don't you find that a little odd?

Respondent: (Long pause) Yes, but I forgot to say some expect you to know something about them already like you've done your research before you get to the stall. So I guess that they must research us so that it's worthwhile for them to do the exhibitions.

Phaedrus: Ah, I see, so you think that if the reputation of the University, the Faculty and the Degree programme is good they can tick that box off so to speak?

Respondent: Yes I think that's right.

Phaedrus: How do you feel about that, doesn't that make you nervous that we, the academics won't get it right?

Respondent: Hmmmm, I haven't thought about that.

Phaedrus: If you follow that to its logical conclusion the employers must already value your degree before you've achieved it due to the reputation of the Faculty.

Respondent: But I've still got to graduate!

Phaedrus: Yes, you've still got to graduate.

The exchange in this example is straightforward with a simple question linking academic outcomes with employability. The interpretation is also simple, through the interlocutory process the student is uncovering some of the underlying normative assumptions of the business community namely that Business Schools deliver pedagogical outcomes that have value and consequently that it is worthwhile for employers to consider recruitment from this community.

Circle three: Question: Do you feel that your degree will be valued by employers?

Phaedrus: I get that you have enjoyed your time at university but do you think that whatever class of degree you finally get will improve your job prospects?

Respondent: I don't think I'm going to get a first class pass but I might a two/one and that should be OK.

Phaedrus: I'm a bit surprised, I didn't think you'd be OK with "OK".

Respondent: I did an internship last year, during the summer and I really enjoyed myself there.

Phaedrus: What were you doing?

Respondent: Marketing for xxxxxxx, some PR work and advertising.

Phaedrus: Did any of the course materials help you?

Respondent: Oh yes, some of the digital business stuff we did in the first year helped, social media and bits like that.

Phaedrus: Again, I'm a bit surprised I thought you didn't like modules like that?

Respondent: I still don't, not for what they are, but I suppose that they show you something. It's important to other people

> and I think that's the whole point of doing an internship or a placement you get to understand what people want.
>
> Phaedrus: But what about the stuff you really like, such as the human resources modules, the more theoretical stuff?
>
> Respondent: I think that's more personal, for you yourself to help you understand things.
>
> Phaedrus: So you make a distinction between what you find valuable from your degree and what other people find valuable?
>
> Respondent: I think we all do that, all the time, there's something that goes on in your head and that's different from the things we have to share.
>
> Phaedrus: Do you think that personal understanding will ever be of use?
>
> Respondent: Oh yes, it already has helped me understand why people sometimes do stupid things and sometimes I write little notes to myself so that I don't do similar things.
>
> Phaedrus: I would advise you to be careful with that.
>
> Respondent: (Laughs) But not many people can speak xxxxxxxx

As with the last example, the exchange is easily understood as an uncovering of what is of immediate utility in the workplace. Equally the interpretation is also straightforward, it is clear that the acquisition of the normative culture of the workplace is facilitated by work experience, but now we have an added dimension; the emergence of what is or is not to be shared as a common understanding. There is a way here in which I can determine the precise elements of what is fused in horizons of understanding and what is not. In this case, the student clearly grasps that some of their skills and techniques relating to acuity and competence in the digital domain can be shared and have value and some are (currently) entirely personal. It may be that in the future this individual's personal understanding will cease to be personal though dint of seniority or wider normative change but it is at this point and at this instance, this is where the boundary of fusion lies. So now in this hermeneutical circle, I have; an evolved and mature process of discursive exchange shaped by Gadamer's work, interpretation along interpretive phenomenological lines, and an understanding that allows me to identify the points at which fusion of horizons occurs.

Beyond Superficial Exchange

One the critical roles of methodology in academic research is to engender a continual sense of doubt and reflection in the mind of the researcher (Lien *et al.*, 2014). If this mechanism were not to exist, or, if I was not to acknowledge it, there is a danger that the method(s) adopted could create their own internal momentum, a narrative direction that becomes thorough its own internal logic an end in and of itself (Atkinson & Delamont, 2006) In any phenomenological based methodology the role of self-questioning is particularly important as the researcher needs to transparently locate their positionality (Hopkins *et al.*, 2017) with clarity. After the close of the third turn of the first hermeneutical circle I made the following note in my personal reflective journal.

> After a slow start and some concerns over how respondents would view the research everything seems to have gone a lot better than I anticipated. In particular my ex-colleague was particularly interested and enthusiastic in participating in the project. The students were also more than happy to engage in the interviews and all the interviews exceeded the time limit I thought might be reasonable. I think in the end I may have many more hours of material than I can handle easily. I am personally surprised at this. I had expected everyone to be like the academics in this first circle, a little more cagey and a little bit defensive. Also, the shared texts (Appendix 1) have been received far more positively than I anticipated. The roots of my concern are what? Why am I

> doubting this? Am I missing something of the innate quality of what is expected in a phenomenologically guided study? Is it because the structure is too limiting on discussion or is it in the nature of the questions?

I hesitate to reproduce this note with its informal style, but it is at this point that I identified that the structure I was using could be used at a superficial level, leading to an almost ritual exchange amongst respondents that stayed within the normative rules of business discourse. What I was truly seeking to uncover was the process of subjectivity/intersubjectivity that uncovered the personal experience of the research participants. By process I mean the point at which internal reflection on the exchange of meaning via both text and discussion changes an individuals' understanding of the matter-at-hand. This is of particular importance to my practice as a teacher in the Business Academy, the identification of the processes that change perception would have an obvious bearing on pedagogical practice and technique. Sharing documents that encapsulated shared understanding was therefore critical to this task. By asking that the respondents consider the same text allows a comparison of response at a multiplicity of levels, functional, intellectual and emotional. In this sense, I approach the meaning of what Gadamer says when he states that, "Who thinks of "language" already moves beyond subjectivity" (Gadamer, 2000 p. 286). The shared texts become the focus of attention and the response of respondents to particular passages has the potential to identify that point at which an individual's subjective understanding of the text moves into an acceptance of inter-subjective meaning. A new consensual reality. Here is an example from Circle two, turn two, where I have identified the point at which some research participants significantly shifted their views and accommodated the shared meaning of the text.

Extract from the shared document – Circle Two, Turn two

> *The quality of the teaching experienced in Business Schools varies considerably. From the perspective of students and alumni from a variety of Schools this appears to be a function of the individual*

> *skill, experience and knowledge manifest by the academic in the classroom or the lecture hall. The academic view is that different disciplines warrant or demand differing teaching styles as more technically demanding fields require a greater emphasis on the transmission of knowledge and an assurance that students have understood the material. Employers find this less problematical as there is an expectation that important gaps in an individuals' knowledge of technical or theoretical issues will be rapidly corrected by workplace practice and knowledge. All agree though that this is not entirely satisfactory as there should be a greater congruence between student expectation of good quality teaching and the employers need to recruit appropriately informed graduates.*

What now follows is a series of responses to this particular extract of text from three differing perspectives. I have tried to identify the point at which the extract moves the research participants' understanding of a position that approaches some form of intersubjective understanding.

> Academic Respondent: Yes, I recognise the difference between disciplines, I imagine it's really difficult to hold the attention of some students when you're teaching accounting principles. In my own field we have a problem with attendance so we are left with the students who are either just good students or those that are genuinely interested in xxxxxxxx. I don't know how you would improve teaching across all subjects? I suppose you could just improve the teaching practice for all subjects maybe thorough better CPD? (Continuing Professional Development)

> Employer Respondent: I suppose this is more important to the students as I don't think they can be prepared for everything. I think from their perspective the better prepared you are the better your chances of a good job, so they must have a leaning to blame poor teaching if they don't get what they want or feel that the teaching has missed something. Sometimes you have to wonder if their teachers understand this. No offence meant. I think it would help if all academics

spent more time talking to business outside the ivory tower, or maybe make it a rule that you can't teach business without having done business. Or talked to business about teaching. Of course, that would mean that we would have to talk to them and I can think of some of my colleagues who think that may be a waste of time. I think that in an ideal scenario we would have to.

Student Respondent: Yes, I agree with this some of my classes are so poorly taught I'm surprised anybody turns up. But for the important stuff like accounts and statistics everyone, well almost everyone, turns up as we all know that that that stuff is important and we have some pretty boring teachers for that. So, I'm not sure really, maybe the other subjects like strategy and organisational studies are more important because they (the employers) won't teach that stuff because they think that we would have automatically got that at Uni. None of us really know do we! Perhaps we should talk more.

Following this exchange of views as facilitated by the shared document the theme of shared concerns over how the pedagogy should respond to the needs of students and employers altered the common understanding of the members of this particular hermeneutical circle on the (perhaps) missing element of communication in the development of both teachers' skills and the pedagogic assumptions made by the Business Academy. The corresponding text for the third document was accordingly re-written as follows with the major alterations highlighted.

The ***perception of*** *the quality of the teaching experienced in Business Schools varies considerably. From the perspective of students and alumni from a variety of Schools this appears to be a function of the individual skill, experience and knowledge manifest by the academic* ***although this may be predetermined by student understanding of what is valuable.*** *Academics recognise that different disciplines warrant or demand differing teaching styles as more technically demanding fields require a greater emphasis on the transmission of knowledge and an assurance that students*

> *have understood the material,* ***however there is a commensurate responsibility on the part of students to engage with material they may not understand that they need.*** *Employers find this less problematical as there is an expectation that important gaps in an individuals' knowledge of technical or theoretical issues will be rapidly corrected by workplace practice and knowledge. All agree though that this is not entirely satisfactory as there should be a greater congruence between student expectation of good quality teaching and the employers need to recruit appropriately informed graduates and* ***this should be facilitated through more open and frequent communication.***

This is a clear example of how shared understanding develops through the medium of language and text.

This raises a major procedural and ethical issue. How far is the personal subjectivity and pre-understanding of the researcher influencing the narrative evolution of the shared documents and the emerging shared horizon of the hermeneutical circle? If this is not addressed it undermines the validity of the research outcomes. I have to ask myself continually am I guiding the responses of the interviewees in the direction of my own prejudice. Fortunately, there is guidance on this in the canon of literature on phenomenological research. Following the guidance of Hopkins, Regher and Pratt, the first concern that need to be addressed is positionality.

> In phenomenology, the researcher is the primary instrument for gathering data and interpreting data. As such, it is necessary for researchers to reflect upon, and state as clearly as possible, the assumptions and beliefs they bring to the research. These beliefs and assumptions are the researcher's positionality (their particular philosophical stance amidst the various perspectives underpinning phenomenology).
>
> (Hopkins, Regher & Pratt, 2017 p. 22)

Whilst I have covered at some length the "beliefs and assumptions" that I bring to the research in an earlier chapter a brief restatement of these is useful. Prior to the research, I assumed that the rise of the Business Academy was a reflection of wider societal perceptions of the primacy of business as the fundamental driver of economic value in society. Furthermore, that the fundamental influences on business pedagogy could be linked to two main strands of pedagogic influences namely the functional and the technical or the scientific view and the humanist stance as manifest in such fields as organisational studies and human resource theory. Finally, that it is my belief that the epistemological congruence amongst participants in the educational process is not perfect and that it can be improved. This pre-judgement in large part led me to Gadamer dues to my belief that I could use his interpretive phenomenology as a vehicle to examine epistemological congruence and perhaps through the use of hermeneutical circles encourage this. This determined the shape and structure of the research design though not its outcomes. In instigating the three hermeneutical circles that formed the key process of the research I was inevitably committed to writing on these themes and through that writing begin to change and evolve my own horizon of understanding. Returning to Hopkins, Regehr and Pratt they correctly situate the importance of writing for reflection on positionality.

> As researchers begin the hermeneutical cycle by reflecting on their own pre-understandings, writing can be used to clarify and crystallize ideas. When starting to gather data in the field, they inevitably start to reflect on and interpret what is observed and what participants have said. Writing these thoughts, reflections and interpretations down helps make sense of what is going on, clarify ideas, develop a sense of what one "knows", and identify what is still unclear and requires further questioning, exploration and reading. As they return to the reflective process, after engaging with a participant or observing in the field, writing helps clarify the meaning of interactions and observations, and facilitates the hermeneutic process of developing a more coherent understanding of the phenomenon. Reflecting through the process of writing then allows the researcher to see things in the

> field that could not be seen before. The unity of research and writing is succinctly summarized by Emerson et al.. (1995)… in that "this process of inscribing, of writing field notes, helps the field researcher to understand what he has been observing in the first place, thus, enables him to participate in new ways, to hear with greater acuteness, and to observe with a new lens" … Thus, the dimension of writing, although highlighted by few, encompasses all of phenomenological work. As such, it is illustrated in the framework as perfusing the entire grid (Figure 1). By foregrounding writing we hope to bring attention to how committing to a regular practice of writing throughout the research process, and not just at the end, enables the researcher to engage more meaningfully with, and understand more deeply, the experiences of participants.
>
> (Hopkins, Regehr & Pratt, 2017 pp. 26,27)

I can claim to have ascribed to the admonition to commit to " a regular practice of writing" through both my own reflective notes and of course the shared texts of the three hermeneutical circles. In my reflective notes, I recorded an important shift in positionality at the close of the first turn in circle 2.

> The added complication of attempting to capture an emotional rather than just an intellectual response to the shared texts has made me consider whether or not the base structure of the research design is wholly relevant. I wonder if I have attempted to force Gadamer into a model that is not entirely deliverable or appropriate. The first circle worked well but said nothing revelatory, adding the emotional vector to the interviews in the second circle has produced more visceral responses that move outside the arbitrary boundaries I have set in my own preconception of the influences on the pedagogy. It becomes difficult to discern what is fusion and what is rapprochement. Students in particular have no firm idea of where subject fields cross other than the definitions that they are given by their schools and for employers the distinction

> between a scientific approach and a humanistic approach is almost risible and has no meaning for them. It is not the bunkers that I have set up that will demonstrate a "fusion or horizons" but where the consensual narrative will lead. My problem is that my pre-conception of what is important is fundamentally in error, these things are important to me but not to my research participants.

This had the consequence of "freeing-up" the subsequent interviews. Whilst I kept to the moderated structure of the interviews I no longer sought evidence of prejudice, synthesis, rapprochement and fusion in the intellectual boundaries I had set. I would now look for them in a less structured manner in the immediacy of the emotional responses to the Business Academy. This more correctly reflected the aim to capture the "pre-theoretical" voice of the interviewees. This "letting-go" of the structure was not that of the operationalised iteration of Gadamer's thought but the structure that I had consciously and unconsciously imposed on the discussions that took place within the interviews. This was in effect a surrendering of authorship which within the context of this research could be argued as part of this process of fusing horizons. The meaning and significance that I derive and deliver from the shared texts is a conduit for a multiplicity of shared experiences and as such, I cannot claim to be its author, just its transcriber. Here then I create the space for Noetic insight.

The Emergence of Noetic Insight

This surrendering of authorship I argue is essential to allow space for noetic insight. This does not invalidate the Gadamerian structure that gives form to the method. Rather it is critical in the uncovering of "Intersubjectivity". If I impose my own boundaries on the evolution of the unfolding discussions I dictate the discursive turn and in effect miss a potential authentic fusion of horizons, and here, I used the term "authentic" in the Heideggerian sense.

> For Heidegger, being authentic does not require some exceptional effort or discipline, like meditation. Rather it entails

> a kind of shift in attention and engagement, a reclaiming of oneself, from the way we typically fall into our everyday ways of being. It is about how we approach the world in our daily activities. Dasein inevitably moves between our day-to-day enmeshment with the they and a seizing upon glimpses of our truer, uniquely individual possibilities for existence. The challenge is to bring ourselves back from our lostness in the they to retrieve ourselves so that we can become our authentic selves.
>
> (Sherman, 2009, p.4)

If I as the lead in the discursive process impose my own prejudice then I become a barrier, an obstacle to the emergence of intersubjective discourse. Here power relationships are an issue. In effect I am the "they" in which the authentic voice of the research participant is lost. In order to uncover an "authentic" voice, I must, consciously throughout the interviews, continually and in real-time reflect on whether or not my voice is approaching dominance of the discussion. This is however a difficult balance to strike, on one hand, I must move the conversation forward to elicit the thematic information I need to make the material relevant to the research design, on the other, I must allow space for the voice of participant which may lead to irrelevant if interesting revelations. I cannot claim to have achieved this with anything approaching perfection. The research technique I adopted is novel, part of my claim to originality for this research and developed during the execution of the method and I can say that my technique, my balancing act improved from the instigation of circle one to the close of circle three. The aim is to uncover the noesis of the participants, to capture the cognitive processes that shape their unique and individual perception of the Business Academy and its pedagogy. In a sense, this is attempting to capture glimpses of authenticity. This uncovering and identification of authenticity is key to a genuine phenomenological enquiry. It means in practice that the balance between structure and space in discussion continually shifts as the exchange between researcher and interviewee unfolds and it requires skill derived from practice to facilitate this with anything approaching competency. By structure I mean the necessity to move the discussion forward and not to digress into tangential narratives and by space I mean the pauses and digressions that are not tangential. This is a matter for personal judgement and all I can do here is to again recommend practice and repetition to develop this acuity. In the context of this research, although it was not planned it was perhaps fortunate that most of the interviews exceeded my anticipated length (some quite considerably) as it allowed me to review early transcripts for those moments that revealed raw perceptions. Reflecting on the research as it unfolded was critical to this. If this research method is adapted and replicated this maintenance of a self-critical journal is essential which I hope I have illustrated above. To move forward beyond the superficial interpretation of the material requires a continual attitude of self-questioning, some examples of which are: Am I overtly directing this conversation? Is my pre-judgement being too selective in attributing significance to this statement? Is this too easy? Have I missed a moment of authenticity?

Accordingly, I attempt to uncover authentic perception, uncovering the noesis of the research participants and identifying which of these can constitute shared experiences for the purposes of answering the research question. Here I return to the fusion of horizons as this noetic insight into shared communalities is the very essence of fusion. And this I will address in some detail in the following chapter that analyses the research material.

The Unfolding of the Research

So far, I have outlined the chronological unfolding of the research method in order to identify how it differs in form and execution from other manifestations of qualitative research. This is important as the implementation of a technique informed by interpretive phenomenology is rare in the context of business research and a careful recounting of the steps that led from simple thematic analysis to noetic insight is important for further development of the method and its replicability by others. In this way, I hope to demonstrate that this a credible and valid technique for business research. In essence, this recounting has four levels of development that record the evolution of the research technique. Starting with the simple mechanics of discourse, this a descriptive account of how the texts were shared, how the interviews were conducted and how this changed with the execution of each hermeneutical circle and how it improved in efficiency with each successive iteration. The second level was the uncovering of meaning where again it was an evolution of technique from circle one to circle three, in which circle one achieved a result which, although received favourably by the members of the circle, remained superficial in its thematic insight. Circles two and three successively improved the depth of insight and analysis thorough the use of reflective self-analysis. This then moves to the third level in this evolution which is the examination of the causes of self-doubt which means that the research goes beyond superficial exchange. The notion of authorship is questioned and is partially surrendered due in no small part to an ethical consideration of how self-reflection is needed to demonstrate transparency and honesty in the core relationship between the researcher and the research participants. This means that structure however well-intentioned must at critical points in the interviews must to surrendered to listen to the authentic voice of the hermeneutical circles. Finally, it is only when there is a constant recognition of the need to balance structure and intended outcome against the space to allow for the unexpected emergence of fragments of authenticity in the research interviews do we eventually arrive at the noetic insights that mark the method as a genuine phenomenological enquiry. Noetic insight is essential if, as intended by the research question we seek to uncover where epistemological horizons are fused and to what extent key actors in the process and outcomes of business pedagogy share common concerns. This reflection and intervention yielded a wealth of material for the metanalysis of the three hermeneutical circles.

Meta-Analysis of Evidence

The material that has been collected in the research process as has been detailed above consists of almost fifty hours of recorded interviews and accompanying notes. This is the raw material that, has been subject to and interpretation and re-interpretation in order to produce the text documents that were the interpretations of the fusion of the participants' epistemological horizons. The research material has therefore been subject to constant analysis prior to this meta-analysis that I am now going to conduct. Before I start on this a brief recap of the outputs as they stand from the three hermeneutic circles will be useful.

Circle one is the one that is most closely recognisable as a form of mainstream qualitative research. The process of interview was predicated on examining the outputs and the utility of the pedagogical process of the business academy to the three stakeholder groups. The final document (above) is recognisable as a palimpsest of some of the core concerns that currently shape the internal and external perception of the academy. In truth I found this to be disappointing as it did not seem to say anything new about academic practice and its effect, it merely supported the normative view of the importance of "soft skills" and crucial base levels of technical knowledge. This disappointment led to a re-emphasis on the centrality of individual experience in the approach I took at the interview stage for the second circle.

Circle two attempted more closely to uncover the pre-theoretical voice of the respondents. In the initial turn, the collective horizon was similar to that of the first circle, but as can be seen above in the description of the process the outputs of the second and third turns began to significantly diverge. By focussing on emotional response and immediacy to experience rather than the reflection on the utility of that experience the fusion of epistemological horizons between the three stakeholder groups becomes far more problematic and interesting. Nevertheless, even in this instance, there was a demonstrable drift towards a communality of goals amongst the respondents and a desire to reach a fusion of understanding.

Circle three in process, execution and outcome was a direct development of circle two in that it more confidently explored the visceral effect of the demands and assumptions of the normative values of business pedagogy. The final turn in outward form was not dissimilar to that of circle two but there was a deeper recognition amongst all the respondents of how wider indirect influences that impinged on their personal perceptions of what they needed from the business academy and how this influenced the fusion of horizons.

So, whilst the process and the execution of the research was consistent in its physical and procedural process there was a noticeable evolution in technique and interpretation and outcome. What this analysis will determine is which elements of the execution of the research process led to this evolution and divergence. The structure and approach I will use is based on Sanders (1982) summary of the process of phenomenological analysis.

> There are four levels of phenomenological analysis. The first level is the description of the phenomena as revealed in the taped interviews. the transcribed narratives identify and describe the qualities of human experience and consciousness that give the person being studied their unique identity and outlook. Level two in phenomenological analysis is the identification of themes or invariants that emerge from the descriptions. Themes refer to communalities present within and between narratives.
>
> (Sanders, 1982 p. 357)

Themes Emergent from the Research

The descriptive accounts of the three circles in the account of how the method was executed uncovers the processes of interview and discourse that are the key procedural processes. These descriptions of experience reveal the "qualities" of the human experience. By simple textual analysis perhaps best exemplified in the final text prepared for the participants in the first circle, a simple collation of common phrases and themes that can be identified in the transcripts yields a comprehensible document that can be shared amongst the respondents and for whom there are clearly concordances that bridge the boundaries of the stakeholder groups. These do not reveal the "invariants or themes that are emergent in these descriptions." For these, I need to turn to my notes made contemporaneously during the interviews and during my post-reflective analysis during the unfolding of the circles to uncover this. To illustrate how these themes were uncovered I will use extracts of the reflective notes I made during each of the hermeneutic circles. Some of these were made during the interview process and some after the interview particularly when reflecting on the meaning of the interchange.

> Note 1 – The theme of disappointment
>
> The interviews are taking much longer than expected and what was envisaged as a short discourse aimed at uncovering the practical response to the efficacy of business pedagogy often diverges into more personal matters of "what was missing" from the retrospective perspective of the usefulness of the curriculum.

This was a common theme amongst all the early respondents from all the stakeholder groups. Students, particularly those who had either been on placement or who were actively seeking one or an internship were largely positive about their experience of the academy, however, most did unprompted criticise the academy for not being more proscriptive in some areas particularly those relating to technical skills such as the use of business statistics, business mathematics and spreadsheets. This was often prompted by a struggle to assimilate into the organisational cultures they encountered during time away from the academy. Even those student respondents that had not yet been on an internship or a placement seemed to have a sense of what was missing from the curriculum and when pressed on this some acknowledged that this was part of the social context of the community of students that applied for such extracurricular enhancements to their studies, a tradition passed from cohort to cohort to aid in the securing of desired positions. The criticism was not trenchant but was often took the nature of a resigned acceptance of the limitations of the academy's curriculum. Academics also acknowledged the technical gaps in the curriculum, but this took a different form, this was more often a more focused and parochial view that what they did, what they taught should have a wider acknowledgment of significance in the curriculum. This was less prevalent amongst those academics that had recently left practice but nevertheless, there was an element of practitioner bias from these respondents that is a close analogue of the views of those academics embedded in their disciplinary fields for longer. Asked when how these gaps should be addressed the responses were not consistent across the stakeholder group and varied from simple resignation "things will not get done" – "no one listens to me" – "this is important, I know" to the more assertive views that the curriculum must be re-organised to reflect the needs of the academic's subject discipline " this is something we must address or our students will struggle" – "our reputation as a business school will suffer unless we devote more resources". There was no consistency across disciplines for this view and seems to be a function of personal bias rather than any communality of academic discipline or length of time in the academic profession. Business respondents were the most consistent group as almost all identified gaps in the Business curriculum that should be addressed. This criticism fell into two categories. Unsurprisingly there was a unanimous view that the Business Academy should be more directly responsible for ensuring that technical and mathematical skills were more thoroughly covered in the curriculum and more subtly that graduates were made aware of the importance of these. It is this latter point that is more interesting and potentially more challenging to the culture of business schools. There seemed to be an expectation on the part of the employers that much of the technical curriculum of business schools prior to the pre-1992 higher education reforms still formed the core of what was taught in higher education in the sense that, for example, most of the respondents expected graduate entrants to be fully familiar with such ubiquitous software packages as Microsoft Office. In conversation during the interviews most accepted that this was not the role of the academy and agreed that higher cognitive outcomes had greater long-term utility both for them and the graduates but many nevertheless thought that Business schools should offer extracurricular activities to improve "STEM" skills. Even when I pointed out that many do including my own, I was challenged on whether we (academics) were doing enough to promote the importance of these. The second curriculum gap that employers identified can best be termed as a lack of cultural awareness amongst graduates. Whilst not unanimous most respondents from this stakeholder group expressed dismay that graduates seemed culturally unprepared for the rigours of organisational environments. This had less to do with the willingness to make an effort to work but a perception amongst employers that new graduate employees were not sufficiently willing to conform to existing normative values. Many employers praised the base work ethic of new graduates but counterbalanced this with an almost mystified observation that there were significant differences normative values between a new and existing employee that sometimes led to misunderstandings about expectations in the common workplace environment. One illustration of this was the issue of organisational loyalty with there being a broad agreement that the rising business school cohorts were much less likely to commit to a substantive career with a single organisation.

There are disappointments across all the stakeholder groups that the Business School curriculum leaves small but critical gaps in preparing students for work. There seemed to be a far greater unanimity in this between the students and the employers and much less with the academic community whose understandable focus lies in the fragmented nature of the subject discipline perspective. This "quality" of disappointment is inevitable. The business curriculum cannot encompass all conceivable requirements of all stakeholder groups. It would also be misleading to characterise this quality of experience as a trenchant failing of the academy as almost all respondents acknowledged their own responsibility for addressing these gaps. In the outcome texts of the hermeneutic circles, this is manifest in the common will towards more effective communication amongst stakeholder groups which should be facilitated by Business Schools. Here then is the first epistemological lesson; base level technical skills and cultural skills should be better understood by academics when reviewing programme content and course curricula and that a co-ordinated and coherent effort should be made across all, subject disciplines to address this in a coherent manner. This does not absolve students and employers from all responsibility, a greater recognition of the necessary fragmentation of knowledge across the academy is needed by these groups. For students, an understanding that there is a commensurate responsibility on them to identify their own skill gaps as early as possible and challenge the Business School to help cover these would aid the communication flow and epistemological coherence. For employers acknowledging that the deepening of subject knowledge is a critical benefit to them in terms of improving our understanding organisational processes at all levels is important and to do this deeper engagement with the academy on the part of the employers would be useful again in the arena of an epistemological understanding.

> Note 2 – the theme of belonging
>
> One of the more emotionally surprising themes amongst the respondents is the sense of belonging. A sense that "we are all in it together" and that there is a desire to be accommodating and welcoming across all the stakeholder groups is palpable in the responses. I am worried that I may be enabling this as the interlocutor and that this reflects my own feelings and values. I need to take care here.

Belonging; the sense that an individual is wanted by a community and in turn wants to belong to that community is a fundamental function of being human, the human species being a social one (Ingram & Zou 2008). However, in the context of Business this is also a cause of conflict colloquially called the "work- life balance". I needed to take care of this particular quality of experience as I have to acknowledge that my own work-life balance in whatever sphere has been skewed towards "work" rather than "life".

Student respondents gave a strong sense that the Business school was a community to which they belonged irrespective of how well or poorly the school itself facilitated this. There was one exception, a student respondent who overtly claimed to disdain both the faculty's and the Student Unions' efforts in this regard so whilst there was no unanimity the sense of belonging was strong. This also extended beyond the student cohort as again most students expressed the belief that the academics irrespective of well or poorly they performed in the classroom were firmly in the same community of interest with the student cohorts. Furthermore, whilst the bridge to communality in the business community was more tenuous there was what could be best described as a desire or wish that this was the social reality; a link of common cause between all three. Even those students that had been on placement or had done internships felt that this was a tangible link, some even more so particularly when their placement organisations had offered them permanent roles following graduation. What is important here is the form of this quality, it was not based on a procedural assumption that business needed graduates and that academics needed to teach graduates. This was not a series of transactional necessities but an emotional bridge between the stakeholder groups. This was difficult to explore in the interview process as student respondents often became defensive when attempting to locate the origins of this belief as often they could not articulate this with precision. What I could determine was this sentiment seemed to have its origins in a wider notion of social interdependence. It is as if students have assumed that there is a social contract between the Business Academy, Business and wider society in which business schools manifest the wider will and desire of society for well-trained managers. This belief is important as there is a core of trust in this, trust that the graduate will be wanted and trust that there will be a positive outcome as a reward for their studies. This does not mean that students feel an entitlement to be wanted, rewarded, or to belong, the competitive nature of the business community is an ingrained and overt theme in the business academy that is taken a self-evident outcome of the nature of economic competition. Belonging from the student's perspective is tempered by the need to maximise their own personal utility to the community, usually expressed through the desire to achieve "good grades" a first or an upper second. This is an important epistemological conduit. If there is a sense of community and common cause that stretches across the stakeholder groups if we can more accurately define this sense of "belongingness" then this becomes a tangible way in which epistemological boundaries can further merge.

The interviews with the employers also revealed a sense of wider community manifest mainly in a sympathy for, and a sympathy with the difficulties facing graduates entering the business and organisational community. When pressed on this point much of this seemed to derive from the respondent's own memories and experiences of their early careers. There was a desire to see rising cohorts enhance and extend the success of organisational life in general, wider societal sense and in particular for the individual parochial concerns of organisations. In the cases where employers had experience of offering placements and internships, for those students that had performed well, there was a real sense of ownership and responsibility for those students and in some cases, this was obviously personal. Even for those students that had not there was still some sense of a desire that they would find a role, a place in which they would belong. Another element of the employer's perspective of "belonging" was a recognition of the need for competence across organisational and commercial communities. A sense that the professional competence of business and management life had to evolve and improve. Nor as this confined to the sectional interests of the respondents. This idea of belonging to a community of competence extended beyond the sectors in which the respondents worked. There was a desire for a general improvement in the entire community. Typically, this was justified by a sense that if the entire business or organisational community drifted in that direction then general economic and social benefits would accrue. Again, though there was a recognition of embedded competitiveness and an expectation that there was a commensurate recognition by graduates that this was a critical element of organisational contexts. In the specific instance of their own experience, particularly amongst those respondents whose careers spanned a number of decades, there was an opinion that the specific belongingness of the individual to the firm – loyalty – has and is being eroded but that this was not a critical problem as the velocity of movement in the employment markets was now a given to be managed rather than a threat to be feared. Nevertheless, even in this subset of the employer respondents, this did not erode the overall sense that communities of interest and common cause continued to be a factor in the evolution and adaptability of business and management practice. The caveat here is that from the employers' perspective the scope of belongingness encompassed all graduates and not just those of business schools, a recognition that was lacking in the student respondents. What I found surprising in analysing this aspect of the responses was not this was not confined to the technical requirements of the various enterprises and organisations. In one instance during an interview with a senior manager of an engineering firm I tried to be specific on the point and said, "of course you have a constant need for well-trained engineering graduates" to which the response was, "yes, but I am referring to our other departments, sales and the like, we have a brilliant graduate in sales who, I think, did English." The conversation continued around this point and it became clear that in this instance at least the sense of belongingness was a far more redolent of a wider embracing of inter-generational movement. It was only when pressed that most employer respondents seemed to acknowledge this wider sense of community as there was an element of both parties, myself and the respondent, marshalling the discourse around the Business Academy. Towards the latter part of the research process in circle two and for the whole of circle three I made a conscious effort during the interviews to ensure that I covered this wider sense of community adequately. This confirmed this early instance of employers feeling that the wider graduate community "belonged" to them. This is a real case of epistemological dissonance between two of the stakeholder groups of the business academy. Resolution is problematic. If business students feel that they do not have some form of competitive advantage by virtue of their subject discipline then there may be an erosion in the confidence in specific business qualifications and this may be counterproductive as in spite of this wider sense of belongingness on the part of employers, business graduates have a much greater chance of securing graduate-level employment than any other humanities discipline (HEFCE, 2018). If on the other hand employers were more transparent regarding their requirements of graduates on a personal level this could have a profound effect on the curricula of business schools. If, for example, as a consequence, the business academy was to compete with other disciplines for those students most likely to develop higher-level critical acuity, then the curriculum would have to be adjusted to accommodate this at all levels and this could mean that the pedagogy devoted to transactional skills (such as presentation skills) that are also highly valued in organisational life is diminished. This would mean that business schools would begin to erode their own distinctiveness and employers would have a much smaller pool of those graduates specifically adept in these fields. If the business academy responds to this dissonance a major factor will be the attitude to belongingness in the academy itself.

Academic respondents had both the least well developed and the most well-developed sense of belongingness amongst the three respondent groups. Any reader of Trowler (2001) will not be surprised that academic respondents had a strong sense of belonging to both school and discipline and a much weaker sense of belonging with the business community. Nor was this linked to whether the academic had had a substantive career in practice. I have reflected on whether this was a function of my own interrogative technique and I have re-analysed the transcripts regarding this quality of experience. I have covered this at some length in the chapter on reflection but a brief excerpt of this may be instructive. "In my self-recognition of being allowed to move out of the world of private enterprise into academia, I have invested in the (business) academy a sense of attachment that is usually manifest in my profession to other people that this is the best job I've had, if not the best paid." Most academics, including ex-practitioners and career academics, have a strong sense of vocational devotion and this was clearly manifest in the research interviews. The quality of belongingness resides primarily in the discipline, the faculty and the school and in that order. Again, this was a quality that became stronger as the research developed and when pressed on this point most academic respondents freely admitted that the focus of belongingness lay with the academy rather than the wider business community. It should be acknowledged however that this is a natural response as human beings are predisposed to have a greater sense of belonging to their immediate communities and this too was also evident in the other stakeholder groups. However, it is especially strong amongst academics and radiates out in circles to the wider communities. This does not mean that there was no recognition of wider belongingness, but this had less of a visceral sense in the discourse and more of an objective recognition that this was something that was functionally good to do. Where academic respondents had undertaken research in organisational communities there was a greater sense of belonging to that specific instance but this did not translate into a wider sense of responsibility. I explored this point with some of the respondents particularly form the aspect of exploring the likely response of students to this inward-facing focus. I was surprised that there was an acceptance on the part of this stakeholder group that "this was the way it is" and "it's university, people do research." I had expected more resentment amongst the responses due to how this might diminish contact time with the teaching staff, but this was largely absent. When asked about contact time with the students, Academic respondents universally accepted the need to provide substantive and good quality teaching content and materials and this went beyond a notion of contractual obligation and some when pressed for "evidence" of concern for student welfare pointed to the formal processes that had been established by their respective faculty management to enhance the student experience. This latter theme was also redolent of the third quality that of apprehension.

Note 3 – The theme of angst

In my conversations with the research respondents across all stakeholder groups there was a detectable underlying sense of incompleteness, a feeling that not was as well as it could be in the relationship between the three stakeholder groups a sense that it could be more complete, which seemed at first pass to support the notion that there should be greater epistemological concordance between academics. I find it tempting to do so but again I must be careful here as "angst" in the phenomenological sense is at the core of Dasein and is

> key driver with the potential to move Dasein from inauthenticity to authenticity. The echoes of this that I find in the transcriptions may be a part of this wider sense of dissatisfaction with the world-as-it-is. Here I must unpick with care what is relevant to the pedagogy of the Business Academy.

Angst in the phenomenological sense does not simply mean anxiety. As defined by Katherine Withy in her paper *The Methodological role of Angst in Being and Time,* Angst is central to the development of human existence and consciousness.

> Heidegger's angst is a rupture in a life. It is a crisis of the everyday. In the experience of angst, my ordinary life collapses – but not in the sense that it falls to pieces and I have to put it back together again. Rather, my life collapses away from me. Engagement in my daily tasks and concerns is suspended, and the day-to-day of life shrinks into insignificance. But unlike anxiety, angst has a positive valence. This breakdown is a legitimate revelation. Where I ordinarily see the myriad tasks ahead of me and the particular entities before me, in angst I see my life as a life, and the whole world as a world. Angst is an experience within a life that provides genuine ontological insight into what it takes to lead a life.
>
> (Withy, 2012, p. 4)

In all respondents, there was a moment of this angst-driven reflection when life "collapses away" a moment, however fleeting when the inauthenticity of much of that which is done in the execution of duty, work, or social ritual is revealed to be superficial and that there are more fundamental problems that underpin the poor working of the world. Echoes of this angst were mainly manifest through a puzzlement at the lack of true communication, a disappointment that "people don't say what they want, I mean plainly." This collapsing away of the superstructure was common to all the stakeholder groups and most often manifest towards the end of a discussion when there was an element of "letting the guard down".

Student respondents were the most hesitant about this "falling away" as understandably they had placed a considerable investment of the personal capital of time and effort into the achievement of a degree that promises social and economic advancement. Who would want to undermine this belief? There were notwithstanding, critical notions even amongst the first-year respondents that not everyone, employers, academics and fellow students were being entirely truthful about the efficacy of the academy. For students whose experience stretched into the final year and particularly those that had been on work placement, this was a much stronger sense of untruthfulness. This may be the growing uncertainty with the world that comes of experience but with care, the transcripts indicate the particular circumstance of angst with the Business Academy. Student respondents in these unguarded moments questioned the relevance and the utility of much academic research, the hyperbole of the marketing materials of the faculty, the promise by employers of rich and rewarding careers and the eventual relevance of the curriculum of their degree programmes. At one level this can be taken as evidence that the pedagogical aim of developing critical acuity has succeeded, on another that the epistemological tensions in wider society are undermining the value of higher education in the field of business. I choose to incline to the former as all student respondents that had been on a work placement or internship could describe circumstances in which the skills and insights acquired through the curriculum aided them in the workplace and the execution of their duties. Nor were these examples confined to the practical or the technical, although these were common, insights into the softer skills of communication, negotiation and persuasion were often cited as most useful. There seemed to be an acknowledgement that the core essentials of the pedagogy held true and that dissatisfaction was specific and often contingent on the individual experience that was acknowledged to be transitory and often just an annoyance. The most specific "falling away" was that of the validity of academic research and a sense of the obscurity and absurdity of some areas of study. This was particularly strong amongst placement students who often volunteered the opinion that the influence of academic research did not reach the workplace and much seemed confined to an internal discussion within the academy. Further exploratory discussions into the application and relevance of such research did alter opinion, particularly when students tried mostly unsuccessfully to cite actual and detailed examples but the notion remained that it could be better, more practical and more tailored to the use of others and in particular employers.

Employer respondents were most sharply critical about the pedagogy of the business school, except again, where the manifest skill of those graduate employees from what were perceived to be the "best" or "elite" business schools transcended any concerns or queries regarding the curriculum. The relevance of much of the curriculum and its efficacy in the workplace often emerged in the early part of the interview and then was tempered over the course of the subsequent discussion. Reflecting on this I argue that the most likely explanation for this reversal of what was prevalent in the pattern of the discussions with the students was a defence mechanism, a way of establishing ground and position to put the interrogator/ researcher on the defensive. Most of this attitudinal response was diffused with an early acknowledgement on my part that much of the curriculum by its nature and manner of deployment and delivery not as responsive as it could be to the immediate needs of contemporary commerce and organisational life. Once this ground had been conceded the respondent (usually) then went through a process of conciliatory responses that sought to re-establish the links between them and me. The falling-away that become most evident when all the transcripts were compared was that of the lack of more formal feedback mechanisms between employers and the academy through which responsiveness could be improved and the curriculum made more relevant to their needs. An underlying current of angst that centred around the feeling that employers themselves were not "doing enough" to support the academy emerged. Support in this sense did not necessarily mean financial or other resources but the more intangible and probably much more difficult notion of direct relationships with the academy that would not be driven by immediate contingency or need. Often this was expressed as "giving something back" but when pressed the motivations were much subtler and not driven by any perceived failing of the academy but by the realisation that a broadening and deepening of individual and organisational knowledge would be a good and useful thing to do in the face of a competitive and hostile environment. A sense that as business people we should stick together. The specific manifestation of angst here is the broken and fragmented nature of the unity of knowledge that can never be fully unified in the business context due to the uncertainties of organisational ecologies. This was emotionally significant as many of the employer respondents were highly successful practitioners and were sharing deeper level anxieties about the fabric of the business world and how this was in their own understanding inauthentic. To look to the academy for assistance in ameliorating this fragmentation is a difficult process for practitioners as it in some sense undermines confidence in personal acuity and competence. Furthermore, this seemed to inverse relation to status, put simply the higher the organisational position of the respondent the more likely they were to question their own failings in maintaining stronger relationships with the academy. When pressed on the practicalities of this relationship there was a falling-back to the traditional manifestations of engagement such as guest lectures or knowledge exchange. One respondent did suggest a cross mentoring scheme almost like a buddy process in which key managers could adopt academics and maintain a professional relationship based on information exchange, but I will discuss this in much more detail later when I talk about how this research will develop. I suspect that the mechanisms needed to enable such relationships for this could be simultaneously d simple and difficult. Not least in respect of the angst of the academics.

Academic respondents most explicitly manifest angst in the discourse, but not for themselves. The falling-away here was directed at student's unwillingness to make connections between the academy and practical application and what was seen as the employer's unwillingness to engage with academic material. Also, unprompted and (almost) unanimously academic respondents were heavily critical of the superstructure of the academy and the "managerial" approach to the design of the curriculum which was both too student-centric and incorrectly weighted in favour of other subject disciplines. Returning to Trowler this is not an unexpected phenomenon due to the entrenched positions of subject disciplines and the building of defensive bunkers of interest. When respondents were prompted in an interview to suggest solutions to these problems not many were forthcoming. When apprised of students and employers own notions of falling-away namely; relevance and communication respectively, academics' own positions became more nuanced partly through a defence of their own positions and partly (and more authentically) through a reconsideration of how their knowledge in their field was ring-fenced in a community of interest. There was a cautious acceptance that the angst of the two other stakeholder groups had merit and if even partially resolved could lead to a more responsive and directly relevant process of teaching and research. What I found surprising here was how far some of the respondents gave ground on the idea of contemporary relevance whilst at the same time warning that such a process of continual renewal would be difficult if not impossible in the bureaucratic context of a business school. The two most often cited hurdles were the rhythm of the academic year with its dynamic of teaching semesters, set points of graduation and resources in all their shapes and forms. Teaching time, research time, financial reward, peer support, office facilities and even car parking. It unsurprising that the academic respondents were the most defensive in their responses as the Academy is where their own sense of position and worth vis-à-vis wider society is located. Criticism of the academy and its pedagogy is an attack and has the potential to undermine position and status. During the discursive exchanges, most academics fundamentally recognised the need to re-examine the superstructures of organisational practice and the established conduits of communication and this indicates that a proto-angst or not well-formed phenomenological angst is forming in the hermeneutical circles.

Subjective Reflection

Now that I have my three key themes, disappointment, belongingness and angst I can now begin my subjective reflection. Here I return to Sander's description of phenomenological analysis.

> Level three is the development of noetic/noematic correlates. These correlates are subjective reflections of the emergent themes...Noetic/noematic correlates represent the individual's perception of the reality of the phenomena under investigation. Interpretation of these correlations is fundamental to the identification of essences or of what an experience "essentially is."
>
> (Sanders 1982, p. 357)

The correlates of the theme of disappointment were in the first turns of all three circles disparate and reflected the immediate practical lived concerns of the respondents. Student respondents were focussed on the importance of the outcome and utility of business pedagogy, employer respondents on cultural misalignment and academic respondents on resources and communication. By the close of all three hermeneutic circles and the three turns of discourse there was more unanimity in opinion and belief as should be expected when enabling a process of communication that seeks common ground. It is here in this subjective reflection on the themes that merge from the research process that Gadamer provides me with a structure to form and shape my subjective reflection on this gradual fusion of noetic/noematic correlates. This is what the text documents promulgated to the three stakeholder groups at each of the turns of the circles facilitated, a coming together of experience and meaning. The research interviews (as has been described above) were semi-structured around Gadamer's ideas of how epistemological horizons can be fused through the interpretation of Text. Applying this structure now to the meta-analysis of the common and emergent themes of the three hermeneutic circles helps with the identification of these noetic/noematic correlates. I am using Gadamer to aid my eidetic reduction. A brief description of the process I use to do this will help here.

In the initial stage of the subjective reflection on the material that indicates the common themes amongst the three circles I first look for "Evidence of Prejudice" in the Gadamerian sense the prejudgement and foreknowledge of the respondent. I then attempt to identify where this prejudice has already been informed by identifiable sources of pre-knowledge that the respondent can identify or which I can reasonably infer. In this instance of the examination of the perceived efficacy of business pedagogy, I then attempt to identify what the respondent believes to be critically effective in this context. I then look for whether the acceptance of the views of others actively responding in the circle is influencing the respondents' opinions and beliefs and finally if there has been an evolution of understanding thorough this acceptance. I will use this structure to aggregate the noetic/noematic correlates of all respondents across the key themes. To more fully explain how this is accomplished I will give an example of how this works for a single respondent who I shall call Acastos.

Acastos - theme one – disappointment.

In the case of Acastos, the evidence of expectation of the business school was mainly derived from the information provided by the school career advisor who guided the respondent to the study of business by what seems to be a pre-evaluation of the Acastos' indeterminate ambition for the future and this has been supported by their own reading of accompanying literature. So here we have prejudice and synthesis of text. This pre-knowledge has rendered Acastos' notion of what is useful in terms of business pedagogy somewhat functional in its essence – what is most useful to get a well-paid job. They have in their subsequent peer interaction in the faculty and externally with students from other disciplines accepted that this pre-judgement was inaccurate and incomplete and through this acceptance of the views of others has evolved a more realistic expectation of the pedagogic process. The noema around Acastos' own experience of "disappointment" is a functional one derived from their simple acceptance of the practical limitations of the educational process as supported by their own experience and the accounts of others, the noesis or meaning of this for Acastos is that there is an *evolving acceptance of limitation* which has application beyond the consideration of the pedagogy of the academy.

Acastos – theme two – belongingness

Acastos has been heavily dependent on the additional support provided by the faculty to navigate the complexities of their new environment. This has manifest itself through a higher than normal engagement with peripheral and extra-curricular activities. Acastos' pre-judgement on the efficacy of this was derived from the opinion of a peer group that they joined/formed at the outset of their time at university, this was supported by the wealth of informal and formal literature provided by the university and the Students Union. This has guided Acastos into an understanding of the importance of "belonging" to the faculty and programme which means that Acastos notion of what should be taught and the faculty's notion of what is taught have a strong overlap. This does not mean that there is a precise alignment of the epistemological boundaries, but these are close. In Acastos' reaction and reflection on the circulated texts in their hermeneutic circle, they have shown a real willingness to consider the idea that not all is as it could be when the academy is challenged by other stakeholders dependent on the outcomes of business pedagogy. There is evidence in the subsequent interviews of a real broadening and fusion of epistemological horizons which almost inevitably segues into a strong sense of rapprochement on Acastos' part. The noema for Acastos is the expanding circle of available opinion which contextualises the role and efficacy of the business school and the correlating noesis is the sense of *business as a definable community*.

Acastos – theme three - angst

As would be expected from Acastos' limited horizon of understanding and experience of business school pedagogy by their own admission there was no sense at the outset of their studies that anything was "wrong" with the whole notion of a degree in business and from their viewpoint business education had considerably greater validity than other degree courses denigrated in the popular media. Acastos' prejudice was biased towards positivity, a belief in the "natural place of business in the economy, which is why business degrees are so popular" Again the limited reading of Acastos of contradictory texts reinforced this view and evidence of synthesis was limited from evidence in the initial interviews to popular and positive views of the role of commerce as a wealth creator in the economy. Again, under examination of the source of this pre-knowledge it was unsurprising that Acastos' family were the owners and founders of a strong and thriving business. Acastos subsequent widening of their epistemological boundaries had a rapid and profound effect on their contextualisation of business in wider society. Of particular interest to Acastos was the observation of the employer stakeholder group. The employer's views on the efficacy or otherwise of business pedagogy were fused into their horizon almost without question into Acastos' individual epistemological horizon so much that at one point in the second interview Acastos became almost hostile towards the academy and its failings. It was only through encouragement on the part of the researcher to widen their reading and understanding of the academic community that Acastos reached any sense of rapprochement on this theme. Even here it was a reluctant acceptance. It is questionable as to whether Acastos developed anything other than a rudimentary sense of angst or the falling- away of certainty it would be better to characterise Acastos' awareness as one of unease. At best the noema in this theme was a vague sense that other negative voices criticising business schools were present and the noesis was a grudging acceptance that *business schools could improve.*

As can be seen from the example above the structure of Gadamer's process of interpretation, reinterpretation, validation and revisiting is a useful means to track how evidence in each individual response supports the emergence not only of the themes of the study but also the mechanisms of the fusion of horizons. The task to apply this to the respondents as an aggregated whole was a little more complex and required the text to be carefully collated under the themes of prejudice, synthesis of text, epistemological boundaries, fusion of horizon and rapprochement. Following the structure above here are the aggregated responses across all stakeholder groups

Aggregation - theme one – disappointment.

Aggregated there were strong commonalties around the "popular" understanding of the function of business schools in the sense that they performed a functional and structural role in supporting the economy. Across two stakeholder groups, namely students and employers this was derived from an unquestioned assumption that this alignment between the academy and the needs of the economy was self-evident. Academic respondents were more challenging in this respect and much of their feedback into the texts used to facilitate connections between the respondents in the hermeneutic circles contributed to the sense of disappointment with the pedagogy. This was not a critical (in the sense of adverse opinion) appraisal of Business Schools from the academic respondents rather a sense of "we could all do better." The common noema of "disappointment" is a functional one derived from the shared knowledge that there is an expectation gap between intent and outcome that has less to do with pedagogic effectiveness and more to do with impossibility of staying fully relevant in a dynamic environment. The noesis of this even on an aggregated analysis is reasonably clear and it is that the limitation of business pedagogy is not the sole responsibility of the academy but that *business schools must be collaborative beyond their current boundaries to develop effective curricula.*

Aggregated – theme two – belongingness

Even when aggregated the influence of the employers in their contributions towards the shared documents had a significant influence. The attitudinal evidence of prejudice was positive across all three stakeholder groups particularly in the sense that there was an unspoken but seamless responsibility to move undergraduates through the educational process and into gainful employment for the mutual benefit of all. The sharing of the text documents reinforced the sense of a wider horizon of opinion and insight for all three stakeholder groups and epistemological boundaries were widened for all. Again the aggregated fusion of horizons was evident particularly by the third turn of all hermeneutic circles and rapprochement was clear. Reflecting on this I believe that this was an inevitable consequence of the process of encouraging discourse across three stakeholder groups and I need to be careful here and consider whether this was an outcome of genuine communication or one which was inevitable due to the design of the research process. I re-examined the source material and identified the aggregated noema as that of facilitated communication and that the noesis of this for most respondents is that the community has something of importance to say and that *no single group of stakeholders holds primacy regarding contextual relevance.*

Aggregated – theme three – angst

I must make an observation/confession before I start my eidetic reduction. Whilst I use the term "angst" in the Heideggerian/Gadamerian sense none of the respondents in the research process had to my knowledge a similar contextual framework in which to frame their unease with some of the issues with the epistemological relevance of business pedagogy. There was a clearer idea of the falling-away of elements of belief, but this was manifest in anxiety over elements of the Business academy's effectiveness. My aggregation of these myriad anxieties into something approximating angst is an entirely artificial construction, albeit one based on transcript evidence.

The falling away of certainty was evident amongst all research respondents as soon as they engaged in the process of discussion. It was evident from the discourse that once I had established trust with the interviewee the easier it became to explore the anxieties and unease that they had with the process of business education at a university level and how relevant and useful this was both for society and individual goals. Aggregated these anxieties fall into three areas. First, and most common was the idea that the complexity and variance of the world make it impossible to fully comprehend the multiplicity of important factors and drivers in the world of commerce and organisation. This was shared equally amongst all stakeholder groups in convictions and opinions that grew stronger and firmer as the circles turned. A prime example of this was the ever-shifting challenge of safely deploying social media in the service of any organisation.

Employers continually pointed out that whilst the medium was proven to be effective for communicating effectively with target markets the legal and regulatory uncertainties made engagement problematic. Academic respondents shared anxieties regarding the competing software platforms and the susceptibility of the medium to changing fashion and public opinion and student respondents in an echo of this uncertainty were unsure as to which skills would have currency in the skills market by the time they graduated. Here unspoken or partly formed unease coalesced as it becomes clear that some of these were shared and confirmed by other members of the circle. Second that as Acastos came to believe that Business Schools were not performing to anything approaching an optimal standard that could begin to explain or unravel this complexity, here there was a slight bias amongst students and employers in this belief. Even so this was grudgingly accepted by the academic respondents. Finally, all respondents were sceptical regarding the ability of the academy to rectify this failure and evolve a process by which at least some evolutionary factors could be contemporaneously understood. This should not be taken as an outright criticism of the academy as there was an acceptance that this issue was inherently complex in its nature and that there could no panacea. Overall the falling-away is one of anxiety in the face of overwhelming complexity. This is a strong common noema of the complexity of the life-world of business and the corresponding noesis that *complexity cannot be managed by the individual.*

Essences – the Why of Experience

> The final step in the process is the abstraction of essences or universals from the noetic/noematic correlates…If noema is described as the what of experience and noesis is described as the how of experience, then essence may be described as the why of experience.
>
> (Sanders, 1982 p. 357)

I now must approach the "why" of this analysis. I have identified three main themes arising out of the hermeneutic circles, disappointment, belongingness and angst, I have also described the noetic/noematic correlates, the task of extracting the universal essence is problematic as I must first acknowledge how the structure of the research process and the use of Gadamer's notions of prejudice, synthesis, epistemological boundaries, fusion and rapprochement have guided the respondents during the research interviews.

The intent of this research was to "operationalise" some of Gadamer's key concepts into a replicable research process and so I can freely acknowledge that this framework gave structure to the discourse, the shared documents and the evolution of the hermeneutic circles. How far this defined and shaped the themes and essences of the responses is a matter for interpretation and judgement and here transparency is key so that a reader of the research can come to their own judgement. This I will do deconstructing the responses against my framework and asking a fundamental question; are the thematic outcomes supportive of my operationalisation of Gadamer?

The first key element was that of attempting to identify amongst the respondent's evidence of prejudgement and prejudice and its origins and causes. As has been described previously the unfolding of the hermeneutic circles was a relatively simple part of the discussion with almost all respondents. Most can clearly articulate their current understanding of what business pedagogy is, what its function is within the context of the Business Academy and why they as individuals valued this. And this remained a constant throughout the circles as they turned even if this ground was shifting. In a sense, this was Dasein exerting its right to be and locating itself in the Lifeworld. This on one level is evidence that the ideas of prejudice and pre-judgment as fundamental to the manner in which an individual places themselves in the world is a constant and useful as an analytical tool. It is less useful though in determining themes or essence. Prejudice is a settled matter at the outset of each individual research discourse and with each subsequent turn of the circle, it evolves, it changes, but it is for each respondent where-they-are at the outset of an interrogative process. Themes and essences have their origins in prejudice as they arise out of this mix of fore-knowledge and pre-judgement and they have a consequential impact on the development of prejudice after interrogative and textual discourse. But prejudice encompasses and enfolds these themes and essences and they become bound-in to the individual's epistemological horizon. It is through the process of challenging this prejudice and changing its shape and content that the themes of phenomenological research emerge.

The first challenge to this under my operationalisation of Gadamer is the uncovering of the textual origins of prejudice, where has this foreknowledge arisen, what was its form and why did this individual bestow validity on this text? This stage in the process is critical in uncovering themes and essences as it begins the examination of how the individual values texts and how their interpretation of these texts contributes to their understanding of the phenomenon at hand. An example from the transcripts will illustrate this. What follows is a verbatim exchange between Phaedrus (the researcher) and a respondent.

> Phaedrus: I know that you went to business school and that you graduated with a first-class degree and I expect that you've kept up with some academic research?
>
> Respondent: No, I don't look at academic research, I find that I am too busy to read all the stuff that crosses my desk during an average day.
>
> Phaedrus: So, you keep up to date…
>
> Respondent: Well I read the broadsheets daily and I spend my Sunday mornings with the FT on Sunday. It's a habit and I guess I'm a bit selective in the columnists I like reading.
>
> Phaedrus: Is that the FT weekend?
>
> Respondent: Yes, I get it delivered on Sunday with the rest of the papers.
>
> Phaedrus: Which are?

Respondent: The Sunday Times and the Mail on Sunday

Phaedrus: Do you ever read the business section of the Mail on Sunday?

Respondent: Yes, it's not too bad, probably the best section in the Mail, apart from the Sport!

Phaedrus: But your main source of wider information is?

Respondent: I have to say the Financial Times

Phaedrus: I just want to unpack that a little, coming back to Business Schools and Business teaching can you remember any recent articles, say over the last six months that offered an opinion on or analysis of Business School teaching and/or Business School graduates?

Respondent: (After a pause) Not really, you get a little bit of indirect stuff, like on MBAs and what comes out of Harvard and some other Big business Schools, most of it is positive I think.

Phaedrus: Sorry to press you on this can you remember anything more specific?

Respondent: (After a pause) I glance at the (Business School) rankings they publish now and then, mainly to check how XXXXXXX is doing in the list. Umm, a lot of the articles are about MBAs and I'm not really interested in MBA students.

Phaedrus: You have an MBA yourself?

Respondent: (Laughs) that's why I don't employ them.

Phaedrus: (Laughs) so coming back to how you track how business schools are doing even if you don't employ MBA postgraduates?

> Respondent: I don't focus on Business Schools as such, I just pick up bits and pieces and generally I think they're doing OK, I mean that they seem a lot better than they were in my day.
>
> Phaedrus: So, despite your view on MBAs you're saying that there is a largely positive view on Business Schools in the media?
>
> Respondent: Yes, I think so, I'm only joking about MBAs, XXXXXXX started about six months ago and she's very bright.

In this extract, the respondent, reveals that the performance of Business Schools is peripheral to their core concerns. When pressed it can be inferred that the respondent's choice of media predisposes them to view Business Schools in a largely positive light. Whilst their own educational background might be a factor, there is an ease and confidence in self-denigration that reveals confidence both in their own skillset and its relevance and the skill set of business graduates. Here the respondent is consciously choosing a text that informs and supports a world view that gives primacy to the role of Business (The Financial Times) and which is largely supportive of Business School education. The prior knowledge that the respondent brings is largely positive and supportive of a world view predicated on the primacy of Business. The relevance and impact of prior knowledge are clear here the respondent is predisposed by education and enculturation to seek texts that support and reinforce their own pre-knowledge.

This was not the case for all respondents; amongst the student group there was more evidence of a more eclectic mix of sources that informed their opinion of business school education and most of these sources were in the general media and by this, I mean social media. Online news feeds social media forums and other online sources. Employer respondents largely followed the pattern of the respondent's consumption of "broadsheet" media sources, whilst Academic respondents had marginally a wider mix and of course a much stronger focus on academic publishing. At the outset of the research, it was clear that sources of prior knowledge in a textual form (and here I include online text-based material, video logs, YouTube opinion pieces and online news sources) were either consciously or unconsciously chosen as they were supportive of pre-knowledge. As the research progressed there was some evidence of wider sources being used to help understand the shared texts of the hermeneutic circles. Here is an extract from Hermeneutic Circle turn 2 that clearly shows this development.

> Phaedrus: You found that section of the document difficult to read?
>
> Respondent: Not after I read up on this
>
> Phaedrus: What did you read?
>
> Respondent: I had a look at that article in the reading list for XXXXXX on graduate employment.
>
> Phaedrus: And?
>
> Respondent: Well I think I understand now why it's so difficult for students to get the placements they really want, I used to think it was the fault of the employers, but I think its 50/50 now, oh and I don't think we (The Business School) offer enough to students for placements. I think the point in the article about guided contact time dedicated to placement applications was a good one but we're never going to do it.
>
> Phaedrus: So how specifically has that changed your understanding?
>
> Respondent: Well its more difficult now, there seems to be more competition and we don't do enough to help students.
>
> Phaedrus: So precisely, why did you choose this article?
>
> Respondent: Well I thought I'd better look at something a bit more, you know, popular.

It is perhaps inevitable that some respondents engaged in a discursive exchange with groups outside their social milieu will begin to extend their sources of information. The simple fact that the research engages different groups facilitates this. Overall the research shows a drift towards this extension of sources across all three hermeneutic circles and as an outcome, this has been largely a positive effect, at least in the opinion of most respondents who noticed that the texts they were reading after the research process were in some cases challenging their opinion and understanding and in most other interesting as they revealed a wider range of opinion and analysis. It must be emphasised here that this was not in the main due to the reading of academic literature but of reading in general. Here was evidence that respondents were responding to the research process by extending their epistemological boundaries.

In the interviews, I specifically tried to uncover the extent and nature of respondents' epistemological boundaries. This is the third element of my operationalisation of Gadamer. The purpose of this was to determine the individuals understanding of what was relevant and appropriate in the context of business. It is useful here to remind ourselves of the centrality of epistemology in Gadamer's philosophy.

> For Gadamer the problem with modern philosophy's epistemological orientation is not to offer a justification or account of our knowledge, Rather, it restricts this "giving of accounts to a legitimation of scientific knowledge. The validity of natural science is both taken as a given and held up as a model for all other forms of knowledge. Epistemology's task then is to show the conditions of this validity and to extend these conditions to show the possibility of similarly rigorous knowledge in other fields as well. To this restricted notion of a "giving of accounts" Gadamer contrasts the older tradition of practical philosophy for which philosophical justification does not simply refer to the uncovering the conditions of the possibility of properly scientific knowledge but is rather concerned to show how different forms of knowledge suit

> our aims and needs in general.
>
> (Warnke, 1987 p. 162)

Gadamer moves the epistemological debate from the technical specificities of philosophical analysis into the realm of the ordinary and commonplace. We all have limits to our epistemological understanding of the world. Our knowledge is limited and consists of a unique mixture of eclectic and fragmentary sources that we combine to make sense of the world. Owing to the fragmentary nature of an individual's epistemological sources and boundaries it would probably be impossible to fully deconstruct these. But we have the possibility of examining a small portion of this complexity when we consider the specificity of a single phenomenon, in this case, the understanding of Business School and their pedagogical functions. In the research process, this was more difficult to identify and define. A key factor in this difficulty was that most respondents simply did not understand the word "epistemology" and after the first turn of the first circle, I used more accessible language to discuss this even amongst academic respondents. In some cases, the very notion that a boundary could be identified between what was or could be "known" and that which could not be "known" was still a difficult concept to grasp for some respondents. The questioning process I adopted that sought to uncover epistemological boundaries had to be approached indirectly in the case of most respondents. Here is an example extract from a portion of an interview on epistemological boundaries using the same conventions as previous extracts.

> Phaedrus: You've never been to business school as I think I remember you did a degree in XXXXX, what do you think, or what do you know Business Schools do?
>
> Respondent: Well I know they teach business courses, degrees and the like. Research into business perhaps like the sort of research the academics did at my university, maybe.
>
> Phaedrus: You must have been aware of the business faculty on your campus when you were an undergraduate, I think

it's the largest faculty in your old university?

Respondent: Well I know they were around, I don't think it was that big back in my day, we were busy with what we were doing. I also played a lot of football.

Phaedrus: Were you in the varsity team?

Respondent: No, well only occasionally for the thirds, it was social football mainly.

Phaedrus: Did you come across business graduates whilst you were playing football?

Respondent: Not that I remember.

Phaedrus: So, it would be fair to say that whilst you were at college (university) you didn't have much of an idea of what the Business School was about and what it taught?

Respondent: That would be fair.

Phaedrus: How about after university, after graduation.

Respondent: I do remember one or two popping up on the milk round, they were Ok I guess, nothing that stood out.

Phaedrus: Graduates applying for graduate jobs with XXXXXX?

Respondent: Yes.

Phaedrus: Did any get through the process with you?

Respondent: No definitely not it was mainly XXXXXXXX graduates like me that succeeded.

Phaedrus: So, it's fair to say that up until you rise through the corporate ranks that you didn't have much dealings with Business School graduates?

Respondent: Yes, that would be true, up until the time I got involved in the assessment centres about (pause) ten/eleven years ago. I was in an assessment team for marketing positions. I had to sit with a clipboard in a room with about a dozen applicants and almost as many assessors writing down everything they (the applicants) said.

Phaedrus: How did you know they were business graduates?

Respondent: It was on the CVs we read for the assessment centre.

Phaedrus: And did they impress you?

Respondent: Some did, most didn't. But there was one guy who was very bright, did his research on us before the assessment centre, knew more about the business than I did. I think he was from XXXXXX so that was not really surprising.

Phaedrus: This candidate impressed you with his knowledge?

Respondent; Yes, he knew a lot about the technical side of the business and I wasn't expecting that.

Phaedrus: What did you expect from a Business School graduate?

Respondent: Some vague stuff about business in general, but this guy seemed clued up on all sorts of things, like HR and customer relationship software.

Phaedrus: Did that change the way in which you thought about Business Schools?

Respondent: I suppose it did a little back then, but it was just the start I guess, a majority of our applicants now come straight from business schools and like that guy they seem to know a lot more than I guessed.

Phaedrus: Did he get the job?

Respondent: (Laughs) I think he got a better offer.

The low expectations of the knowledge taught in business schools of this respondent evolved as they encountered more business graduates. This portion of this interview ended with an almost grudging acceptance that the evidence of the depth and breadth of the Business Academy's curricula has more utility than the respondent first assumed. This is a micro-historical record of how one individual's epistemological boundary in respect of business school pedagogy has unfolded and evolved; widened by the encounters with recruits and other colleagues. In aggregate from non-business school graduates amongst the employer group of respondents, there was an acceptance of the validity of the business school curriculum. Here communication with and exposure to business school graduates was key, the more that employers had come into contact with the product of the pedagogy the greater the chance that it was accepted as being relevant to their context. There were exceptions but these were on minor and mainly centred around specific technical knowledge. Across all stakeholder groups, the epistemological boundaries were widened through engagement with the research process. The most profound development of the epistemological reach was evident amongst the student respondents. Here is an extract from an interview with a respondent from Circle three, turn two.

Phaedrus: What surprised you most about the last shared text, you know the document that I sent you about a week ago?

Respondent: I didn't know how much basic skills were valued by employers, I mean we covered most of this in year one, it's like basic stuff.

Phaedrus: Why does that surprise you?

Respondent: I thought everybody could use spreadsheets, I thought everybody could understand Stats (Statistics).

Phaedrus: So you weren't aware before that that was important?

Respondent: I suppose I just took it for granted that everyone knew.

Phaedrus: Will some of that affect the way you look for a placement year?

Respondent: (Pause) Not really I just think that some of the things we covered in the first year are not wasted.

Phaedrus: Is there anything form the text document that will?

Respondent: Oh yes, I am definitely going to tell people about my work as a XXXXXX that stuff seems important to employers and I wasn't expecting that.

Phaedrus: So no regrets taking the course you're on?

Respondent: Some I think, but it's too late now and it doesn't seem that important now.

Phaedrus: Why not?

Respondent: It seems more important just to a get a good grade, a good degree and demonstrate you're, like, more than that. That you've done more things.

Phaedrus: Haven't we been telling you that from induction week?

Respondent: (Laughs) These guys (the employers) know more about the real world though.

Phaedrus: (Laughs) I guess they do.

Here in this example the respondent's epistemological boundary shifts from recognising a form of words – extracurricular activities are important – to knowing or believing that this is actually true within the context of employment. The words now have meaning beyond simple comprehension, they are now imbued with value and import and have a consequence that can be measured in the altered belief of the respondent. This movement and change is the precursor of the fusion of horizons.

The fusion of horizons or the overt acceptance of the views of others is different in quality to an individual shifting their own epistemological boundaries; it is the formal acknowledgement that the view of the other has merit and meaning. In the interview process and the subsequent analysis, this is much easier to identify and to interrogate. There are two factors at play here and we return to Gadamer's exposition of the interplay of subjectivity/intersubjectivity to understand this.

> The way Heidegger had developed the preparation of the question of Being, and the way he had worked out the understanding of the most authentic existential structure of Dasein, the Other could only show itself in its own existence as a limiting factor. In the end, I thought, the very strengthening of the Other against myself would, for the first time, allow me to open up the real possibility of understanding. To allow the Other to be valid against oneself – and from there to let all my hermeneutic works slowly develop – is not only to recognize in principle the limitation of one's own framework but is also to allow one to go beyond one's own possibilities, precisely in a dialogical, communicative, hermeneutic process. When I conveyed this to Heidegger, he nodded, if not entirely approvingly, but then said: "Yes, but what about thrownness?" Obviously Heidegger meant that that which I wanted to make valid would for him all be included in the fact that the existing of Dasein is not only a projection, but also thrownness. This means that Dasein must take itself up, in a way which never becomes completely penetrable.
>
> (Gadamer, 2000 p.284)

Here, Gadamer in conversation with Heidegger acknowledges that for an authentic sense of self, of location in the world Dasein needs to understand how the other limits and challenges the limits of Dasein's horizons and how it is only through a "dialogical, communicative and hermeneutic process" that we uncover a sense of self. Furthermore, following Heidegger's own philosophical development Gadamer himself develops this further by placing this fusion of the other in the primacy of language as an exchange of meaning.

> Later on, after his abandonment of the transcendental self-conception to which he held so strongly in Being and Time, Heidegger left behind the dimension of subjectivity and also the structure of care in Dasein even more fundamentally, even eliminating the concept of understanding and of hermeneutics from his thought after the "turn." Those of my own works which are oriented towards the primacy of speech, and which found their first expression in the sketch of the third part of Truth and Method, were an attempt to move in this direction. Who thinks of "language" already moves beyond subjectivity.
>
> (Gadamer, 2000 p. 286)

The fusion of horizons, the acceptance of the other and the expression of this in the exchange of meaning in interpreting the language of the other is core to Gadamer's hermeneutical structure of interpretation. This goes further than just "changing one's mind" it is the fundamental acceptance that the life-world is not as it was but is now changed. Dasein's orientation and relationship with what is real have been altered. In its effect, it is intellectual, aesthetic and emotional and changes inter-relationships. It is not just an opinion that it changed it is belief and being. In the first turns of all three circles, there was some evidence of this process already at play due to the engagement in the research project itself. Initial interviews with respondents who had read and considered the opening statements on the efficacy or otherwise of business education already showed signs of a shift in position, a premonition that there might be other possibilities of understanding the academy and its role in a wide context and to them as individuals. I have to consider here whether or not my pre-selection of research participants had an unconscious bias to those who would perhaps be more receptive to this process than the general population and I will cover this in my chapter reflecting on the research process and my subjective analysis of my role as a researcher. Briefly, on reflection, it was my role of interlocutor that prompted this beginning of the fusion of horizons and in examining the pattern of my questions I acknowledge that I encouraged this process. As the research unfolded this process accelerated.

During the launch of all three circles, the acceptance of the views of others was limited as practically those views had not yet been circulated. The notion that the role and understanding of the Business Academy could be re-examined and questioned nevertheless prompted some initial questioning of positions, particularly my own.

> Respondent: If you're not sure about teaching business, why do you work in a business school, isn't it a little dangerous to be doing this?
>
> Phaedrus: It's not that I am unsure about teaching business, I just want to make it more effective.
>
> Respondent: What if you change your mind about that, what will you do? What if you find that the whole thing is nonsense. (Laughs)
>
> Phaedrus: Then I'll have to deal with that, perhaps you could give me a job.

None of the respondents showed any resistance at the outset of the research to the possibility of changing their views and belief and most seemed eager to gain new insights. I had made a conscious effort at the outset of the research to include in the research, representatives from as wide a range of colleges, industries and faculties that I could manage. A small minority were known to me, but most were strangers before the research. On reflection and checking my notes this openness was largely similar in nature across the whole respondent sample. In subsequent turns of the circle, this openness changed in character.

In the first turn of all three circles when the first substantive documents were circulated most of the respondents reacted positively to the collated texts with a few dissenters questioning the balance between the voices represented in the text. Even amongst the dissenters, there was an acceptance that there was still some validity and that new insights into the motivations and concerns of others. Also, there was some surprise at the confluences of opinion amongst the stakeholder groups with some of the student respondents almost relieved that some of their concerns were shared with what they assumed to be the employers. Most resistant to acceptance of the views of the others were the academic participants which showed more evidence of being defensive but even here there was a manifest interest in how they were perceived outside the academy. The feedback from the subsequent interviews led directly to a significant feature of the second iteration of the documents which can best be described as a blending of voice where it was necessary to identify which group said what so that the other groups could reflect on their positionality. It was clear even at this stage that acceptance of common cause and common problems were growing amongst the respondents in all three circles. Admittedly in the first circle, this was more functional in character than the more emotive connections made in circles two and three but it was evident nevertheless. In the third iteration of the documents, I decided to blend the voices in the documents to see if respondents could still recognise the voice of their stakeholder group within the text. There were no objections to this from any respondent which could be indicative that horizons were being genuinely fused. One participant spoke explicitly on this.

> Respondent: I think that the latest article you have put together sums up some of the problems we have. I was a little depressed at the beginning I didn't think anyone understood us and what we're going through. I thought people of your age had it easy, but I don't think that now and I think that there is an understanding of how difficult it is for us.
>
> Phaedrus: In what way difficult, could you be more specific?
>
> Respondent: (Rustling of paper) (Pause) This paragraph here which says that the "velocity of change is a factor that

creates an emotional strain on the student, on the business community and anxiety amongst the academics who must teach them. It may be impossible to understand this perfectly and the best we may able to do is to just understand the difficulties of comprehending this." (Pause) I think that's right.

Phaedrus: So how will you use that insight in future? How has it changed what you knew then (at the outset of the research) to what you know now?

Respondent: I think I'll be able to talk with more confidence at interviews because I know the people on the other side of the room have the same problems.

Phaedrus: I'd be a little careful with that as not all have your insight and you must assume that the people who interview you for jobs do have some quite detailed and technical knowledge that is appropriate and effective in the context of the sector they compete.

Respondent: (With a note of annoyance) Well I don't mean the specifics of jobs I mean how they feel generally about things!

I am still unsure as to what extent this facilitation of the fusion of horizons was due to my own ability to bridge these voices through my writing but the result was that there was unanimity amongst the participants that the final text documents were a fair reflection of their emerging beliefs and opinions.

The final element of the operationalisation of Gadamer is the goal of rapprochement, the synthesis and evolution of understanding through the acceptance of the views of others. This I discerned mainly in the final round of interviews in all three circles after the promulgation of the third and final document to each group of participants. There were two reasons for this. First, there was an element of knowing the final destination on the part of all the research participants. By this, I mean that all knew that the process was bound and that it had a finite goal. This meant that all the participants knew that there would be an opportunity for a final reflection on the materials and the process and an opportunity, to sum up, their reflection. To have something of significance to say at this endpoint does perhaps limit the feedback on rapprochement earlier in the research process. The second factor was the final blending of the participants' voice in the end documents. This meant that the respondents could ascribe to an aggregation of views that embedded elements of their own understanding seamlessly throughout the text. And here we return to the themes and essences uncovered by the research and Gadamer's development of subjectivity/inter-subjectivity. The entire process of initiating, facilitating and interpreting the data produced by the research process is in its own essence a process of rapprochement as the hermeneutic exchange is designed to place before others views and evidence that will encourage the fusion of epistemological horizons.

Themes, Subjective Reflection and Thematic Essences

By adopting a structure for qualitative enquiry based on Gadamer's ideas on hermeneutic interpretation and exchange I must acknowledge that I may be entering a self-referencing circle with an internal logic but no external application or utility. Ultimately it is for the readers of this text to judge from their own interpretation if this has sufficient merit to warrant replication or further development. In defence of the method and methodology, I point out that on a superficial level the nineteen participants in the research did (in the final interviews that closed the circles) aver that the research had merit, had influenced their understanding of the interplay and interconnectedness between the stakeholder groups and had altered their epistemological horizons. The structure of the research and its subject matter inevitably generated the thematic outcomes. By design, PHAEDRUS sought to deconstruct the effectiveness of Business Pedagogy by using interpretative hermeneutics. It succeeded in uncovering three themes, disappointment, belonging and angst which were used in turn to generate the noetic correlates which I will summarise as collaboration, context and complexity.

To understand why these themes and correlates have been revealed by the research process and to look for the underlying essence of these themes I returned to the transcripts of the research itself and attempt to aggregate the outcomes of each turn of the circles as they unfolded. The first phase of the deconstruction, the establishment and observation of the hermeneutic circles provide a vehicle for the noematic recounting of the experience of the Business Academy and its pedagogic practices, outcomes and consequences. This shaped the data and provided boundaries for interpretation and reflection.

By re-examining the transcripts of the research, it became clear that the key themes and their noetic correlates identified in the first thematic analysis of the material could be aligned to key stages in the interview process. From discussing with the research participants, the roots of their Prejudice (pre-knowledge) a theme of disappointment emerged which was reinforced as the circles turned and participants became more confident in expressing their reservations about business education. The noetic correlate of this was that business schools must be collaborative beyond their current boundaries to develop effective curricula and this has a natural corollary, progress on improvement to act on disappointment must be predicated on *the sharing of dissatisfaction amongst key stakeholder groups as a necessary precursor to the uncovering of what must be done to improve* this situation. In uncovering where participants had Synthesised text and where their epistemological boundaries lay the reading of the shared texts indicated a common cause or belonging as the respondents "see" traces of their own pre-knowledge within these documents. The noetic correlate of this that no single group of stakeholders holds primacy regarding contextual relevance naturally leads to the conclusion that the *mechanism for change must be a collaborative act and that no stakeholder group holds a primacy of knowledge regarding the epistemological relevance of business school pedagogy. Effective change lies a shared process of renewal.* Finally, in the unfolding fusion of epistemological horizons and in evidence of rapprochement I see evidence of Angst in the Heideggerian sense as a validator of shared concern and an underpinning of the fusion of horizons and rapprochement. With the noetic correlate that complexity cannot be managed by the individual and the current structures of collaboration are inadequate. *In essence, this means that the Business Academy must (if it is to remain relevant in intent and effective in outcome) continually renew itself and its pedagogical approach through an un-bunkered contextual understanding.* By un-bunkered, I mean that it must face its own fragmentation of knowledge by subject discipline and examine how coherence amongst these fields of knowledge can be led from within the academy and reinforced by interests outside the academy. Using Gadamer's provides both a means for shaping a hermeneutical study and a means to analyse its outcomes along phenomenological lines. A final note on subjectivity/inter-subjectivity reveals to us why in an ontological sense that this has validity.

> In Heidegger's approach, with regard to the question of Being the primacy of subjectivity is ruled out so radically that the Other cannot even become a problem. Dasein is, of course, not subjectivity. Thus in Heidegger's approach the concept of subjectivity is replaced by the concept of care. Here it becomes clear that the Other does not remain only at the margins, seen only from a biased perspective. Heidegger speaks, then, of care and also of solicitude. Solicitude receives a particular accent when he calls real solicitude "freeing solicitude." The word indicates what its significance is. True solicitude is not to care for the Other, but rather to let the Other come freely into one's own being self – as opposed to taking care of (Versorgung) the Other, which would take away from him care for Dasein (Daseinsorge)… Here again, Heidegger is concerned only with the preparation of the question of Being, which can only be posed beyond all metaphysics.
>
> (Gadamer, 2000 p. 24)

I contend that this operationalisation of Gadamer is a clear demonstration of how Dasein can "let the Other come freely into one's own being self" or as "Acastos" puts it.

> I didn't think that people would listen to me, but I can see in the text echoes of my thoughts and my opinions its added to my confidence, it also made me think about why I wanted to study business in the first place.

Chapter 7

The Implications for Pedagogical Practice

Introduction

This discussion is in three parts, the first deals with the findings from the research, the evidence it generated and the conclusions of the analysis. The second part deals with the outcomes of the research itself and how these changed from the original intent during its execution. Finally, I summarise the impact of this research project for my professional practice; the methods' validity and its further development and application. The original research aim was a simple one, to establish if the pedagogy of Business Schools was delivering an epistemological fit between three key stakeholder groups, students, employers and academics. This was underpinned by the assumption that the closer the overlap between the epistemological horizons of these three groups the more effective the pedagogy of the Business Academy would be. The execution of the research and the phenomenological analysis of the results yielded a far more complex relationship. As the hermeneutic circles unfolded and the shared text documents were absorbed and altered the prejudice of each research participant the recounting of the life-experience of the participants moved the discussion and consideration of the effectiveness of Business Schools pedagogy beyond the epistemological. The notion that I could map the borders of knowledge ceased to be central to this study. The act of exploring the life-world of the individual even from this narrow perspective brings an emotional engagement into the research mix. Echoes of hope, fear, belonging, concern for the future and companionship all were uncovered by the discursive process and this is not an exhaustive list. In some sense, the epistemological horizon of the research project itself has fused with this emotional dimension and moved forward itself as if it had a life-world of its own. The net result of this is that on one level the analysis of the research has yielded three thematic perspectives on the pedagogy of the academy and its effectiveness and on another methodological level it has contributed the relationship between business research and the relevance of Phenomenological enquiry. I will deal with the implications for business pedagogy first.

The Sharing of Dissatisfaction

Arising from the uncovering of prejudice/pre-knowledge and the use of a semi-structured discursive process it was clear that disappointment over the fragmentary nature of business pedagogy was a key concern felt strongly amongst the research participants. This is not a finding unique to this study as other researchers have identified this as a key concern for the Business Academy.

> Once we accept that management is not about neutral techniques but about values, it is possible to have a conversation about what those values should be. It will inevitably be an open-ended conversation for, almost by definition, it will be to engage with keenly contested and ultimately insoluble arguments about, to put it at its most general, the "good society." In this sense, what is at stake is the underlying philosophical premises held by managers and the ways that these are established and transmitted so as to impact upon behavior (Boyatzis, Murphy, & Wheeler, 2000). These premises go beyond ethics to encompass the ontological and epistemological assumptions associated with, for example, the manageability of human relations and, indeed, the very notion of what it is to be human.
>
> Such might be seen, and traditionally have been seen, as well beyond the competence and responsibility of business schools and confined, perhaps, to departments of philosophy or politics. Yet, as management and business are more than ever integral to the contemporary world, why should this be so?
>
> (Grey, 2004 p. 180)

Christopher Grey highlights here what he sees as a fundamental gap in the pedagogic scope of the Business Academy, the failure to address the "very notion of what it is to be human." This is criticism of untrammelled scope and it is joined by a myriad of other concerns about what it is we should teach in Business Schools from Dayun's (2006) concerns on failings in vocational education to Chandler & Teckchandani's (2015) plea for better use of social constructivist pedagogy. The Business academy seems particularly vulnerable to such criticism and this research suggests why this should be so from a phenomenological perspective. Business as a practice, as the medium through which human society and human individuals exchange value is ubiquitous (Hill & Hernández-Requejo 2008). It is difficult to envisage a scenario in which even the remotest human tribe does not engage in some form of Business relationship. There may be some uncontacted tribes in the remote area of the world for whom the notion of business is alien and unknowable but even the Bushmen of the Kalahari now wear Nike branded t-shirts (Bleek, 2011). Here lies the problem, the transaction of value amongst individuals is so infinitely varied and complex that it is an impossible task for Business Schools to cover the technical processes involved in all business, it must respond to this complexity by building curricula around generalisable principles and processes, key theoretical constructs and a historical sense of what management is (Starkey, Hatchuel, & Tempest, 2004). Dissatisfaction with this in-escapable limitation is inevitable and yet when we return to the deconstruction of this thematic essence ameliorating solutions suggest themselves. The noetic correlate, the theme that informs this essence, that business schools must be collaborative beyond their current boundaries to develop effective curricula, is derived directly from a sharing of this dissatisfaction amongst stakeholder groups. So here whilst we may have a problem beyond solution because of its uncontrollable complexity we do have the suggestion of a way of managing this pedagogic uncertainty. It is to simply acknowledge that there is a problem and address with enough transparency to acknowledge that visceral concerns of those with a stake on the academy are known and that they are being addressed. In the Business Academy, we do acknowledge that we have to manage complexity with resilience (Pucciarelli & Kaplan, 2016) and collaboration.

> Businesses commercializing complex goods can attempt to overcome the difficulties by operating independently or by relying on collaborative relationships with other organizations to carry out business activities. A business with an independent approach carries out some development, production, and marketing functions itself and acquires other components through hands off relationships with other organizations.
>
> (Mitchell & Singh 1996 p. 170)

But this research questions whether we do so with enough honesty. The base theme that underpinned the essence of Dissatisfaction with the pedagogy was that the sharing of unease with the effectiveness of Business School pedagogy amongst key stakeholder groups is a necessary precursor to the uncovering of what must be done to improve it. And this is indicative of the fact that we are not doing this well, if at all. Yet this is a natural response as the Business Academy as an established discipline in Global Higher Education Culture should be the repository of knowledge and authority (Alajoutsijärvi, Juusola & Siltaoja, 2015) to admit otherwise has the potential to undermine legitimacy. One of the key contemporary themes in practical business education is a focus on encouraging and developing resilience in business graduates. This is a quality seen as essential for survival, endurance and prosperity in the modern business context both for the individual and the organisation (Ortiz-de-Mandojana & Bansal, 2016). Uncovering dissatisfaction as a key issue for the Business Academy and its relationship with at least two of its major stakeholder groups indicates that the Academy should adopt its own lessons of resilience and engineer and implement processes that can address this. Furthermore, the research was not silent on what process might be appropriate to manage this dissatisfaction it also uncovered a counterbalancing theme/essence; that of Belonging

Shared Processes of Renewal

One of the strongest emotional undercurrents present in the transcripts of the research and in the subsequent hermeneutic circles and their outcomes was the feeling that "we are all in it together." This again is a natural human response to identification with a community that has common cause. The promotion of community and the establishment of a cohort identity amongst business students is an ongoing effort (Darwish, LaVenia, & Polkinghorne, 2018). Cohort identity is a seen as a positive factor that enhances the student's learning experience (Mårtensson & Bild 2016). Also, external engagement is promoted as a way in which the academy stays connected to developments in the wider context of business and society (Driscoll and Sandmann, 2016). More explicitly Michael Hitt (1998) claims that strategic partnerships should be established.

> We must reach out to and build bridges with our constituencies to include business school deans and executives. We must translate research for managers and executives, making the basic research that we do more easily accessible for and usable by them (i.e., we must place more emphasis on the Academy of Management Executive). We must also continue the process created several years ago of ensuring that this research reaches executives through the popular business press. They need our help, and we need their support. Thus, we should pursue cooperative strategies; alliances with executives/ managers and deans can and should be mutually beneficial.
>
> (Hitt, 1998 p. 223)

What is moot here is not the intent or the desire for external engagement with stakeholders on the part of the academy but whether we do this effectively.

> We would argue that, too often, these benefits have not been communicated to the vast majority of practitioners, and we are left with unhelpful stereotypes. One stereotype is of the ivory tower academic, out of touch with practice. Another is of the professor as an all-knowing guru. This latter view can be seen as an uncomfortable conspiracy between practitioners, who are looking for expert help in solving difficult problems, and academics, who want to boost their credibility.
>
> (Hughes et al., 2011 p. 53)

We (the academy) recognise that we need to engage externally, to create communities of interest and that we have the theoretical frameworks that could enable this process. Yet when we begin to examine the roots of pedagogic practice it is clear from the sample of respondents used in this research that the willingness to listen to emerging concerns appears to be less than effective in informing our own pedagogic development. The essence of the primacy of knowledge and its relationship to the epistemological relevance of business school pedagogy is perhaps better accomplished through a shared process of renewal. To do this though requires mechanisms that build confidence across stakeholder groups. But this uncovers a deeper problem which is the fragmentation of the Business Academy into subject disciplines that compete for the same ground. A business issue can be analysed from a variety of subject perspectives, Strategy, Operations, Human Resources, Organisational studies and so on. It would be wrong to assume that there is some form of unifying discipline that could unite these perspectives as there is not. So, when the academy reaches out it does so in a variety of guises. This is not to say that there is some alignment as Human Resources academics, for example, will in the main look at the human resource perspective in organisational life but it could be argued that this further encourages fragmentation and a bunker mentality. This process creates a tautological loop in which the knowledge that is shared in external engagement becomes self-referential and self- regarding distorting the views of the participating academics and the specialist practitioners. Theodore Zorn in his paper on organisational communication, *Converging within Divergence* (2002) recognises this.

> …our research and teaching can be enriched by seeing the multiple perspectives on the same event and by the more comprehensive analysis of the event that could be attained from these different perspectives. The problem is that we too seldom see such events from other than our own subdisciplinary lenses.
>
> (Zorn, 2002 p. 45)

He goes on to suggest a remedy.

> Perhaps the most radical and long-term action is to work towards structural realignment within our universities.
>
> (Zorn, 2002 p. 51)

This suggestion could also be a potential remedy to the Noetic Correlate of this theme/essence in that no single group of stakeholders holds primacy regarding contextual relevance. If we admit that this is a possibility, then this principle extends into the fragmentation of subject disciplines within the Business Academy and suggests that the beginning of a remedy to manage complexity begins with closer and more effective interdepartmental communication and a fully coherent cross-disciplinary pedagogic approach. If we remember where this sense of common cause to manage complexity and build resistance originated from the propensity of the research participants to "see" traces of their own pre-knowledge within the texts shared in the unfolding of the hermeneutic circles than we can reasonably suppose that the wider business community would welcome the acknowledgement by the academy that it needs to manage this fragmentation with a coherent pedagogic strategy. Zorn goes further and suggests in his paper a number of mechanics and techniques to enable this management of subject fragmentation, but this in my contention would only partly address the problem. My own research indicates that even if we accomplish this modicum of academic coherence we would still need to encourage and embrace the active participation of other stakeholder groups in pedagogic development and implementation. Business cannot escape its vocational centre, we are embedded in and are of the world outside the academy. We are expected as a discipline to educate graduates that will be effective and value-creating in the widest societal contexts, our graduates are expected to have significant transferable skills that are of value to the graduate and their putative employers. As Business Schools we cannot resile from this, but we also need to challenge or encourage our own stakeholders to participate in the process of developing pedagogic tactics that will help us manage fragmentation and complexity.

Angst and Renewal

The third theme or essence uncovered by the research which has direct relevance to the epistemological and pedagogical "fit" of Business Schools is that of the feeling of angst in the phenomenological sense amongst the research participants. As I have mentioned above I must confess here that I am aggregating a wide spectrum of anxiety amongst the transcripts here ranging from mild unease of a successful employer to the profound paranoia of the student not convinced that their degree programme would yield a useful outcome. This essence of the research outcomes is different in form and consequence from the essence of belonging. Belonging was indicative of the notion that as part of a wider business community we should all have common cause and cooperate to manage context, this is the how of what we should do, Angst is the why it should be done at all. Angst in the phenomenological sense of the word is a positive and illuminative concept. Recognition by the individual that the world is not as it should be, the falling away of certainty is the beginning of authentic existence. I argue that my research has encouraged in its unfolding of the hermeneutical circles a common feeling amongst the participants that Academy must continually renew itself and its pedagogical approach through un-bunkered contextual understanding. It is important to explain what I mean by un-bunkered. The bunkering of "academic tribes" (Trowler, 2001) is a phenomenon observable within the business academy. As mentioned above the establishment and development of the subject disciplines within the Business Academy is well documented and perhaps an inevitable consequence of the way business itself organises its functionality (Barnes, 2001). The bunker is the boundary that encompasses the modes of research, teaching and scope of enquiry that define the subject discipline. This is not to say that there are no cross-disciplinary modes of research or pedagogy and as a teacher who has led modules that had cohorts of over nine hundred students drawn from the entire faculty intake I can say with authority and experience that these are effective and deliver demonstrable and beneficial pedagogic outcomes for most if not all students. But this does not mean that we have un-bunkered ourselves even on these cross-disciplinary initiatives, boundaries still exist under this module-level that identify and protect the peculiar character of these subject disciplines. It may be that beyond this we cannot go in collaboration if as the Noetic Correlate for this Theme/ essence tells us *complexity cannot be managed by the individual and the current structures of collaboration are inadequate* we may have to consider more radical ways in which business pedagogy can renew itself. If we consider it to be a desirable thing that the epistemological reach and nature of Business School teaching should consider stakeholder views in order to make itself relevant and responsive we may need to further understand the nature of anxiety within the wider business community. Returning to the research outcomes, although this was a small sample of nineteen people this sense of Angst was a recurrent and common theme a direct result of the shared concern which underpinned the of horizons and rapprochement. Here is an extract from one of the shared documents that illustrates this, and which was subsequently validated in the post-publication interviews that brought this circle to a close.

> If we are to effectively erode the boundaries of knowledge that divides stakeholder groups from each other and from the Business School, we must identify instances in which our teaching has not been effective for the students or their employers. This however has consequences that reach beyond the Business School into post-academic environments. It may be that employers and graduates in employment have not effectively communicated their needs or failings. Academics cannot deal with problems that they either, don't know exist or which have been unacknowledged by those affected by them. Honesty and transparency are required by all.
>
> (Circle 3, Turn 3 penultimate paragraph)

In the subsequent interviews, none of the respondents disagreed with this, which indicates a strong rapprochement amongst this group regarding the failure of the wider community to address issues of pedagogic and epistemological relevance. This is an uncertainty, a falling-away of the current normative structure which may not be "fit for purpose".

This theme is close in form to belongingness and it is probably the case that without this common cause, this community, we cannot have the confidence to develop an effective feeling of angst. The differences between the two are best discerned in the outcomes they suggest. The outcome of belongingness is that we need to collaborate to manage subject fragmentation and contextual complexity, the outcome of Angst is that we may need to re-think the fundamental roots of Business pedagogy as it suggests the possibility that we are simply following an erroneous curriculum. To re-think how and why we teach business would necessitate a radical un-bunkering of academic boundaries. We already see evidence in the current pedagogical practice of this idea. The teaching of the principles and the practices of entrepreneurial behaviour is a current area of interest and development in the Business Curriculum (Murray et al., 2018) and in contrast to the "traditional" modes of teaching the idea that students could be best inculcated with these values and behaviours by experiential-based learning or – team entrepreneurship – has been gaining traction and credibility. Here is an extract from the description of one of these programmes.

> On this course you'll train on the job, writing reports, delivering presentations, form filling and managing cash flow. By joining this with academic work, you'll develop the habits of lifelong learners.
>
> Throughout the course you'll provide evidence of how you have learned from your projects and your study. You'll work within your Team Company, supported by your team coach, to share and develop your learning.
>
> Get used to keeping work hours, managing day-to-day challenges, dealing with customers and clients and learn how a real business works. Learn by doing real work on real projects, alongside other members of your Team Company.
>
> You'll be provided with an extensive list of relevant books and journals. Read up on topics such as sales and marketing, leadership and entrepreneurship so you can apply these

> skills to your own projects. Develop insight into how these ideas work in practice. You will join professional workshops and mentoring sessions as you explore the issues involved with setting-up and running your own ventures. There are no lectures on this course, though you can attend selected lectures offered on other courses.
>
> Your team coaches will support and guide your Team Company through the duration of the course. Where you need more specialist guidance, your coach will help you find a suitable source. You'll demonstrate your learning by completing projects and project reports, making presentations and by undertaking research and writing reflective essays. Your learning will be enhanced by giving and receiving feedback with fellow team entrepreneurs and your Team Coach.
>
> (UWE, Anon, Business Team Entrepreneurship, 2019)

This course is unstructured and allows the student participants to collate their own materials and gives them a great deal of freedom in considering what is or is not relevant. This a truly un-bunkered approach and could be considered for other subject disciplines. Widening the boundaries of pedagogical input as team entrepreneurship does by nature of its structure engages with a wider epistemological base and it may be here that achieving the goal of closer epistemological overlap between the academy and its stakeholders lies.

In summary, the direct pedagogic outcomes of the research indicate that the sharing of dissatisfaction amongst key stakeholder groups is a necessary precursor to improvement and that the primacy of knowledge regarding the epistemological relevance of business school pedagogy lies a shared process of renewal which the academy can best address through the renewal of its pedagogical approach and an un-bunkered contextual understanding.

The Research Process and its Effect on Intended Outcomes

The original intent of the research project, PHAEDRUS, was to answer the following question. Is the pedagogical approach adopted by Business Schools in the Higher Education Sector in the UK appropriate for: Students, business and other organisational stakeholders and the maintenance of a coherent pedagogy in the context of Higher Education. These, as I have said, are not original questions but I had intended that the answering of these through the methodology and the attendant method had the potential to deliver a unique insight. When I was considering the context of this research I had anticipated that an examination of the life-world of respondents and the merging of their epistemological horizons had the potential to resolve the bifurcation between these two dominant perspectives (Of business pedagogy -Scientific Management and Humanism) and bring the individual as the embodiment of meaning and the carrier of relevance into focus as the true object of pedagogical effort. In retrospect that was an ambitious aim for a relatively small-scale project. The research did nevertheless yield insights into the relevance and application of phenomenological research in the context of the Business Academy and its perceived effectiveness. The original predicted or desired outcomes were that the operationalization of Gadamer's interpretive phenomenology could provide an understanding of the nature and form of what epistemological congruence was. Through the conduct and the unfolding of the project, these outcomes changed as the research process unfolded. Here it is useful to remind ourselves of my original speculation on the research outcomes.

> The prime outcome is to answer the research question(s) from a new perspective and to provide a further detailed demonstration of the applicability of a phenomenological ontology in the context of business academia. The final (third) turn and observation of the Hermeneutic cycle will point towards specific actions that could inform curriculum design and pedagogical intent. Ultimately the aim is to inform action that increases the overlap between the epistemological understanding of the three major stakeholders and

to provide a process by which the "Zone of Epistemological Congruence" is monitored for efficacy and furthermore, that the amount of overlap or its size is maximised. Such outcomes would generate a wealth of material for wider academic engagement in the form of publication and formal discourse. In this case, there is the potential for an important secondary outcome; the testing and possible establishment of a hermeneutical methodology and method in the context of research into Business Pedagogy; which would, in turn, lead to the establishment of a cycle of discourse for post-doctoral research and the development of a new form of textual coding based on phenomenological principles

On the other end of the scale of ambition is an appraisal that the methodology, method and ontological stance are not applicable in this context. Similarly, though, this will also generate further academic discourse, formal or otherwise around the issue of why phenomenological analysis is not contextually appropriate.

I will deal with each of these in order.

Answering the key question

The notion that there is, or that there can be a definable "Zone of Epistemological Congruence" has to some personal embarrassment been revealed as at base an erroneous idea. The multi-layered and nuanced responses from the hermeneutical circles reveal a far more complex picture which could be described as a continual and shifting negotiation of what actually counts as "knowledge". By this, I mean that the response and evolution of Businesses and organisations to the challenges of a competitive and changing context demands that knowledge itself must similarly change and evolve to retain validity and applicability. What became apparent through reflection on the themes of Angst, Disappointment and Belonging was what actually was needed or desired an attitudinal-emotional congruence rather than an epistemological congruence. If I take the example of technical "Spreadsheet" skills or the ability to use and apply some common software techniques, these were assumed to be a "given" a base process and that the value to be added by Business Schools lay not so much in the extension and deepening of these skills but having the attitude to adapt and apply software skills as tools to solve unexpected or unanticipated challenges and opportunities. It did not matter where these skills were acquired, what mattered was the ability to understand when it was appropriate to use them. This is a much harder skill to teach as it is fundamentally undefinable, open-ended and open to subjective evaluation on the part of the interested parties. So what was needed in the context of base computer skills was not the knowledge of technique but knowing how and when to apply the technique and having the confidence to do so. And this is an important distinction. It extends to other disciplinary skills, for example the skills needed to be an effective manager of people, whether these be derived from an understanding of organisational dynamics or human resources theory also change in reaction to wider contextual forces that are largely beyond the remit of any single organisation or business to influence. The attitudinal shift in the millennial generation to the workplace had been documented by this research and it has also been confirmed by other studies.

> The new generation, called the Net generation or millennials, face three potential problems in relation to management learning. The first problem involves the challenge of sustaining concentration during studies or lectures, given that millennials seem to be addicted to technology gadgets (Marcus, 2011). Second, students are challenged with engaging in instructor-led lectures (Graves, 2001) and traditional evaluation methods such as paper-and-pencil exams (Volkema, 2010). Third, difficulties associated with social isolation or alienation (Nie, 2001) is becoming pervasive among millennials. To address these challenges, this paper develops the concept management learning at the speed of life, which suggests management educators provide reflective, creative, and collaborative spaces for students.
>
> (Karakas, Manisaligil & Sarigollu, 2015 p. 1)

Generational shifts in attitude not only demand commensurate attitudinal shifts in managers but may also require major structural responses in the organisation itself, with, for example, the manner in which employment contracts are sufficiently flexible to meet employee expectations. Soon there will be a generation entering the workplace moulded by new sociological factors and they too will make significant demands on the perceptions and skills of those that manage them. No amount of epistemological congruence at any given point will fully deliver the requisite skills. The challenge for the business academy is to provide an attitudinal change in business graduates so they understand the malleability of knowledge and accept epistemological boundaries are indeterminate and ever-shifting.

So at best, the idea of a "Zone of Epistemological Congruence" is simply a snapshot of what might be extant at that particular time and that even if I were able to map the precise boundaries of knowledge across multitudinous subject disciplines, businesses and student cohorts it could only claim validity for that precise moment. This is not an entirely useless visualisation though as it does graphically demonstrate that there will always be an epistemological dis-congruence between those who have an interest in the pedagogy of business. As an aide-memoire in this context, it underlines the need for vigilance and reflection on the relevance of what we teach, particularly on the part of the academy. One point to note is that this is particularly relevant to higher education as there will always be a demand for the secondary sector to deliver solid and testable base skills.

In terms of the research process then, the key model which visualised the research question was flawed due to the assumptions it made regarding what was measurable and whether this was subject to research enquiry and this was highlighted by the conduct of the research method and its identification of noetic themes as a binding factor amongst the business community rather than epistemological congruence.

The Relevance of Phenomenological Enquiry

In contrast to the limited model that originally framed the research the potential for interpretive phenomenology in general and business research, in particular, has (at least in part) been demonstrated by this project. Key to this is the reflective process that forces me as a researcher to continually challenge my pre-conceptions and determine where my own prejudicial filters are distorting the authenticity of the voice of the participants. Unlike other qualitative techniques, it is not designed to deliver a workable theory, test a hypothesis or provide instructional guidance for similar scenarios, it is designed to provoke thought and to instigate action. My own action arising out of the project is to re-evaluate as a teacher how I embed pedagogical techniques that encourage and engender improvements in critical acuity and attitudinal flexibility amongst my students. This is a direct response to the experience of conducting the interviews, writing the shared documents and reflecting on the evolution from one turn to the next of the hermeneutical circles. In this one important respect has had a critical outcome; the improvement of my professional reflectivity as a professional educator. This is a laudable effect in itself. As Angela Brew points out in her 2003 paper "Teaching and Research: New Relationships."

> The Boyer Commission (1999) suggests that research-based learning should be standard and that the first year should be inquiry-based. Brew and Boud (1995) suggest that teaching and research are part of the same enterprise; that they can be brought together by employing the concept of learning. Both research and learning, they suggest, involve personal growth and are, in this sense, developmental.
>
> (Brew, 2003 p. 17)

Brew makes an important point here about personal development and the role that engaging in research plays in the development of a professional teacher in the context of higher education. Furthermore, she goes on to say,

> Both teaching and research involve exploring existing knowledge and trying to go beyond it. Both involve the human act of making sense of the world (Brew & Boud, 1995). This is essentially the layer conception of research since in this conception, research is interpreted as a process of discovering or generating underlying meanings.
>
> (Brew, A. 2003 p. 18)

I can with some confidence say that engaging in research has, for me, uncovered new meaning and generated a new personal conceptualisation of the role of teaching in the wider business and organisational community, namely that it should not be delivered as holy writ but that it should be negotiated with key actors, constantly checked for "real-world" efficacy and delivered in a manner that stimulates thought and constructively challenges behaviours and beliefs. The immediate and physical manifestation of this for my practice is an ongoing conscious need to keep a continual and deepening link with those outside the academy who have a direct interest in the outcomes of our teaching in Higher Education.

On the wider question of relevance to the practice of research in Business, in general, I hope to have demonstrated that this method and methodological approach has an unbounded potential to deliver new insights into all aspects of research in our field and not just pedagogy. It is difficult and time-consuming and I would caution that it takes practice and patience to approach the possibility of uncovering moments of authentic insight but the real-world impact of this has the potential to be significant. The peculiar contribution of a phenomenological approach is the uncovering of the meaning that lies beyond the ritual exchange of normative discourse, in other words asking respondents what they really mean. This aspect of the research process is as challenging in the context of business research as it appears to be in other disciplines such as nursing and psychology. Whilst I do not claim here to be engaging with such profound life-changing phenomena as ill-health or mental trauma, I am nevertheless dealing with an aspect of Dasein's life-world that has a profound impact on personal economic survival, social status, fears for the future and individual effectiveness. Also, if we recognise that this pre-theoretical sense-making of the world has an impact on individual perception and action in the business context then it has quite profound implications. If the use of business theory is in any way used as a post-hoc justification for decision making and action by individuals in any organisational context then we need to identify with some clarity when and where this takes place. This indicates that further research along phenomenological lines may not just be desirable but essential. One of the key predicates of business pedagogy, particularly at higher levels is that it encourages a conceptual link between theory and practice and in this way stimulates the emergence of critical acuity in students. However, if all we are truly accomplishing is adding to a tool-kit of post-hoc justification then we are failing to achieve this pedagogic goal. The research process in this context has highlighted this danger and if nothing more warrants further investigation. The difficulty of this is that Business Theory is attractive as a sense-making tool for the business practitioner, academics and students. The language of theory adds to the professional mystique of management as a practice. It can act as an exclusionary barrier to the non-initiated, a private language to be shared with colleagues and a demonstration of an individual's right to belong to a private club. Theory has a multiplicity of uses in the context of Business, it is used as a how-to guide, a sense-making explanatory tool, a process of communication and a resource for continuing research. All of these things are laudable and useful and to challenge this and say that there is something that underpins theory and has a more authentic voice is a controversial hypothesis. This is one of the questions that phenomenological enquiry asks, is this authentic, has the theory been truly understood as a call to action and not a simple validator of action.

Whilst it had been one of my original intents to contribute to a way in which the positivist-rational and the humanist strands of Business pedagogy could be bridged, I cannot make this claim. With this challenge to the applicability of theory in business discourse what I am left with is an admonition for care in the use of theory rather than a mechanism that can act as an arbiter of validity. The uncovering of an authentic voice using the method I have used is a difficult one to implement as it is time-consuming; in the execution of the Hermeneutic circles, the transcription of evidence, the reflection on the material and the authorship of shared texts. In a business environment where decisions have to be made continually in the short term often in response to malleable contexts the instigation of this method in the format I have used it to judge the validity of action is impractical. All I can reasonably say is that we will continue to use those theoretical models that we most easily comprehend to inform research into pedagogical effectiveness, research into business issues and post-hoc evaluations of business phenomena. The place of phenomenological enquiry in this context is to judge the effects of this myriad of decisions and to gauge what effect this un-analysable environment has on the sentiment, the emotion and the attitude of individuals involved in the business world to emerging challenges and opportunities. It is in this space that I would argue that ongoing hermeneutical discourses are an important examination of practice across the whole spectrum of the business field from its pedagogy to its practice.

Phenomenology and its Place in the Academic Discourse on Pedagogy

I will start here with a perspective on this from Karen Ilse van Heerden's thesis entitled *"A phenomenological investigation into undergraduate students' experience of acquiring the discourse of engineering"*. Here she "introduces" what she regards as the four distinguishing concepts of phenomenological enquiry in the context of qualitative research.

- Lebenswelt, because it allows the researcher to understand the phenomenon from the subject's point of view;
- intentionality, because it accommodates the uniqueness of perception;
- description, because it allows the data to speak for themselves;

- reflection (and transformation), because it allows me as researcher access to the subject's experience.

(Van Heerden, 2000 p. 69)

The underlying assumption in all phenomenological research is that the personal and unique perception of the individual has a validity prior to their unique voice being aggregated into larger data sets or subsumed to support a theoretical construct. The observations that van Heerden was able to make from the data arising out of her study on multiple identities in a multi-cultural society provided valuable insights for academics working in other fields including that of business (Robinson, 2002) and education (Bengesai, 2012). This illustrates how phenomenological research has its own distinctive validity and that it can contribute to other discourses. In the context of business, in almost, every widely published and used text on the nature and implementation of Business Research has at least some passing reference to phenomenological technique usually placing it in the context of qualitative research. Specifically, for research into education and pedagogical practice, it has an identifiable profile (Bogdan & Biklen, 1997, O'Donoghue & Punch, 2003, Johnson & Christensen, 2008) and unsurprisingly so. If we return to the four "distinguishing concepts" it would be difficult for an educator teaching at any level to deny the validity and importance of the individual voice. In the particular case of my own pedagogical research, I fully acknowledge through my research design that this is of critical importance to my own personal understanding of my practice as a professional and that has important insights that will impact on the understanding and the practice of others. The hermeneutical circles may have conflated the voices of students, academics and practitioners but this process does not diminish the uniqueness of contribution but aggregates it into a shared fusion of horizons that are mutually supportive of each other. The text itself becomes an individual voice.

> Gadamer also uses face-to-face conversational terms to describe how a reader experiences a text. For Gadamer, the text is like a "Thou" -which "is not an Object; it relates itself to us" (358). For every claim the reader makes, the Thou of

> the text makes a counter-claim. And interpretation can only develop through the I's revision of the thou's claim.
>
> (Sotirou, 1993 p. 368)

As a professional educator, I am admonished to listen to the student voice, accommodate the needs of the real world and engage in cross-disciplinary co-operation (Barritt, 1985) and I argue that a hermeneutic circle is almost an ideal vehicle for facilitating this. Accordingly, in respect of the academic discourse on the maintenance of an effective pedagogy hermeneutical phenomenology has a critical role to play. And there is already evidence for this in a number of studies on such diverse issues as classroom practice in higher education (Ramezanzadeh, Adel & Zareian, 2016) and the career choices made by technical education students (Hioki, Lester, & Martinez, 2015). The use of hermeneutical circles that facilitate the sharing of voice amongst a number of actors has the potential to make this discourse even richer. This is dependent though on whether the method is replicable.

In chapter five I have recounted in some detail and with some key examples, the practical processes and analytical techniques that have led to the outcomes of the research project and I believe that this, together with the examples of the shared documents and the moderation form gives sufficient detail to allow another to reshape and reinterpret the method. It should be noted that as with any phenomenological enquiry there is no claim to be made here for the universal applicability of the findings of this research. I can only claim that for this circumstance and for this set of research participants that this was their collective insight. It is an inevitable consequence of the thrownness of human perception that this will already have moved on and changed in response to changes in the life-world of Dasein and changes in the life-world of the They. This is a critical point for any research based on phenomenological principles, it is the moving execution of the technique that uncovers fragments of authenticity that is important and not the generalisability of the research findings themselves. This does not mean that others may choose to generalise the findings but that I counsel against this. This leads to a critical challenge which is to question the purpose of the phenomenological enquiry if it is not "generalisable". My response to this starts with a quote by Stan Lester from his paper, "An Introduction to Phenomenological Research".

> Phenomenological studies make detailed comments about individual situations which do not lend themselves to direct generalisation in the same way which is sometimes claimed for survey research. The development of general theories (i.e. which apply to situations beyond the participants or cases which have been studied) from phenomenological findings needs to be done transparently if it is to have validity; in particular, the reader should be able to work through from the findings to the theories and see how the researcher has arrived at his or her interpretations.
>
> (Lester, 1999 p. 2)

I hope that I have provided such transparency and that for the reader that it supports the implications and the conclusions that I draw upon for the development of my own pedagogical practice and for continuing studies in this area. In retrospect what was most surprising was the unanticipated shape of the outcome, a multi-layered combination of Gadamer's hermeneutical phenomenology and the use of some of the basic principles of phenomenological interpretation to uncover and better describe the layers of Gadamer's thought. In effect, this is a synthesis of technique and it gives rise to three key questions. First, is this a valid technique that can be replicated, second does it have the potential to uncover new insights and finally can this research method be used in contexts other than this particular study.

In conclusion, I argue that the use of hermeneutical circles based on this particular interpretation of Gadamer's interpretive phenomenology can be used for further study and the outcomes from discourses built around these can be both valid and actionable in their own right and a make a credible contribution to other academic discourses. The experience of conducting this research has also had a significant influence on my own personal professional practice as a teacher. This has manifested itself as a heightened ethical awareness of what I do as a teacher and what I do as a researcher as Murray and Holmes (2014) warn;

> The radical implication for a research methodology is that only as phenomenology is ethical analysis possible. For ethical responsibility must shift its gaze toward the context in which a subject finds him/herself, the scene that is constitutive of his/her subjectivity.
>
> (Murray & Holmes, 2014 p. 26)

Chapter 8

EHP and the future of the Business School

Contribution

The contribution I have made to the development of new insight into the pedagogy of the business school is twofold. I have demonstrated that *Existential Hermeneutic Phenomenological* (EHP) research can deliver a new understanding of how business pedagogy is perceived by key actors. This has profound implications for the business school not least in the realm of curriculum design and curriculum content. My research clearly shows that we need to establish open and transparent modes of communication across all actors in the business community to make our curricula effective and relevant. By this, I do not mean such narrow activities as knowledge transfer partnerships that focus on the generation of revenue or the creation of market share or the temporary secondment of academics to organisations or even guest teaching from business practitioners. These activities are laudable in their own right but they are fragmentary and such traffic does not have a profound effect on either pedagogy or curriculum (Trank & Rynes, 2003). I have demonstrated that we need a continual continuum of communication, the establishment of conduits that genuinely exchange information and meaning seamlessly and which do this in real-time. In this way, business can contribute to a relevant curriculum and the academy can aid in tackling challenges and opportunities.

Significance of the Study

In order to contextualise my claims to contribution, I will re-visit salient features of other contemporary phenomenologically driven research in the practice of Business and the pedagogy of the Business Academy.

The indissoluble link between what we do and what we are was emphasised by Gloria Dall'Alba and Jorgen Sandberg in their article,

A phenomenological perspective on researching work and learning (2014). In this article, they challenge the notion that the act of work can be separated from the process of learning in a subject/object duality. Their idea of the "entwinement" of the life-world with practice finds clear echoes in the outcomes of this research. The life-worlds of the participants within the hermeneutic circles as revealed through the fusion of horizons are indissolubly linked with the communality of perception of what the practice of Business is and how they are situated within this community. Entwinement binds all with the promise of Business could be and what it is not, particularly though the theme of *Disappointment* and its potential essential remedy, the *Sharing of Dissatisfaction*. In this sense, the Phaedrus research is complimentary to their call for using the perspective and understanding of the significance of the phenomenological term life-world as a motivating insight into the potential creation of new pedagogical techniques.

Where the significance of this study departs from previous applications of Interpretive phenomenology is in its scope. Previous studies have focussed on aspects of, most commonly, organisational dynamics or research techniques. In contrast, this study questions our fundamental understanding of what business actually is. When what I define as the business academy aggregated a multiplicity of subject disciplines such as strategy, human resources, accounting and organisational study it did so a result of external influences such as governmental concerns over economic performance and a mimesis of extant business schools primarily in the United States of America. What it did not do was aggregate these topics under a unifying theoretical structure as such a thing does not exist. Nor, perhaps, should it exist. As has been illustrated in the literature review the Business Academy is an academy that has evolved in response to external pressures. Successive governments focussed on the importance to the economy of a well-educated managerial class and looked to Business Schools, particularly post Dearing to fulfil this need. What was being asked though of this Business Academy was simply no less than the aggregation of a wide range of human activity that encompasses a spectrum that stretches from the market trader and the manufacturer of passenger aircraft. As much of the modelling for apparently successful behaviours came from the USA it is unsurprising that the curricula that emerged in Business Schools showed a high degree of mimesis. Although UK Business Schools have considerable flexibility within the general process of mimesis to configure their own peculiar mixtures of the core curriculum, their task to deliver a fully coherent Business education is probably impossible. As what we think of as Business, not only has a wide variety of activity that sits under this umbrella term, it is also continually evolving and reconfiguring. Reconfiguration of Business activity is an inevitable response to change in whatever vector we might wish to consider. This does not invalidate the existence of the Business Academy but it does argue for an acceptance of that this open-ended generality is an inevitable consequence of the manner in which we currently aggregate this area of human activity. This means that the differing perceptions of what constitutes a valid pedagogic approach whether this is positivist rationalism or subjective humanism will always continue and will always be debated. This is not in itself a bad thing as discussions within the Business Academy on the robustness of its approach is both a consequence of Business's continual evolution and a response to it. However, this is unhelpful to any individual student, employer or academic seeking to resolve what it is about "business" that is unsatisfactory or what could actually be improved.

A Phenomenological approach to how we understand the social phenomenon of what we call Business resolves this difficulty. The Existential Hermeneutic Methodology (EHP) I have used in this research is a demonstration of this possibility. This research with its emphasis on identifiable underlying essences unifies the conceptualisation of "business" outside the confines of the bunkered fragmentation of pedagogical approaches found within the Business Academy. For example, the aggregation of the theme of *Belongingness* and its essence, its call to action, of a *Shared Process of Renewal* is applicable both to how we approach accounting processes and how we treat with other actors in an organisational context. With development, EHP could be the start of an intimation of a unifying approach to why we aggregate the subject disciplines that sit under the Business Academy that goes beyond happenstance, convenience and the arbitrary application of benchmarks.

The Impact on a personal pedagogic understanding

The second contribution that I make to the development of business pedagogy is my own more contextually rich understanding of the ethics of that which I do and which I have covered in the previous chapter. I argue here that this deepened understanding of the ethical dimensions of that which we do as teachers should be a profound part of a reflective process in which all pedagogues in the academy should engage. This is not simply a function of a phenomenological approach. Considering the centrality of an individual's experience may have highlighted this but the admonition for care goes beyond my own method and methodology and reaches across subject disciplines. Where we teach, we must consider ethics. Returning to the original contextualisation of this research I would argue, unlike Martin Parker that we do not need to "Bulldoze the Business School" but that we do need to re-orient the academy's pedagogic strategy. We need to re-emphasise the importance of communication with the wider business community and develop new forms of communication that are not episodic or asymmetric or prey to the "bunkering" of subject discipline parochial interests. Furthermore, the primacy of individual experience also needs to be re-examined particularly if we are to acknowledge that the pre-theoretical voice has as much influence on the immediacy decision making in business as the post-theoretical one. These contributions were not what I expected and this has re-shaped not only my understanding of how to apply Phenomenology but what the form and nature of the continuation of my research activity.

My personal subjectivity in this context lies within my role as a professional educator in the Business Academy. The fulfilment of the research project has a reflective outcome; how has the research affected me in my view of myself as a teacher and as a researcher and I will deal with these in turn. The two are linked as research in Higher Education has a critical role in informing pedagogy (Coate,

Barnett, & Williams 2001) but for the purposes of clarity, I will disaggregate these.

The Emergence of a New Ethical Understanding of Practice

One of the most radical effects of conducting this research was the emergence of a new personal epistemological boundary. Hitherto I had considered that that role of business pedagogy lay firmly in the realm of functionality and task-oriented learning. In this, I included the theoretical understanding of organisational and interpersonal dynamics as a process that could be observed and acted upon. This impersonal view was derived in part from decades as a business practitioner and in part from my intellectual understanding of the importance of social dynamics as an educator. This is not to say that I was entirely immune to the emotional vectors of practice or the importance of teaching the value of empathy in the classroom. It is to underline that at the outset of the research I had not anticipated the emotional and visceral insights that the research process would deliver and how this would have a significant effect on my personal epistemological boundary. This is important as an extension of what I regard as valid and credible knowledge has an ethical corollary; if I extend that which I consider to be valid as knowledge then my ethical understanding of the nature of that knowledge and its ethical effects must also extend to match my new understanding. In the case of facilitating hermeneutical circles and the emergence of the unexpected noetic themes and their validity as demonstrated by the reception of the shared texts meant that I gained new ethical as well as epistemological insights into the consequences of my personal pedagogic practice and the wider pedagogy of the Business Academy. Here is a note from my reflective journal.

> In failing to understand that the difficulties of the business environment has an emotional vector in terms of angst and the falling away of certainty I have failed to properly address the full meaning of the necessity of teaching resilience and that resilience itself lies beyond the merely transactional process of moving careers or jobs and has a real psychic and physiological effect on students and practitioners alike.

Resilience or how we teach it was not I realised a simple admonition to move on with the functional process economic survival but that it had an emotional vector that I was not fully addressing in my own teaching practice. This had a profound impact on my personal professional understanding of my role as a teacher and also my responsibility as a facilitator of communication with the wider business community. First, in my re-appraisal of my role as a teacher, I now feel that it is important to embed a notion of the interdependency of the wider business community into my pedagogic materials. It could be argued that on a superficial level at least this is already being done as most modules and most programmes delivered in the Business School emphasise the interconnectedness and complexity of the contemporary business ecology. However, even when we (the academy) talk about reaching out to the business community and that wider community itself talks about the importance of education and life-long learning we fall short of considering the empathy that could be developed to strengthen these bonds. Typically, when we consider links between business practice and the business academy we think primarily about function, task and outcome, rather than connection, consequence and empathy. Here is an example from Harrington and Kearney (2011) where they talk about building new relationships between the business community and higher education.

> In order to cultivate entrepreneurial knowledge, business and academic communities should collaborate to provide a practice-based perspective in leadership education and training. In the longer-term there is a need to focus attention on stimulating awareness of the relationship between management practitioners at all levels and the wider research community. The challenge of developing relevant actionable knowledge that prepares and enthuses university students not just to observe, but to lead and drive business activity must address the academic-practitioner interface. Management education should be constructed to reflect both academic and practitioner perspectives, by balancing in-class training, rooted in academic knowledge, with the experiential knowledge of

> business leaders and greater attention and investment needs to be made to better understand this dynamic.
>
> (Harrington & Kearney, 2011, p. 134)

Here Harrington and Kearney talk quite correctly about "practice-based perspectives", "actionable knowledge" and the need to "drive business" as these are essential outcomes. But all of these vectors have human consequences. Can we, for example, fully understand the impact that these communities will have on each other if they are brought together to solve problems or exploit opportunities. A new or re-imagined practice-based perspective has the potential to both encourage and erode the confidence and commitment of individuals involved in this re-constructed way of doing things. Will "actionable knowledge" undermine the embedded institutional knowledge of an organisation and will the over-arching need to "drive business" drive the element of social belonging from an organisation? Phenomenological perspectives on this form of academic/ practitioner co-operation have the potential to examine some of the unforeseen consequences on individuals and perhaps better inform action and ameliorate the trauma of structural change.

The challenge to me as an educator is to solve the problem of operationalising the consequences of my new ethical understanding in my professional practice. This is not a simple matter of perhaps introducing materials on ethical challenges into the curriculum, it rather strikes to the issue of classroom practice and what I say to regard the consequence of action in any management context. I should articulate with as much reason and coherence to students the interconnectedness of all business: That it is the responsibility of business practitioners to consider that all aspects of their behaviour have ethical consequences and not just on those issues they will encounter that have an obvious ethical dimension, such as care for the environment and employment equity across gender, ethnicity, disability etc. It is to emphasise how personal experience and perception is the basic unit of the construction of a mediated reality and that equanimity in the treatment of others is fundamental to building productive business communities. So my future practice must bring ethical considerations into the heart of my teaching.

To do this effectively I must have a technique that reminds me of my ethical duty and I return to the findings of my research to aid me with this.

> The theme of disappointment
>
> The interviews are taking much longer than expected and what was envisaged as a short discourse aimed at uncovering the practical response to the efficacy of business pedagogy often diverges into more personal matters of "what was missing" from the retrospective perspective of the usefulness of the curriculum.

I must be more transparent and honest about the limitations of the curriculum and its scope, we in the business school cannot possibly approach the full extent of knowledge and insight that graduates will need in order to pursue successful careers. We can provide route maps to find the resources that they need and we can deliver the skills of effective research but we cannot provide all the knowledge and the analytical perspectives they could in all eventualities need. I can bridge this aporia by focusing on attitudinal reactions to gaps in knowledge and reassurance of their innate ability to find what is needed both in terms of raw data and the tools (and perhaps people) needed to understand this.

> The theme of belonging
>
> One of the more emotionally surprising themes amongst the respondents is the sense of belonging. A sense that "we are all in it together" and that there is a desire to be accommodating and welcoming across all the participant groups is palpable in the responses. I am worried that I may be enabling this as the interlocutor and that this reflects my own feelings and values. I need to take care here.

Given my concern that my positionality as a researcher may have some interlocutory influence on this theme, the ethical manifestation of this finding needs to be considered carefully. I do not want to over emphasise the sense of community against the inevitably of competition in the practice of business. All businesses, all organisations given a long enough timeline will either change beyond recognition or fail. It is an inevitable consequence of the inherent disequilibrium caused by extraneous factors in any business sector. Competitiveness does not mean however that there is no communality of experience on a personal level. So the ethical vector here is to reassure students that they will almost certainly face failure as well as success and that this is a common human experience in the context of business and that there should only be opprobrium levelled at an individual that fails when there is a clear case of wilful malfeasance.

> The theme of angst
>
> In my conversations with the research respondents across all stakeholder groups, there was a detectable underlying sense of incompleteness, a feeling that not was as well as it could be in the relationship between the three stakeholder groups a sense that it could be more complete, which seemed at first pass to support the notion that there should be greater epistemological concordance between academics. I find it tempting to do so but again I must be careful here as "angst" in the phenomenological sense is at the core of Dasein and is a key driver with the potential to move Dasein from inauthenticity to authenticity. The echoes of this that I find in the transcriptions may be a part of this wider sense of dissatisfaction with the world-as-it-is. Here I must unpick with care what is relevant to the pedagogy of the Business Academy.

This theme is the most difficult to translate into an actionable response. Research participants clearly manifested within the various discourses a sense that business practice is failing in its full potential. Against this there is no sense within academic writing that business as a practice is perfectible; there is no golden utopian state to which we, as business people can aspirc. Even the allied discipline of economics acknowledges that there is no point at which markets can reach perfect equilibrium as market knowledge can never be spread equally across all participants in the market (Chamberlain, 1948; Stigler, 1957; Kononenko & Kugai, 2019). Nevertheless, academics freely admit that all aspects of business practice can be improved such as Business Ethics (Crane *et al.*, 2019), Marketing (Hanssens & Pauwels, 2016), Strategy (Kaplan & Norton, 1996) and Human Resource Management (Noe, et al., 2017). This list can be extended to every subject discipline within the field of business. There is a universal consensus that we can all work and move towards something better. We emphasise in the business academy that management and business practice has clearly defined goals and whether these be the maximisation of profit or the attainment of optimum operational efficiency the successful practitioner will continually work towards the attainment of these. This key driver of pedagogy is not dissimilar to any to be found in any of the disciplines of Higher Education. Robert Thompson (2014) succinctly summarises the challenges of contemporary Higher Education.

> To realise the goals of a formative liberal education, colleges and universities must adopt a developmental model of education to guide and structure undergraduate educational experience to go beyond a focus on enhancing students' capacities for reasoning and tolerance. Opportunities must also be provided for students to develop a personal epistemology that includes a commitment to evaluative thinking, their capacity for empathy, an integrated identity that includes values and a commitment to constructively engage differences.
>
> (Thompson, 2014 p. 147)

The engendering of "angst" is an inevitable consequence of these multi-layered pedagogical goals, it is embedded in a mindset that is encouraged to foster "evaluative thinking". My ethical responsibility here lies in how I advise or guide students in the management of "angst" or how they should embrace this "falling -away" as a natural consequence of a professional self-reflective attitude. Graduates of the business school, will unless they are extremely fortunate or lack cognitive acuity, encounter innumerable moments of disappointment regarding the imperfectability of business processes. Recognition of the imperfectability of business is an important personal epistemological tool and whilst I cannot embed this formally in the curriculum I can use the admonition "memento mori" to remind them of the limitations of personal perfectibility.

The Emergence of a New Ethical Understanding of Research

It is incumbent on any researcher who participates in research that claims to give voice to the individual to consider at length the ethical implications what they do (Burgess, 2005, Simons & Usher, 2012). I will however start with some general ethical considerations applicable to all pedagogical research in a higher education context. In any research proposal that addresses pedagogical issues in the UK, the British Education Research Association (BERA) provide an essential set of principles and procedural guidance (Halpin, 2005, Thomas, 2013) the current document being published in 2018. Of note is a BERA commissioned paper Ethics and Educational Research (Hammersley & Traianou, 2012) which is particularly useful in the context of this project, as it gives procedural guidance on appropriate communicative processes with respondents in qualitative studies. However, as the methodology of this project is specific and has its own particular ethical topography it has been necessary to draw (as indicated in Chapter 2) from ethical perspectives in which phenomenological research is more common, such as Nursing. And here I give a brief restatement of some of the critical advice from this discipline.

As I have observed Ethical considerations in Nursing arise from the intensely personal relationships that must be engaged in to become a professional nursing practitioner. The profession and the discipline has an extensive canon of literature on this (Benner, 1994; Walters, 1995; Usher & Holmes, 1997; Goethals, et al., 2010) and on the application of phenomenological methodology itself (Caelli, 2001; Walker, 2007). This includes the use of phenomenology including consideration of the implications of applying a Gadamerian methodology. (Walker, 2007; Häggman-Laitila, 1999) that puts at its heart the importance of critical self-reflection.

Bound up in the phenomenological method is a process that clearly identifies the voice of the researcher in the discourse. Noting Hägg-man-Laitila's admonition to identify and describe my own view in each stage of the research process I kept a reflective journal to do just that and from this, I was able to make the following critical ethical observations. First, that I have a tendency to lean towards and to favour those statements and opinions that are confirmatory of my own understanding: Second, I am conscious of giving more weight to the opinions of those respondents that I personally like and the longer the personal relationship I have with a respondent the more likely I am to give credence to their opinions. I will address both of these with the ameliorative actions I took to counterbalance these effects.

One of the key purposes of research is to extend understanding and knowledge and any personal prejudice that limits the openness of this aim must be addressed with transparency and seriousness. Statements and opinions that are confirmatory of pre-existing positions must be identified and challenged continually through reflection. The keeping of a reflective journal is for me the most critical discipline in following a phenomenological method and adhering to a phenomenological methodology. At the outset of the research, my note keeping was perfunctory and took the form of additional commentary made in the columns of the moderation forms I used to structure the interviews with the research participants. When the research was stalled by circumstance and a lack of personal energy this changed. In a moment of clarity, I realised that I had been making unwarranted excuses for my lack of progress. At this point, I returned to Donald Schön's seminal text, The Reflective Practitioner: How Professionals Think in Action. Schön makes a valuable observation on the nature of reflection and how it is not bound by any specific notion of time, space or form.

> When a practitioner reflects in and on his practice, the possible objects of his reflection are as varied as the kind of phenomena before him and the systems of knowing-in-practice which he brings to them.
>
> (Schön, 1983 p. 62)

As I also have a background in Art and Design I began to experiment with different forms of recording my reflections on the research process, including at one point drawing a series of self-portraits interspersed with text notes on a particular emotional aspect of the research process. This had a dual effect, the nature and density of my reflective observations grew, and the research process was given a fresh momentum. This was due to the fact that the conscious recording of my inner observations revealed that I had in fact been leaning towards material that was confirmatory of my own pre-conceptions. Giving these preconceptions physical form in a reflective journal gave them an existence independent of my own thought processes and had the effect of making them obvious. I cannot claim that in the subsequent execution that I was entirely free of them, but now I was fully conscious of this aspect of my prejudicial understanding and I could use this to sense check my receptivity to the voice of others. I came to the conclusion that in the pursuit of any form of phenomenological research the keeping of a reflective journal is essential.

Having personal affinities towards people is a natural human trait and we are predisposed to seek fellows whose views, opinions and attitudes reflect our own as they confirm the validity of our life-world (Berger & Luckmann, 1991). Whilst interviewing the research participants I would always spend some time in the social niceties of greeting and conversational exchange, particularly when I reached the third occasion when I was interviewing the participant. Through the process of transcribing the first round of interviews conducted in the first circle, I notice that two of the interviews were considerably longer than the other four. These were with people I had known in contexts prior to my career in academia and whilst neither of which could be described as close friends, both were more than passing acquaintances. The effect of this was that their material contribution to the shared narrative was considerably skewed in their favour. Whilst this may be taken as a straightforward admonishment not to include friends or acquaintances in any form of qualitative study it is also a practical warning to sense check through checking transcribed material to see if bias is manifest in the over attribution of validity to key individual participants. This is also perhaps, why such intensive qualitative studies such as those predicated on phenomenological methodology should restrict the discursive and interrogatory process to a limited number of participants. The remedy of this was reasonably straightforward a simple time limit reminder on each section of the moderation form helped to even out the length of each discussion. Again, I cannot claim that my research and findings are wholly devoid of conscious or unconscious bias we must admit as phenomenological researchers that they never can be. This does not though invalidate the research as a contributor to knowledge it has a vital a continuing contribution to make.

Continuation

Before I discuss the continuation of the method for future research projects and indeed, the continuation of this project here is a reminder of my original intentions in a passage I had written at the outset of the project.

> The PHAEDRUS research project aims to adapt a new hermeneutic method and use this to engage specialist practitioners in the exchange of complex discursive themes in a new form of asymmetric "social" media. By adapting the work of Georg Gadamer a new analytical process has been developed to deconstruct the deeper meanings and origins of discourse. This will enable participants in expert hermeneutic circles to rapidly fuse individual understandings of critical thematic issues in order to reach new and synergistic agreements on identifying challenges and the solutions to these. Meanings and discourse will be exchanged through an asymmetric social forum facilitated in part by a new class of cognitive algorithm coded specifically to engage participants in hermeneutic exchange. Primarily this will take the form of a continually modified text which evolves as subscribers to the forum offer comments and suggestions.

I am somewhat embarrassed to admit that at one point that I thought that the hermeneutic circles and the discursive exchanges embedded within it could be subject to deconstruction and replication in an automated process. It may well be that in the future that I could, in collaboration with others, build a cognitive algorithm that could approach some of the analytical depth I have used in this research, but now I find this an unlikely prospect due to the emotional and empathetic elements of communication that are critical to the identification of noematic themes. Even if such a project was possible it would not have the same quality of nuanced exchange which is of particular importance in the uncovering of the authenticity of interpersonal human exchange. Even when Gadamer ascribes an independent voice to a text it is still the voice of human communication that is assumed in the text, even when this does purport to echo the voice of the divine. In its original iteration, PHAEDRUS was an acronym; Phenomenological Hermeneutical Analysis Extending Discursive Reach Utilising Subjectivity/Inter-subjectivity, now it is not. The operationalisation of Gadamer's hermeneutical process revealed in its execution that it defied a simplification of function and reduction to a rules-based process. It demanded emotional attention, human reflection, the revisiting of prejudicial attitudes. Also, there had to be a continual evaluation and re-evaluation of the transcribed material and the development of new skills of listening and questioning. Nor were these skills perfectly transferable from one respondent to another, each respondent had to be treated and talked to in a unique manner that reflected their own needs for the building of trust and confidence. The human interlocutor and facilitator of the hermeneutic circle is (currently) essential.

I have retained the title Phaedrus for two reasons, first as a reminder of the original intent as outlined above and the second reason is that Phaedrus, the titular character of Plato's treatise recounting Socratic technique whilst (probably) a fictional construct remains a key actor in the development of western rhetorical exchange. As both Gadamer (Dostal, 2002) and his teacher Heidegger (Adkins, 1962) were grounded in the discipline of Greek Philology there is a direct link between Gadamer's belief in the contribution of discourse as a key contributor to the emergence of rational exchange to the manner in which discourse has been used in this research project.

> Gadamer champions a genuine rhetoric that concerns the "discovery and transmission of insight and knowledge, "an event that is exemplified in the "art of leading a conversation." Gadamer invokes Plato's account of rhetoric in the Phaedrus, but he steadfastly argues against an attempt to constrain rhetoric by linking it to certainty and unchanging truth. He looks to Plato's activity of writing the Socratic dialogues rather than Plato's philosophical self-understanding, insisting that what we learn from the Platonic dialogues is that it "is more important to find the words which convince the other than those which can be demonstrated in their truth, once and for all."
>
> (Hackforth, 1972 p. 4)

Gadamer is pointing here to the criticality of convincing the other, of encouraging intersubjectivity, through a continuing discursive exchange and thereby a fusion or horizons. The shared documents of the hermeneutic circles are an example of this "convincing of the other" a shared understanding that most of the participants in the research were keen to continue. This then is the first avenue of continuation for the method; a continuing dialogue on the efficacy of the pedagogy of the business academy. This in itself has a multiplicity of opportunities for further research. I could continue with the main narrative thread, and /or encourage new threads of interest to be opened. Using the same strictures of anonymity for participants, respect of their voice and as accurate an accounting of the communalities amongst the circle members as I can reasonably facilitate there is no barrier to continuation. Here perhaps, I have a moral duty to continue this hermeneutical discussion. I have piqued interest and delivered insight to the members of the three circles and there may be much more to uncover here. By conflating the three circles I could possibly extend the uncovering of insights into personal authenticity and continue to develop my own understanding of the pedagogy of business into the context of higher education. In this way, I can contribute to the ongoing discussion concerning the efficacy and relevance of business schools.

The developed and mature iteration of the method can also be transferred to other issues that could also contribute to the development of business education. Here is an observation made by Professor Martin Parker on one possible development of the business school curriculum.

> ...the sort of research and teaching that happens within the business school can be enriched by the inclusion of methodologies and topics not commonly seen to be part of its remit.
>
> (Parker, 2018 p.71)

The use of Gadamerian inspired hermeneutics and the insights it delivers by the use of phenomenological principles of analysis are precisely that, a methodology not commonly seen in the business school. Placing the individual at the heart of the meaning of business as a practice and the conflation of the noesis of actors within the business community delivers new insights not simply on the pedagogy of business schools but also on the wider impact of what we teach on the business community at a societal level. Accordingly, my first extension of the method I have developed will be to examine the nature and meaning of business itself. As I have mentioned throughout the text, we do not have a settled or satisfactory definition of what business is. From the responses of my research participants even on this relatively narrow topic the import and effect of business practice extends beyond simple transactional exchange or the single-minded pursuit of profit it has, perhaps, unexplored vectors of meaning, empathy and belonging that we have not yet begun to understand. As hubristic a metaphor as it sounds this may the missing "Dark Matter" of the business universe that explains the irrationality that bedevils economic theory and its inability to model the future (Orrell, 2010).

The second extension conflates two of my research interests and returns to the application of cognitive technologies as alluded to above. If one of the key issues in analysing business activity is that we do not in sufficient depth, consider the primacy of individual action and its emotional vectors then we cannot fully comprehend how new cognitive technologies will be used or misused. If we accept that business practice lies beyond two-dimensional transactional relationships then the application of such technologies to automate tasks, to drive efficiencies and to extend analytical reach may not be simply driven by economic concerns but deeper motivations that we cannot begin to understand as we have not yet applied methodologies that will uncover these. So, another key project will be to use a hermeneutical circle that follows the techniques I have developed to gauge if there are other motivations in the adoption of what we inaccurately term Artificial Intelligence.

The third and most important extension is a direct acknowledgement that the purpose of this research is to improve my professional practice as an educator. The execution of the research encouraged me to reflect on not just what I teach students via the curriculum but how I teach students. Returning to the key noetic themes of Angst, Belongingness and Disappointment I will need to continue at a personal level address how these underlying tensions impact on student's perception of what business is and how it should be conducted. I will need to devise forms of narrative description that draws on my own experience as a professional business practitioner that demonstrate that a feeling of Angst is a positive motivator in the pursuit of a state of praxis. Also, to reassure students that Disappointment is a natural result of attempting to achieve excellence in practice and that again it should be used as a motivational force and finally that we all nevertheless have Belongingness to a wider community that has common cause and concerns. To crystallise these themes into something that be considered and evaluated by others will mean the writing of an independent paper and this in all probability will be the first direct and tangible outcome of this research. Returning to Djleic's assertion that "management has reached a status of taken-for-grantedness that makes it essentially transparent and invisible to us" (Djelic. 2016 p.1) it is my intention to contribute to a process of stepping –away from this taken-for-grantedness and to reinforce a process reflective activity that looks at the pedagogy of business holistically as the noetic themes of Angst, Disappointment and Belongingness cross-subject discipline boundaries.

In conclusion, the journey that engaging in interpretative phenomenology takes you is not an easy one. It challenges perceptions about yourself as a professional and others as key actors in your community. Such research can point towards dark and troubling issues that lie outside the normative understanding of what is acceptable to the community to which you belong, but is and always will be, worthwhile. I had started this research journey with what I now realise to be a naïve notion of simply applying a mechanistic process based on a topographical reading of Gadamer's work. This took me on a journey in which an acronym – PHAEDRUS – became a deeper discursive and analytical role in I became an embodiment of a contemporary Phaedrus, a role which revealed that it may be possible through questioning and discussion to uncover a process that could point towards a unifying principle for "Business".

I leave the final words to Gadamer.

> What man needs is not just the persistent posing of ultimate questions, but the sense of what is feasible, what is possible, what is correct, here and now. The philosopher, of all people, must, I think, be aware of the tension between what he claims to achieve and the reality in which he finds himself.
>
> (Gadamer, 1957 p. 623)

References

Ackerman, D. S., Gross, B. L., & Perner, L. (2003) Instructor, student, and employer perceptions on preparing marketing students for changing business landscapes. *Journal of Marketing Education*, 25(1), 46-56.

Adkins, A.W., (1962) *Heidegger and language*. Philosophy, 37(141), pp.229-237.

Ainley, S. (2014) A Phenomenological Study of Agritourism Entrepreneurship on Ontario Family Farms. *Tourism Planning & Development*, 11(3), 317-329.

Alajoutsijärvi, K., Juusola, K., & Siltaoja, M. (2015) The legitimacy paradox of business schools: losing by gaining?. *Academy of Management Learning & Education*, 14(2), 277-291.

Allen, D. and Simpson, C. (2019) Inquiry Into Graduate Attributes: Reviewing the Formal and Informal Management Curricula. *Journal of Management Education*, *43*(4), pp.330-358.

Amann, W., Pirson, M., Dierksmeier, C., Von Kimakowitz, E., & Spitzeck, H. (2011) *Business schools under fire: Humanistic management education as the way forward*. Palgrave Macmillan.

Anderson, D., Sweeney, D., Williams, T., Camm, J., & Cochran, J. (2015) *An introduction to management science: quantitative approaches to decision making*. Cengage Learning.

Anderson, J. C. (1995) Relationships in business markets: exchange episodes, value creation, and their empirical assessment. *Journal of the Academy of Marketing Science*, 23(4), 346-350.

Anderson, L., Thorpe, R. and Coleman, C. (2020) Reviewing Management Learning: The field and the journal. *Management Learning*, *51*(1), pp.17-34.

Andrews, J., & Higson, H. (2008) Graduate employability, 'soft skills' versus 'hard' business knowledge: a European study. *Higher Education in Europe*, 33(4), 411-422.

Anosike, P., Ehrich, L.C. and Ahmed, P. (2012) Phenomenology as a method for exploring management practice. *International Journal of Management Practice*, 5(3), pp.205-224.

Antoniadou, M., Sandiford, P. J., Wright, G., & Alker, L. P. (2018) Workplace Fear: A Phenomenological Exploration of the Experiences of Human Service Workers. *In Individual, Relational, and Contextual Dynamics of Emotions* (pp. 271-297). Emerald Publishing Limited.

Atkinson, P. and Delamont, S. (2006) Rescuing narrative from qualitative research. *Narrative inquiry*, 16(1), pp.164-172.

Audretsch, D.B. and Thurik, A.R. (2004) *A model of the entrepreneurial economy* (No. 1204). Papers on Entrepreneurship, Growth and Public Policy.

Augier, M., & March, J. (2011) *The roots, rituals, and rhetorics of change: North American business schools after the Second World War*. Stanford University Press.

Badua, F. (2015) The ROOT and STEM of a Fruitful Business Education. *Journal of Education for Business*, 90(1), 50-55.

Bam, K. (1992) *Research methods for business and management*. academia.edu

Bandura, A. (1977) Self-efficacy: toward a unifying theory of behavioral change. *Psychological review*, 84(2), 191.

Barnes, D. ed., (2001) *Understanding business: processes*. Psychology Press.

Barnett, C. (1972) *The collapse of British power*. William Morrow & Company

Barney, J. B. (2002) Strategic management: From informed conversation to academic discipline. *The Academy of Management Executive*, 16(2), 53-57.

Barritt, L. (1985) *Researching educational practice*. ERIC

Baskerville, R., & Myers, M. D. (2004) Special issue on action research in information systems: Making IS research relevant to practice: Foreword. *MIS quarterly*, 329-335.

Bengesai, A.V. (2012) *Critiquing representation: the case of an academic literacy course in an engineering faculty in a South African university* (Doctoral dissertation).

Benner, P. (Ed.). (1994) *Interpretive phenomenology: Embodiment, caring, and ethics in health and illness*. Sage publications.

Bennis, W. G., & O'Toole, J. (2005) How business schools lost their way. *Harvard business review*, 83(5), 96-104.

Bercovitz, J., & Feldman, M. (2006) Entrepreneurial universities and technology transfer: A conceptual framework for understanding knowledge-based economic development. *The Journal of Technology Transfer*, 31(1), 175-188.

Berger, P., & Luckmann, T. (1966) *The Social Construction of Reality: A Treatise in the Sociology of Knowledge*. Penguin

Berglund, H. (2015) Between cognition and discourse: phenomenology and the study of entrepreneurship. *International Journal of Entrepreneurial Behavior & Research*, 21(3), 472-488.

Billett, S., Harteis, C. and Gruber, H. eds. (2014) *International handbook of research in professional and practice-based learning*. Dordrecht, The Netherlands: Springer.

Bishop, P., & Deason, C. (2013) A phenomenological exploration of the mentoring experiences of women business owners in Central Florida. *Journal of Women's Entrepreneurship and Education*, (3-4), 28-50.

Black, S. (1971) Thoughts on management education. *Industrial Relations Journal*, 2(4), pp.34-62.

Bleek, D. F. (2011) *The Naron: a Bushman tribe of the central Kalahari*. Cambridge University Press.

Bogdan, R. and Biklen, S.K. (1997) *Qualitative research for education*. Boston, MA: Allyn & Bacon.

Boland, R. J. (1989) Beyond the objectivist and the subjectivist: learning to read accounting as text. *Accounting, Organizations and Society*, 14(5), 591-604.

Bombała, B. (2012) Phenomenology of management–didactic aspects. *Management and Business Administration*. Central Europe, 116(3), pp.50-59.

Bourke, Patricia E. (2007) Inclusive education research and phenomenology. In *Proceedings Australian Association for Research in Education*. Research impacts:

Proving or improving?, Fremantle, Western Australia.

Bradbury-Jones, C., Irvine, F., & Sambrook, S. (2010) Phenomenology and participant feedback: convention or contention? Caroline Bradbury-Jones, Fiona Irvine and Sally Sambrook consider the use of member checks to improve the rigour of phenomenological research. *Nurse Researcher*, 17(2), 25-33.

Bratti, M. (2006) : Social class and undergraduate degree subject in the UK, IZA *Discussion Papers, No. 1979*, Institute for the Study of Labor (IZA), Bonn

Bresnahan, T.F., Brynjolfsson, E. and Hitt, L.M. (2002) Information technology, workplace organization, and the demand for skilled labor: Firm-level evidence. *The quarterly journal of economics*, 117(1), pp.339-376.

Brew, A. (2003) Teaching and research: New relationships and their implications for inquiry-based teaching and learning in higher education. *Higher Education Research & Development*, 22(1), pp.3-18.

Brown, P., & Hesketh, A. (2004) *The mismanagement of talent: Employability and jobs in the knowledge economy*. Oxford University Press.

Brunnquell, C. and Brunstein, J., 2018. Sustainability in Management Education: Contributions from Critical Reflection and Transformative Learning. *Metropolitan Universities*, 29(3), pp.25-42.

Brydon-Miller, M., Greenwood, D., & Maguire, P. (2003) Why action research?. *Action research*, 1(1), 9-28.

Burgess, R.G. ed., (2005) *The ethics of educational research*. Routledge.

Cabantous, L., & Gond, J. P. (2011) Rational decision making as performative praxis: explaining rationality's Eternel Retour. *Organization Science*, 22(3), 573-586.

Caelli, K. (2001) Engaging with phenomenology: is it more of a challenge than it needs to be?. *Qualitative Health Research*, 11(2), 273-281.

Cartter, A. M. (1977) *The Cartter report on the leading schools of education, law, and business*. Educational Change.

Chamberlin, E.H. (1948) An experimental imperfect market. *Journal of Political Economy*, 56(2), pp.95-108.

Chandler, J. D., & Teckchandani, A. (2015) Using social constructivist pedagogy to implement liberal learning in business education. *Decision Sciences Journal of Innovative Education*, 13(3), 327-348.

Channon, D. F. (1973) *The strategy and structure of British enterprise*. Pub. Harvard Business School

Chapman, J. W., & Tunmer, W. E. (1997) A longitudinal study of beginning reading achievement and reading self-concept. *British Journal of Educational Psychology*, 67(3), 279-291.

Cheit, E. F. (1985) Business schools and their critics. *California Management Review* (pre-1986), 27(000003), 43.

Chia, R. (2014) From relevance to relevate: How university-based business school can remain seats of. *The Journal of Management Development*, 33(5), 443-455.

Chong, Y. S., & Ahmed, P. (2014). A phenomenology of university service quality experience. *International Journal of Educational Management*.

Clarke, C., Knights, D. and Jarvis, C. (2012) A labour of love? Academics in business schools. *Scandinavian Journal of Management*, *28*(1), pp.5-15.

Coate, K., Barnett, R. and Williams, G. (2001) Relationships between teaching and research in higher education in England. *Higher education quarterly*, 55(2), pp.158-174.

Cole, C., Couch, O., Chase, S., & Clark, M. (2015) Hermeneutic Exploration, Analysis and Authority: Phenomenology of Researcher's Emotions and Organizational Trust. In *Proceedings of the 14th European Conference on Research Methods 2015*: ECRM 2015 (p. 153). Academic Conferences Limited.

Comer, D. R., & Vega, G. (2015) *Moral courage in organizations: Doing the right thing at work*. Routledge.

Conklin, T. A. (2013) Doing phenomenology, becoming phenomenological: The evolution of person and practice. In *Academy of Management Proceedings* (Vol. 2013, No. 1, p. 13905). Briarcliff Manor, NY 10510: Academy of Management.

Conklin, T.A. (2014) Phenomenology redux: Doing phenomenology, becoming phenomenological. Organization Management Journal, 11(2), pp.116-128.

Crane, A., Matten, D., Glozer, S. and Spence, L. (2019) *Business ethics: Managing corporate citizenship and sustainability in the age of globalization*. Oxford University Press.

Crang, P. and Martin, R.L., 1991. Mrs Thatcher's vision of the 'new Britain' and the other sides of the 'Cambridge phenomenon'. *Environment and Planning D: Society and Space*, *9*(1), pp.91-116.

Crockett, G. and Elias, P. (1984) British managers: a study of their education, training, mobility and earnings. *British Journal of Industrial Relations*, 22(1), pp.34-46.

Creed, P. A., & Hughes, T. (2013) Career development strategies as moderators between career compromise and career outcomes in emerging adults. *Journal of Career Development*, 40(2), 146-163.

Cupchik, G. (2001) Constructivist realism: An ontology that encompasses positivist and constructivist approaches to the social sciences. In *Forum Qualitative Sozialforschung/Forum: Qualitative Social Research* (Vol. 2, No. 1).

Curtis, S., & Lucas, R. (2001) A coincidence of needs?: Employers and full-time students. *Employee relations*, 23(1), 38-54.

Darwish, R. H., LaVenia, K. N., & Polkinghorne, F. W. (2018) Sense of Belonging: International Student Enrollment in Business Programs. *International Journal of Business and Applied Social Science* (IJBASS), 4(2).

Datar, S. M., Garvin, D. A., & Cullen, P. G. (2011) Rethinking the MBA: Business education at a crossroads. *Journal of Management Development*, 30(5), 451-462.

Darics, E. (2019) Critical language and discourse awareness in management education. *Journal of Management Education, 43*(6), pp.651-672.

Dayuan, J. (2006) Thoughts on Fundamental Problems of Vocational Education Pedagogy [J]. *Vocational and Technical Education*, 4(8), 8.

Deer, S. and Zarestky, J. (2017) Balancing profit and people: Corporate social responsibility in business education. *Journal of Management Education, 41*(5), pp.727-749.

De Gagne, J.C. and Walters, K.J., 2010. The lived experience of online educators: Hermeneutic phenomenology. *Journal of Online Learning and Teaching*, 6(2), pp.357-366.

De Klerk, J. (2015) Exploring the Use of a Business Simulation to Teach Business Concepts to Emirati Students. *Developments in Business Simulation and Experiential Learning*, 42.

De Vita, G., & Case, P. (2014) 'The smell of the place': Managerialist culture in contemporary UK business schools. *Culture and Organization*, (ahead-of-print), 1-17.

De Witt, L., & Ploeg, J. (2006) Critical appraisal of rigour in interpretive phenomenological nursing research. *Journal of advanced nursing*, 55(2), 215-229.

Dearing, R. (1997) The Dearing Report. The National Committee of Enquiry into Higher Education, *London. Retrieved May, 3, p.2006.*

Debesay, J., Nåden, D., & Slettebø, Å. (2008) How do we close the hermeneutic circle? A Gadamerian approach to justification in interpretation in qualitative studies. *Nursing Inquiry*, 15(1), 57-66.

Dictionary, O. E., & Idioms, E. (2019) *Oxford References Online.*

Djelic, M.L. (2016) History of management–what is the future for research on the past?. In *A research agenda for management and organization studies.* Edward Elgar Publishing.

Doherty, B., Meehan, J., & Richards, A. (2015) The business case and barriers for responsible management education in business schools. *Journal of Management Development*, 34(1), 34-60.

Dore, R. (1995) The end of jobs for life?: corporate employment systems: Japan and elsewhere.

Dostal, R.J. (2002) Gadamer: The man and his work. *The Cambridge Companion to Gadamer*, pp.13-35.

Dowling, M. (2004) Hermeneutics: an exploration. *Nurse Researcher*, 11(4), pp. 30-9.

Dreon, O., & McDonald, S. (2012) Being in the hot spot: A phenomenological study of two beginning teachers' experiences enacting inquiry science pedagogy. *Teachers and Teaching*, 18(3), 297-313.

Driscoll, A., & Sandmann, L. R. (2016) From maverick to mainstream: The scholarship of engagement. *Journal of Higher Education Outreach and Engagement*, 20(1), 83-94.

Drucker, P. F. (1973) *Management: Tasks, Responsibilities*. Harper & Row

Dubé, L., & Paré, G. (2003) Rigor in information systems positivist case research: current practices, trends, and recommendations. *MIS quarterly*, 597-636.

Durepos, G., Maclean, M., Alcadipani, R. and Cummings, S. (2020) Historical reflections at the intersection of past and future: Celebrating 50 years of Management Learning. *Management Learning*, *51*(1), pp.3-16.

Edwards, M., Brown, P., Benn, S., Bajada, C., Perey, R., Cotton, D., Jarvis, W., Menzies, G., McGregor, I. and Waite, K. (2020) Developing sustainability learning in business school curricula–productive boundary objects and participatory processes. *Environmental Education Research*, 26(2), pp.253-274.

Egri, C. (2014) Introduction: Reflecting on the Epistemological Beliefs and Dialogical Pedagogy in Management Education, *Academy of Management Learning and Education*, 13(2) 244

Ehrich, L. (2005) Revisiting phenomenology: Its potential for management research. *Challenges of Organisations in Global Markets: BAM2005*, pp.1-13.

Elley-Brown, M.J., Pringle, J.K. and Harris, C. (2018) Women opting in?: New perspectives on the Kaleidoscope Career Model. *Australian Journal of Career Development*, *27*(3), pp.172-180.

Elzinga, A. (1997) The science-society contract in historical transformation: With special reference to "epistemological drift". *Social Science Information*, 36(3), 411-445.

Eury, J.L. and Treviño, L.K. (2019) Building a Culture of Honor and Integrity in a Business School. *Journal of Management Education*, *43*(5), pp.484-508.

Fernández-Balboa, J. M., & Stiehl, J. (1995) The generic nature of pedagogical content knowledge among college professors. *Teaching and Teacher Education*, 11(3), 293-306.

Field, J. (2000) Governing the ungovernable: why lifelong learning policies promise so much yet deliver so little. *Educational Management & Administration*, 28(3), 249-261.

Forida, R. and Cohen, W. (1999) *Engine or infrastructure? The university role in economic development. Industrializing knowledge: University-industry linkages in Japan and the United States. MIT Press*, Cambridge, MA.

Foucault, M. (1972) *Archaeology of Knowledge*. Pantheon Books

Fourcade, M., & Khurana, R. (2013) From social control to financial economics: the linked ecologies of economics and business in twentieth century America. *Theory and Society*, 42(2), 121-159.

Fred, H. L., & Cheng, T. O. (2003) Acronymesis: the exploding misuse of acronyms. *Texas Heart Institute Journal*, 30(4), 255.

Gadamer, H. G. (1972) *The science of the life-world. In The Later Husserl and the Idea of Phenomenology* (pp. 173-185). Springer Netherlands.

Gadamer, H. G. (1996) *Truth and method* (2nd rev. ed. Joel Weinsheimer & Donald Marshall, Trans.). New York: Continuum.

Gadamer, H. G. (2000) Subjectivity and intersubjectivity, subject and person. *Continental Philosophy Review*, 33(3), 275-287.

Gadamer, H. G. (2008) *Philosophical hermeneutics*. Univ of California Press.

Gentile, M.C. (2017) Giving voice to values: a pedagogy for behavioral ethics. *Journal of Management Education, 41*(4), pp.469-479.

Gibson, S.K. (2004) Mentoring in business and industry: The need for a phenomenological perspective. *Mentoring & Tutoring: Partnership in Learning, 12*(2), pp.259-275.

Gibson, S.K. and Hanes, L.A. (2003) The contribution of phenomenology to HRD research. *Human Resource Development Review, 2*(2), pp.181-205.

Gill, M. J. (2014) The possibilities of phenomenology for organizational research. *Organizational Research Methods*, 17(2), 118-137.

Gill, M. J. (2015) A Phenomenology of Feeling: Examining the Experience of Emotion in Organizations. In *New Ways of Studying Emotions in Organizations* (pp. 29-50). Emerald Group Publishing Limited.

Goethals, S., Gastmans, C. and de Casterlé, B.D. (2010) Nurses' ethical reasoning and behaviour: a literature review. *International journal of nursing studies*, 47(5), pp.635-650.

Goldkuhl, G. (1998) *The six phases of business processes: Business communication and the exchange of value*. Jönköping International Business School.

Gray, D.E. (2007) Facilitating management learning: Developing critical reflection through reflective tools. *Management learning, 38*(5), pp.495-517.

Grayson, C. J. (1973) Management science and business practice. *Harvard Business Review*, 51(4), 41-48.

Grey, C. (2002) What are business schools for? On silence and voice in management education. *Journal of management education, 26*(5), pp.496-511.

Grey, C. (2004) Reinventing business schools: The contribution of critical management education. *Academy of Management Learning & Education*, 3(2), 178-186.

Groenewald, T. (2004) A phenomenological research design illustrated. International journal of qualitative methods, 3(1), pp.42-55.

Grugulis, I., Bozkurt, Ö., & Clegg, J. (2011) 'No place to hide'? The realities of leadership in UK supermarkets. *Retail work*. Palgrave: Houndsmill, 193-212.

Gummesson, E. (2003) All research is interpretive!. *Journal of business & industrial marketing*, 18(6/7), 482-492.

Hackforth, R. ed., (1972) *Plato: Phaedrus* (No. 119). Cambridge University Press.

Häggman-Laitila, A. (1999) The authenticity and ethics of phenomenological research: How to overcome the researcher's own views. *Nursing Ethics*, 6(1), pp.12-22.

Halpin, D. (2005) *Researching education policy: Ethical and methodological issues*. Routledge.

Hammersley, M. and Traianou, A. (2012) *Ethics in qualitative research: Controversies and contexts*. Sage.

Hanssens, D.M. and Pauwels, K.H. (2016) Demonstrating the value of marketing. *Journal of Marketing*, 80(6), pp.173-190.

Harkavy, I. (2006) The role of universities in advancing citizenship and social justice in the 21st century. *Education, citizenship and social justice*, 1(1), 5-37.

Harlos, K.P., Mallon, M., Stablein, R. and Jones, C. (2003) Teaching Qualitative Methods in Management Classrooms—. *Journal of Management Education, 27*(3), pp.304-322.

Harrington, D. and Kearney, A. (2011) The business school in transition: New opportunities in management development, knowledge transfer and knowledge creation. *Journal of European Industrial Training,* 35(2), pp.116-134.

Hart, C. (2018) *Doing a literature review: Releasing the research imagination.* Sage.

Harvey, L., & Knight, P. T. (1996) *Transforming Higher Education.* Open University Press, Taylor & Francis, 1900 Frost Road, Suite 101, Bristol, PA 19007-1598.

Heidegger, M. (1962) *Being and time* (J. Macquarrie & E. Robinson, trans.).

Heidegger, M. (2014) *Introduction to metaphysics.* Yale University Press.

Henderson, R., Jaffe, A.B. and Trajtenberg, M. (1998) Universities as a source of commercial technology: a detailed analysis of university patenting, 1965–1988. *Review of Economics and statistics,* 80(1), pp.119-127.

HESA Statistics, https://www.hesa.ac.uk/data-and-analysis/students/whos-in-he [Accessed 02 September 2019]

HESA, (2013) What Do Graduates Do? Pub. Higher Education Statistics Authority.

Hill, C. W., & Hernández-Requejo, W. (2008) *Global business today.* New York: McGraw-Hill Irwin.

Hioki, W., Lester, D. and Martinez, M. (2015) Predisposition factors of career and technical education transfer students: A hermeneutic phenomenology study. *The Community College Enterprise,* 21(2), p.9.

Hitt, M. A. (1998) Twenty-first-century organizations: Business firms, business schools, and the academy. *Academy of Management Review,* 23(2), 218-224.

Holloway, J. and Francis, G. (2002) Implications of subject benchmarking in United Kingdom higher education: the case of business and management. *Quality in higher education, 8*(3), pp.239-25

Hopkins, R.M., Regehr, G. and Pratt, D.D. (2017) A framework for negotiating positionality in phenomenological research. *Medical teacher,* 39(1), pp.20-25.

Hughes, T., Bence, D., Grisoni, L., O'regan, N., & Wornham, D. (2011) Scholarship that matters: Academic–practitioner engagement in business and management. *Academy of Management Learning & Education*, 10(1), 40-57.

Hughes, M.Ü., Upadhyaya, S. and Houston, R. (2018) Educating future corporate managers for a sustainable world: recommendations for a paradigm shift in business education. *On the Horizon*. Emerald

Humphrey, C., & Hugh-Jones, S. (Eds.). (1992) *Barter, exchange and value: an anthropological approach*. Cambridge University Press.

Hunt, S. D. (2002) *Foundations of marketing theory: Toward a general theory of marketing*. ME Sharpe.

Ingram, P., & Zou, X. (2008) Business friendships. *Research in organizational behavior*, 28, 167-184.

Ironside, P. M. (2006) Using narrative pedagogy: learning and practising interpretive thinking. *Journal of advanced nursing*, 55(4), 478-486.

Ivory, C., Miskell, P., Shipton, H., White, A., Moeslein, K., & Neely, A. (2006) The future of business schools in the UK. London: *Advanced Institute of Management Research.*

Jayawardhena, C., & Foley, P. (2000) Changes in the banking sector–the case of Internet banking in the UK. *Internet Research*, 10(1), 19-31.

Jensen, M. D., & Snaith, H. (2016) When politics prevails: the political economy of a Brexit. *Journal of European Public Policy*, 23(9), 1302-1310.

Johnson, B. and Christensen, L. (2008) *Educational research: Quantitative, qualitative, and mixed approaches*. Sage.

Kaler, J. (2003) What Is a Business?. *Philosophy of Management*, 3(2), 57-65.

Kalleberg, A. L. (2013) *Globalization and precarious work*. Sage

Kaplan, R.S. and Norton, D.P. (1996) *Using the balanced scorecard as a strategic management system*. Jackson

Karakas, F., Manisaligil, A. and Sarigollu, E. (2015) Management learning at the speed of life: Designing reflective, creative, and collaborative spaces for millennials. *The International Journal of Management Education*, 13(3), pp.237-248.

Khurana, R. (2010) *From higher aims to hired hands: The social transformation of American business schools and the unfulfilled promise of management as a profession*. Princeton University Press.

Kononenko, A.I. and Kugai, K. (2019) Competitive market types development and market concept for competitive position formation. *Conceptual aspects management of competitiveness the economic entities.*

Koontz, H. (1961) The management theory jungle. *Academy of Management Journal*, 4(3), 174-188.

Koslowski, P. (2010) *Elements of a Philosophy of Management and Organization*. Springer.

Kuepers, W. (2016) Phenomenology of embodied and artful design for creative and sustainable inter-practicing in organisations. *Journal of Cleaner Production*, 135, pp.1436-1445.

Küpers, W.M., 2007. Phenomenology and Integral Pheno-Practice of Wisdom in Leadership and Organization. *Social Epistemology, 21*(2), pp.169-193.

Larson, M.J. (1992) Practically academic: Forming British business schools in the 1960s. *Management, 1890*(1990).

Laughton, D. (2005) The development of international business as an academic discipline: Some implications for teachers and students. *Journal of Teaching in International Business*, 16(3), 47-70.

Lester, S. (1999) *An introduction to phenomenological research.* Stan Lester Developments, Taunton

Lien, B.Y.H., Pauleen, D.J., Kuo, Y.M. and Wang, T.L. (2014) The rationality and objectivity of reflection in phenomenological research. *Quality & Quantity*, 48(1), pp.189-196.

Lilley, K., Barker, M., & Harris, N. (2014) Educating global citizens in business schools. *Journal of International Education in Business,* 7(1), 72-84.

Locke, R.R. (1989) *Management and higher education since 1940: The influence of America and Japan on West Germany, Great Britain, and France*. Cambridge University Press.

Lukka, K., & Granlund, M. (2002) The fragmented communication structure within the accounting academia: the case of activity-based costing research genres. Accounting, Organizations and Society, 27(1), 165-190.

Macfarlane, B. (1995) Business and management studies in higher education: the challenge of academic legitimacy. *International Journal of Educational Management*, 9(5), 4-9.

Macfarlane, B., & Ottewill, R. (Eds.). (2013) *Effective learning and teaching in business and management*. Routledge.

Mäkinen, M. (2013) Becoming engaged in inclusive practices: Narrative reflections on teaching as descriptors of teachers' work engagement. *Teaching and Teacher Education*, 35, 51-61.

Mancuso, M. S., & Tonelli, M. (2014) The phenomenological approach: a framework to design markets. *Eprints*: 4437-4451.

Mårtensson, P., & Bild, M. (2016) *Teaching and learning at business schools: Transforming business education*. Routledge.

Maslow, A. H. (1943) A theory of human motivation. *Psychological review*, 50(4), 370.

Mason, J. (2017) *Qualitative researching*. Sage.

Masrani, S., Williams, A. P., & McKiernan, P. (2011) Management education in the UK: The roles of the British Academy of Management and the Association of Business Schools. *British Journal of Management*, 22 (3), 382-400.

Mathias, P. (1975) Business History and Management Education. *Business History*, *17*(1), pp.3-16.

McCabe, D. L., Butterfield, K. D., & Trevino, L. K. (2006) Academic dishonesty in graduate business programs: Prevalence, causes, and proposed action. *Academy of Management Learning & Education*, 5(3), 294-305.

McLaren, P., & Jaramillo, N. (2007) *Pedagogy and praxis in the age of empire: Towards a new humanism*. Rotterdam: Sense Publishers.

Miles, M.P. and Munilla, L.S. (1993) The eco-orientation: an emerging business philosophy?. *Journal of Marketing Theory and Practice*, pp.43-51.

Minocha, S., Hristov, D., & Reynolds, M. (2017) From graduate employability to employment: policy and practice in UK higher education. *International Journal of Training and Development*, 21(3), 235-248.

Mintzberg, H. (2004) *Managers, not MBAs: A hard look at the soft practice of managing and management development*. Berrett-Koehler Publishers.

Mitchell, W., & Singh, K. (1996) Survival of businesses using collaborative relationships to commercialize complex goods. *Strategic management journal*, 17(3), 169-195.

Mitroff, I. I., Alpaslan, C. M., & O'Connor, E. S. (2015) Reflections: What's Wrong with Business Schools and Why they Need to Change. *Journal of Change Management*, (ahead-of-print), 1-7.

Mootz III, F.J. (2011) Gadamer's Rhetorical Conception of Hermeneutics as the Key to Developing a Critical Hermeneutics. Gadamer and Ricoeur: *Critical horizons for contemporary hermeneutics*, pp.83-103.

Moriarty, J. (2005) On the relevance of political philosophy to business ethics. *Business Ethics Quarterly*, 15(3), 455-473.

Mulligan, T. M. (1987) The two cultures in business education. *Academy of Management Review*, 12(4), 593-599.

Murcia, M.J., Rocha, H.O. and Birkinshaw, J. (2018) Business schools at the crossroads? A trip back from Sparta to Athens. *Journal of Business Ethics*, 150(2), pp.579-591.

Murray, A., Crammond, R. J., Omeihe, K. O., & Scuotto, V. (2018) Establishing successful methods of entrepreneurship education in nurturing new entrepreneurs. *Journal of Higher Education Service Science and Management* (JoHESSM), 1(1).

Murray, S.J. and Holmes, D. (2014) Interpretive phenomenological analysis (IPA) and the ethics of body and place: Critical methodological reflections. *Human Studies*, 37(1), pp.15-30.

National Committee of Inquiry into Higher Education (Great Britain) and Dearing, S.R., (1997) The National Committee of Inquiry into Higher Education: main report. NCIHE.

Nilson, H. (2015) 12. Critical pedagogy theory and the family business. Theoretical Perspectives on *Family Businesses*, 211.

Noe, R.A., Hollenbeck, J.R., Gerhart, B. and Wright, P.M. (2017) *Human resource management: Gaining a competitive advantage*. New York, NY: McGraw-Hill Education.

O'Leary, M. and Cui, V. (2018) Reconceptualising Teaching and learning in higher education: challenging neoliberal narratives of teaching excellence through collaborative observation. *Teaching in Higher Education*, pp.1-16.

Oblinger, D. G., & Verville, A. L. (1998) What Business Wants from Higher Education. *American Council on Education/Oryx Press Series on Higher Education*. Oryx Press, PO Box 33889, Phoenix, AZ 86067-3889.

O'Donoghue, T. and Punch, K. eds. (2003) *Qualitative educational research in action: Doing and reflecting*. Routledge.

O'Hair, D., Friedrich, G. W., & Dixon, L. D. (2007) *Strategic communication in business and the professions*. Allyn & Bacon.

Oldham, M. (1978) Interdisciplinarity in higher education business studies courses. *The Vocational Aspect of Education*, 30(76), 53-58.

Olkkonen, R., Tikkanen, H., & Alajoutsijärvi, K. (2000) The role of communication in business relationships and networks. *Management Decision*, 38(6), 403-409.

Olssen, M., & Peters, M. A. (2005) Neoliberalism, higher education and the knowledge economy: From the free market to knowledge capitalism. *Journal of education policy*, 20(3), 313-345.

Orrell, D. (2010) *Economyths: ten ways economics gets it wrong*. John Wiley & Sons.

Ortiz-de-Mandojana, N., & Bansal, P. (2016) The long-term benefits of organizational resilience through sustainable business practices. *Strategic Management Journal*, 37(8), 1615-1631.

Parker, M. (2016) Towards an alternative business school: A school of organizing. In *A Research Agenda for Management and Organization Studies*. Edward Elgar Publishing.Powell, W. W., &

Parker, M. (2018) *Shut down the business school.* University of Chicago Press Economics Books.

Parks-Leduc, L., Rutherford, M.A., Becker, K.L. and Shahzad, A.M. (2018) The professionalization of human resource management: Examining undergraduate curricula and the influence of professional organizations. *Journal of Management Education, 42*(2), pp.211-238.

Pernecky, T. and Jamal, T. (2010) (Hermeneutic) phenomenology in tourism studies. *Annals of Tourism Research, 37*(4), pp.1055-1075.

Perriton, L. and Reynolds, M. (2004) Critical management education: From pedagogy of possibility to pedagogy of refusal?. *Management Learning, 35*(1), pp. 61-77.

Petriglieri, G., & Petriglieri, J. (2015) Can business schools humanize leadership?. *Academy of Management Learning & Education*, amle-2014.

Pfeffer, J., & Fong, C. T. (2002). The end of business schools? Less success than meets the eye. *Academy of Management Learning & Education*, 1(1), 78-95.

Piekkari, R., Welch, C., & Paavilainen, E. (2009) The case study as disciplinary convention: Evidence from international business journals. *Organizational research methods*, 12(3), 567-589.

Pietkiewicz, I. and Smith, J.A. (2014) A practical guide to using interpretative phenomenological analysis in qualitative research psychology. *Psychological journal*, *20*(1), pp.7-14.

Pucciarelli, F., & Kaplan, A. (2016) Competition and strategy in higher education: Managing complexity and uncertainty. *Business Horizons*, 59(3), 311-320.

Ramezanzadeh, A., Adel, S.M.R. and Zareian, G. (2016) Authenticity in teaching and teachers' emotions: a hermeneutic phenomenological study of the classroom reality. *Teaching in higher education*, 21(7), pp.807-824.

Raven, J. (1989) British history and the enterprise culture. *Past & Present*, (123), pp.178-204. JSTOR

Reed, M. and Anthony, P. (1992) Professionalizing management and managing professionalization: British management in the 1980s. *Journal of Management studies*, *29*(5), pp.591-613.

Rennie, K.D., Byrum, K., Tidwell, M. and Chitkara, A.K. (2018) Strategic Communication in MBA Curricula: A Qualitative Study of Student Outcomes. *Journal of Management Education*, *42*(5), pp.594-617.

Richardson, K. A. (2008) Managing complex organizations: Complexity thinking and the science and art of management. *Emergence, Complexity & Organization*, 10(2), 13-26.

Richardson, T., Elliott, P., & Roberts, R. (2015). The impact of tuition fees amount on mental health over time in British students. Journal of Public Health, 37(3), 412-418.

Rippin, A., Booth, C., Bowie, S., & Jordan, J. (2002) A complex case: Using the case study method to explore uncertainty and ambiguity in undergraduate business education. *Teaching in Higher Education*, 7(4), 429-441.

Robbins, L.R.B. (1963) *Higher Education: Report of the Committee appointed by the Prime Minister under the chairmanship of Lord Robbins*, 1961-63 (No. 2). HM Stationery Office.

Robinson, D.A. (2002) *A phenomenological study of how South African entrepreneurs experience and deal with ethical dilemmas* (Doctoral dissertation, Rhodes University).

Roy, A., & Starosta, W. J. (2001) Hans-Georg Gadamer, language, and intercultural communication. *Language and intercultural communication*, 1(1), 6-20.

Sanders, P. (1982) Phenomenology: a new way of viewing organizational research. *Academy of management review*, 7(3), 353-360.

Sarasvathy, S. D. (2001) Causation and effectuation: Toward a theoretical shift from economic inevitability to entrepreneurial contingency. *Academy of management Review*, 26(2), 243-263.

Schein, E. H. (2010) *Organizational culture and leadership (Vol. 2)*. John Wiley & Sons.

Schön, D. (1983) *The Reflective Practitioner*, Basic Books

Schweiker, W. (1993) Accounting for ourselves: accounting practice and the discourse of ethics. *Accounting, Organizations and Society*, 18(2), 231-252.

Schipper, F. (1999) Phenomenology and the reflective practitioner. Management Learning, 30(4), pp.473-485.

Segal, S. (2010) A Heideggerian approach to practice-based reflexivity. *Management Learning*, *41*(4), pp.379-389.

Seymour, R.G. (2006) Hermeneutic phenomenology and international entrepreneurship research. *Journal of International Entrepreneurship*, 4(4), pp.137-155.

Sherman, G.L. (2009) Martin Heidegger's Concept of Authenticity: A Philosophical Contribution to Student Affairs Theory. *Journal of College and Character*, *10*(7).

Simon, H. A. (1960) *The new science of management decision*. PsycBOOKS

Simons, H. and Usher, R. (2012) *Situated ethics in educational research*. Routledge.

Slaughter, S., & Rhoades, G. (2004) *Academic capitalism and the new economy: Markets, state, and higher education*. JHU Press.

Small, L., Shacklock, K. and Marchant, T. (2018) Employability: a contemporary review for higher education stakeholders. *Journal of Vocational Education & Training*, 70(1), pp.148-166.

Smith, J., 2009. A., Flowers, P., & Larkin, M. (2009) Interpretative Phenomenological Analysis. Theory, Method and Research. *Qualitative Research in Psychology*, *6*(4), pp.346-347.

Smith, J.A. and Shinebourne, P. (2012) *Interpretative phenomenological analysis*. American Psychological Association.

Smith, S., Kempster, S. and Wenger-Trayner, E. (2019) Developing a program community of practice for leadership development. *Journal of Management Education*, *43*(1), pp.62-88.

Snellman, K. (2004) The knowledge economy. *Annu. Rev. Sociol.*, 30, 199-220.

Sotirou, P. (1993) Articulating a hermeneutic pedagogy: The philosophy of interpretation. *Journal of Advanced Composition*, pp.365-380.

Starkey, K., & Tempest, S. (2005) The future of the business school: Knowledge challenges and opportunities. *Human Relations*, 58(1), 61-82.

Starkey, K., Hatchuel, A., & Tempest, S. (2004) Rethinking the business school. *Journal of Management Studies*, 41(8), 1521-1531.

Steiner, C. J., & Gaskin, P. (1999) Educating leaders: From the abstract and rational to the concrete and personal. *Journal of Leadership & Organizational Studies*, 5(2), 83-102.

Stigler, G.J. (1957) Perfect competition, historically contemplated. *Journal of political economy*, 65(1), pp.1-17.

Stroh, L. K., & Brett, J. M. (1994) A decade of change: Managers' attachment to their organizations and their jobs. *Human Resource Management*, 33(4), 531-548.

Stromquist, N. P., & Monkman, K. (Eds.) (2014) *Globalization and education: Integration and contestation across cultures*. R&L Education.

Taylor III, B. W. (2015) *Introduction to management science*. Prentice Hall.

Taylor, S. (1980) School experience and student perspectives: a study of some effects of secondary school organisation. *Educational Review*, 32(1), 37-52.

Thomas, A. B. (1980) Management and Education: Rationalization and Reproduction in British Business. *International Studies of Management & Organization*, 71-109.

Thompson Jr, R.J. (2014) *Beyond reason and tolerance: The purpose and practice of higher education*. Oxford University Press.

Thorne, K., & Pellant, A. (2007) *The essential guide to managing talent: How top companies recruit, train, & retain the best employees*. Kogan Page Publishers.

Tiratsoo, N. (2004) "The "Americanization" of management education in Britain." Journal of Management Inquiry 13, no. 2: 118-126.

Todres, L. and Galvin, K.T. (2008) Embodied interpretation: A novel way of evocatively re-presenting meanings in phenomenological research. *Qualitative Research*, *8*(5), pp.568-583.

Tomás Gómez Arias, J., & Bello Acebron, L. (2001) Postmodern approaches in business-to-business marketing and marketing research. *Journal of Business & Industrial Marketing*, 16(1), 7-20.

Trank, C.Q. and Rynes, S.L. (2003) Who moved our cheese? Reclaiming professionalism in business education. *Academy of Management Learning & Education*, 2(2), pp.189-205.

Trowler, P. R. (2001). *Academic tribes and territories*. McGraw-Hill Education (UK).

Turok, I. (2004) Cities, regions and competitiveness. *Regional studies*, 38(9), 1069-1083.

Tuschling, A., & Engemann, C. (2006) From education to lifelong learning: The emerging regime of learning in the European Union. *Educational philosophy and theory*, 38(4), 451-469.

Usher, K. and Holmes, C. (1997) Ethical aspects of phenomenological research with mentally ill people. *Nursing Ethics*, 4(1), pp.49-56.

UWE, *Business Team Entrepreneurship* (2019) https://courses.uwe.ac.uk/N191/business-team-entrepreneurship [Accessed 09 February, 2019]

Van Fleet, D.D. and Wren, D.A. (2005) Teaching history in business schools: 1982–2003. *Academy of Management Learning & Education*, 4(1), pp.44-56.

Van Heerden, K.I. (2000) *A phenomenological investigation into undergraduate students' experience of acquiring the discourse of engineering* (Doctoral dissertation, Rhodes University).

Van Manen, M. (1990) *Researching lived experience: Human science for an action sensitive pedagogy*. Routledge

Vandenberg, D. (2002) Phenomenology and fundamental educational theory. In *Phenomenology World-Wide* (pp. 589-601). Springer, Dordrecht.

Vauterin, J. J., Linnanen, L., & Michelsen, K. E. (2013) A university–industry collaborative response to the growing global demand for student talent: Using interpretive phenomenology to discover life-world knowledge. *Industry and Higher Education*, 27(1), 41-54.

Vickers, M.H. and Parris, M.A. (2003) January. Telling it how it really is?: life in organisations revealed using Heideggerian phenomenology. In *AEPP 2003 Conference Proceedings: the 11th Annual International Conference 2003* (pp. 29-35). Association on Employment Practices and Principles.

Viney, C. (1995) A phenomenological study of ethical decision-making experiences among senior intensive care nurses and doctors concerning withdrawal of treatment. *Nursing in Critical Care*, 1(4), 182-187.

Vu, M.C. and Burton, N. (2020) Mindful reflexivity: Unpacking the process of transformative learning in mindfulness and discernment. *Management Learning*, 51(2), pp.207-226.

Walker, W. (2007) Ethical considerations in phenomenological research. *Nurse researcher*, 14(3).

Walters, A.J. (1995) The phenomenological movement: implications for nursing research. *Journal of Advanced Nursing*, 22(4), pp.791-799.

Warnke, G. (2013) *Gadamer: Hermeneutics, tradition and reason*. John Wiley & Sons.

Warnock, M. (1970) *Existentialism*. Oxford University Press

White, D. and Heslop, R. (2012) Educating, legitimising or accessorising? Alternative conceptions of professional training in UK higher education: a comparative study of teacher, nurse and police officer educators. *Police practice and research*, 13(4), pp.342-356.

Whitley, R. (2008) Universities as strategic actors: Limitations and variations. *The university in the market*, (No. 557). Manchester Business School Working Paper.

Wicks, D. (2014) What do Business Schools Really Teach? The Role of Critical Management Studies in Business Education. In *Getting Things Done* (Dialogues in Critical Management Studies, Volume 2) Emerald Group Publishing Limited, 2, 195-202.

Wilkins, S. and Huisman, J. (2012) UK business school rankings over the last 30 years (1980–2010): Trends and explanations. *Higher Education*, 63(3), pp.367-382.

Williams, A. P. (2010) *The history of UK business and management education*. Emerald Group Publishing.

Willis, P. (2019) Retroduction, reflexivity and leadership learning: Insights from a critical realist study of empowerment. *Management Learning*, 50(4), pp.449-464.

Willmott, H. (1994) Management education: provocations to a debate. *Management learning*, 25(1), pp.105-136.

Winch, P. (2008) *The idea of a social science and its relation to philosophy*. Routledge.

Withy, K. (2012). The methodological role of angst in Being and time. *Journal of the British Society for Phenomenology*, 43(2), 195-211.

Wilson, D.C. and Thomas, H. (2012) The Legitimacy of the Business of Business Schools: What's the Future?.(2012). *Journal of Management Development*, 31(4), pp.368-376.

Wooster, H. A. (1919) University Schools of Business and a New Business Ethics. *The Journal of Political Economy*, 47-63.

Worthy, J., & Broaddus, K. (2001). Fluency beyond the primary grades: From group performance to silent, independent reading. *The Reading Teacher*, 55(4), 334-343.

Wren, D. A., Halbesleben, J. R., & Buckley, M. R. (2007) The theory–application balance in management pedagogy: A longitudinal update. *Academy of Management Learning & Education*, 6(4), 484-492.

Wright, R.E. (2010) Teaching history in business schools: An insider's view. *Academy of Management Learning & Education*, 9(4), pp.697-700.

Zorn, T.E. (2002) Converging within divergence: Overcoming the disciplinary fragmentation in business communication, organizational communication, and public relations. *Business Communication Quarterly*, 65(2), pp.44-53.

Index

I

K

L

M

N

O

P